TRYING TIMES
Keighley's Amateur Rugby Teams
1876-2011

Rob Grillo
© 2011 & 2017

This is a reprint of the original 2011 edition, which was produced as a limited edition and sold out very quickly.

CONTENTS

Page

INTRODUCTION

Following the publication of my books on the history of soccer in Keighley a few years back, I originally planned the same with the oval ball game, but despite finishing most of the research back in 2002 and writing it all up, I never really got round to doing anything with it. The whole thing was promptly forgotten about, save for a few reminders from friends who knew I had untaken the work, and as I've moved further away from sport history over the last few years it looked as if I might never get round to sharing the research. A couple of queries from people wanting gaps filling in their own knowledge led to me filling in what has happened in the local game since 2002, although in less detail than the rest of the town's amateur rugby history. Someone else can do that. As I am in no way involved in the sport in any way, all research has been done from a neutral viewpoint throughout, and invariably there will be errors that have crept in. A number of local rugby players & officials have looked through the text, so some errors have already, hopefully, been wiped out.

This is a book about rugby teams, not players. It's the towns sporting teams, and venues, that have always held my interest rather than the individuals who have represented them, whether it be football, rugby or even athletics clubs over the last couple of hundred years, so hopefully I have not missed out any of these fine groups of men in error. Saying that, I have mentioned individuals when it has been appropriate to do so.

Many of the photos were provided by John Heald (former sports editor at the Keighley News), several of which were taken by Trevor Smith, who is credited in the appropriate places.

THANKS TO (in no particular order)
John Heald & Malcolm Hoddy at the Keighley News newspaper for again allowing access to their archives, David Ingham, Barry Mitchell, Jack Riley, James Pressley, the patient & tireless staff of Keighley Reference Library (2000-2002), Bob Gillard (Cougar Cubs), Tim Cooper (Keighley Albion), David Kirkley (Keighley Albion), Trevor Delaney, Peter Lush (London League Publications), Steven Wood, Ian Dewhirst, the late Terry Hollindrake, the late Andy Bennett (Pennine Rugby League), Chris Kelly (Keighleyweb.co.uk), Barbara Klempa & Trevor Smith.

EARLY DAYS

Football was nothing new to Keighley when the 'Keighley rugby and association club', was formed on the 17th October 1876. An early version of the game of football, described as *'riotous'* is claimed to have been played between local villages before the mid 1800's. Dozens of young men would attempt to force a ball of sorts into a 'goal' placed in an opposing village, possibly located several miles away. Although games such as this have been described as *'crude'* and without rules, they were actually quite an organised pastime, occurring often on feast days, although there was little regard for property or indeed for human suffering! Broken bones, and even deaths, were reported in such games around the country. The authorities were clearly not impressed by this ritual, such games becoming illegal, and, in common with other towns & cities across the country, by 1824 the Keighley Improvement Commissioners' Act had prohibited the playing of 'football' on public highways. In fact as late as May 1905, several Keighley youths, residing in Leeds and Turkey Streets were each fined 3 shillings plus costs for playing soccer in the street.

By the time Keighley rugby & association club had banded together, Victoria was almost 40 years into her long reign as monarch, Benjamin Disraeli had temporarily taken over as prime minister – before handing it back to Gladstone's liberals two years later, while Alexander Graham Bell was writing his name in history with his patenting of the telephone ! The oval ball game was the formative club's preferred form of recreation from the start, and the club's association section never really took off. A growing fixture list in its formative months included its first fixture against a side from Crosshills, on 18th November 1876 on a rented field on Lawkholm Lane (this field really was on Lawkholme Lane, not far from the current rugby ground). The occasion ended in a draw, although in the 'visitors favour'. What subsequently happened to the Crosshills side is anyone's guess, with no more references to what may well have been a 'scratch' outfit.

A first fixture against the better-established Bingley club took place on January 13th the 1878. Not surprisingly Bingley won by 2 tries and 2 touchdowns to 2 touchdowns, despite fielding only 14 men, one less than Keighley. A measure of the complicated scoring system of the times was illustrated in Keighley's opening match of the 1877-78 season, when on 6th October 1877 they defeated Bradford Juniors by 1 goal, 1 touchdown & 1 dead ball to Bradford's 2 disputed goals & 4 touches down!

Another local Keighley 'derby' took place on 7th October 1877 when Keighley met, and defeated, Kildwick by 1 goal to 5 touchdowns. The Kildwick side were never heard of again and, like Crosshills before them, were more than likely formed as a scratch side to play this match only. The victorious Keighley XV side on the day was: *A.Rishworth (captain), A.E.Sale (backs), E.Laycock, J.Craven (three-quarter backs), J.B.Wilson, W.H.Clapham (half backs), T.Wale, H.Wale, J.W.Darling, C.H.Foulds, H.Summerscales, W.Clapham, L.Ramsden, F.Rishworth, T.Butterfield (forwards).* Kildwick could only muster only 14 men for the game, although both sides clearly had sets of brothers in their line-ups! (The Kildwick team is included in the clubs section later in the book.)

In the absence of organised league and cup competition, Keighley generally played friendly fixtures against other sides from around the West Riding - Skipton, Cleckheaton, Otley, Manningham & Bradford, then based at Apperley Bridge, and the long gone Bradford Zingari among them. Keighley were certainly not among the leading lights on the local scene, but they were much stronger than many other 'junior' sides of the time such as Gargrave and Giggleswick, who could only hope for fixtures against the second teams of the top clubs in the area.

By the start of the 1878-79 campaign, Keighley had added a second string, a practice match being on October 5th of that season when the first twelve took on 'the next 18'. April 5th 1879 the club actually played a challenge match against a Keighley & District representative side. Sadly, given the lack of other clubs in town, the representative side could muster only 11 men for the fixture and not surprisingly they went down by 1 goal and 2 touchdowns to 2 tries and 3 touchdowns.

The district XI for this fixture was: *W.H.Watson (back), G.Hastings (captain), J.Hastings (three-quarter backs), A.H.Peart, W.F.Frost (half backs), J.Laycock, W.T.Booker, E.Skirrow, W.Asquith, S.Asquith & J.Gott (forwards).* It is possible that the J.Laycock referred to here is the same man who had played for Kildwick against Keighley 12 months earlier.

1879 saw the formation of another club in Keighley. 'Keighley Athletic and Football Club' was founded in October of that year as a football section of Keighley Cricket Club. Playing on a field adjacent to that of the cricket section on Lawkholme Lane, they merged with the better-established Keighley club (who had since moved their home games to a field on Dalton Lane) in April 1881. Ironically the combined Keighley rugby club then merged with the cricket club in April 1885, the club taking up residence at what is the Lawkholme Lane ground on Hard-Ings Road! The cricket club had again attempted to form their own rugby side and had spent £250 preparing an enclosure suitable for the game.

The Keighley Athletic and Football Club line-up was generally thus: *Anderton, Slater (backs), Haggas (captain), Hall (three-quarter backs), Dunderdale, Smith (half backs), Richardson, Shuttleworth, Feather, Gledhill, Whitehead, Riley, Craigie, Whiteoak & Wild (forwards),*

By the time the 1880-81 season commenced, it was clear that the oval ball game was catching on in the town. On November 4th 1880, two new sides were in action against each other - Keighley Juniors and Sutton taking the field, each for possibly the first time, on the ground of the latter (result unknown). With the Athletic Club side newly merged at Dalton Lane, Keighley Juniors were to play home fixtures at Lawkholme during the following season and they actually met Keighley's third team in October 1881. The following month saw them play Sutton Mills, in all probability the same side they had faced the previous season. The same day, a Keighley Parish Church side were reported in the local press to be due to meet Bingley Grammar School 'A' (again, no indication the following week what the result was).

A small number of local clubs continued through the 1882-83 season, with Keighley Juniors and Sutton/Sutton Mill continuing their fixtures against other junior sides or second teams of better established clubs. However, an interesting series of 14-a-side matches took place that season involving the previously unheard of Red Star club. On October 21st 1882 they met Keighley Parish Church at Dalton Lane, their home ground. The result was *'a draw in favour of the home team...2 minor touchdowns to nil'*. The teams lined up like this: *Red Star: B.Hey (back), Bradley, Carr, Slater (three-quarter backs), Crabtree, Smith (half backs), Ambler, Ogden, Haygarth, Walmsley, Walbank, O'Hara, Murgatroyd, W.Sunderland (forwards) Keighley Parish Church: Sellars (back), Calvert, Thomas, Haw (three-quarter backs), Mellor, Shuttleworth (half backs), Welsh, West, Atkinson, Walton, Hanson, Mitchell, Lonsdale, Smith (forwards).*

The following week Red Star met Keighley Zingari at the same ground. Another draw resulted, again 'in favour' of Red Star by 3 touchdowns to one. Interestingly, the Zingari side included many of the faces that featured in the Parish Church side seven days previously, which suggests that this series of matches was against rather informal clubs in the town. The third match of the series saw Red Star defeat Parkwood Wanderers, winning easily by 3 goals, 2 tries and 3 touchdowns to nil. No other mention was made in the local press of this Wanderers side, possibly substantiating the conclusion that one off-informal sides were in contest. Red Star and Zingari met again, in December, Red Star winning this time, the final recorded match of the series taking part after Christmas, Parish Church defeated by Red Star who thus ended their campaign undefeated! There seems to have been no fixtures between the opponents of Red Star, which suggests that this strange club may have sent out challenges to other informal groups of rugby playing men around town. A brief look at the senior club in town saw Keighley lose heavily at Wakefield Trinity in the first round of the Yorkshire Challenge Cup this season - the score being 2 goals, 8 tries, 11 touchdowns and 2 dead balls to nil.

1883-84 saw only Keighley and Keighley Juniors matches reported in the local press, although it is possible that Sutton (at least) were still operating at a very minor level. Things could not have been more different the following season however. The summer of 1884 saw the emergence of a number of new clubs in and around town, a clear indication of the rising popularity of the sport. The 1884-85 season saw the emergence, alongside Keighley and Keighley Juniors, of

Stockbridge-based Keighley Hornets, who would in later years lead a rather nomadic existence. In October 1884 they had an eventful game at home to another new side - Silsden. Their opponents were said to have disputed nearly every point, walking off, fighting, after 20 minutes. The Keighley Herald reported that the cobbydalers *carried on in a very disorderly manner*. This is not the first time that a Silsden side would be accused of going 'over the top', although to be fair to them this label would be applied to thousands of other clubs nationwide over the ensuing century and a quarter!

One of the prime movers behind the new Silsden club was Dr.John Purcell, a native of Ireland, yet a very much respected 'off-cum-dun' in the village. A GP by trade, he was also instrumental in the formation of a 'soccer' club in Silsden several years later, and was a member of the local cricket and bowling clubs too.

Other new names this season included the first village clubs from Morton and Haworth, as well as a more formal Keighley Zingari C&FC. The nearby villages of Cullingworth and Denholme had also been new clubs emerge over the summer, and they were regular opponents of Keighley teams. More informal sides continued to operate - Park Lane Roebush, Keighley Free Wanderers and Keighley Tradesmen among them. It appears that no less than three 'informal' games took place at Keighley Juniors' new Worth Village ground in January 1885 - Worth Village Free Wanderers met Cullingworth, R.Brooksbank Works played Holmes Pearson Employees and Hattersleys Works promoted a Fitters-v-Turners match.

Over the next three seasons there was an astonishing rise in the number of rugby teams in Keighley. Many clubs ran two sides, although some disappeared as quickly as they had at first appeared - 'one-off' in effect. In addition, the number of local fields procured for the sport grew, and several sides occupied different sites each season. Local villages saw the emergence of their first teams - other villages and areas around town had more than club, and no doubt local enthusiasts continued to play for more then one team. In addition to the main Haworth club, Haworth Albion, Mill Hey Wanderers & Haworth Trinity appeared in the 1885-86 season, followed by Haworth Rangers and Haworth Rovers before the end of the decade - all of which were short lived. At the same time, Silsden had Silsden Rangers to compete with, and a strong Ingrow side had Ingrow Rangers to contend with. Many of these clubs had their seeds sown in local places of worship. These same religious institutions that had objected to the supposed violence and lawlessness of the early forms of football were prime movers behind the new 'muscular Christianity', which actually encouraged the playing of physical sport, partly through a need to closely establish young men in their community with the local church, and also to gain spiritual fulfilment through 'manly' exercise. There was already a plethora of local church-based cricket teams operating and now the many religious institutions in town turned their hand to the promotion of rugby in order to further their cause.

New clubs such as Keighley Shamrocks began to make a name for themselves. Shamrocks' first season - 1885-86 - saw them playing on Highfield Lane, although twelve months later they had procured a new ground at Oakworth Road, which was also referred to as the Holycroft ground. In their first season their first team played 18 fixtures, winning 11 and drawing two; in 1886-87 winning 12 and drawing 6 of 22 fixtures, scoring 8 goals, 22 tries and 57 minor points. In this, their second campaign, three teams were run - their second team winning 12 out of their 16 fixtures, the third team winning all five of their games without having a single point registered against them. Shamrock's third team actually decided to 'go it alone' in December of 1886, renaming themselves Keighley Alexandra for the remainder of the season. The Keighley Shamrocks club was started in the old Shamrock Club, which itself was begun by the town's growing Irish community. It was located near the bottom of Turkey Street. The Angel Inn, located opposite, was initially used for changing. The region had seen a large influx of Irish migrants mainly as a result of the failure of the potato crop there for three consecutive years from 1845. By 1951, one person in twenty in Keighley was Irish, many of these migrants having taken poorly paid jobs within the community, other taking on the role of hawker or journeyman tailor. The Irish Kellys, Flynns, Durkins & O'Haras could be found within their own densely populated, crowded, communities based around Damside and the long-gone Pinfold and Baptist Square with open drains as sewerage. That a Shamrock club should grow up so close to these streets was almost inevitable and it is an indication of their sense of community that the name should live on even into the 21st century. With their rugby players taking the field so close to the areas they predominated, it is reasonable to assume that the club would have a loyal and vociferous support.

The 1887-88 season saw Shamrocks join the senior Keighley club in the first round of the Yorkshire Challenge Cup, but while Keighley themselves progressed to the second round at the expense of Bowling (going out in round 2 at home to Pontefract), Shamrocks went out by 1 goal and one minor point to three minor points against Greengates (Bradford). Twelve months on, both Ingrow and Silsden joined Shammies in the preliminary round of the same competition.

Keighley rugby club played a practice match at the end of September 1885 against and Ingrow & district select. This quickly gave rise to an Ingrow team, and within a short space of time they had established themselves as one of the foremost outfits in the town. Their 1886-87 campaign saw them win 14 of their 17 fixtures, with only one defeat, their home ground above the Knowle Spring Brewery, 'commanding a good view of the surrounding country' according to the Keighley Herald.

With the number of new clubs, all trying to attract the best players around, there were the inevitable casualties. Morton, despite securing a new ground in the village in the summer of 1886, disbanded in December 1887, while Keighley Juniors also went to the wall. In their final season - 1886-87 - they had changed their name to Keighley Free Wanderers (the second team to use that title) in order that their

'Juniors' title would no longer debar them from obtaining fixtures with reputable sides. Many of the club's former players went on to play for Silsden. It was hoped that some of the surviving clubs would actually pack up too - the local press describing a *'rough and disgraceful game'* played by Thwaites Brow / Long Lee (the club was known by both names) against the Airedale Free Wanderers in October 1886. The Herald went on to say *'If this is their way of playing against respectable clubs, the sooner they sell their jerseys and goal-posts the better'*. This comment provoked an angry response from the club in question, but was not an extraordinary occurrence at the time!

By this time the local press was also bemoaning the fact that too many local players preferred to shine for smaller clubs in town, rather than raising their aspirations and uniting to help the town club become a major force. The senior Keighley club at this time had a long way to go if it wanted to be a major force in the sport, fixtures against the top clubs in the county being few and far between.

By 1888 there were fewer 'informal' or 'scratch' sides around, as the better clubs in town became more established and attracted the better player. There had been over 30 in the town in 1886-87 - although there were reported to be over 100 at this time in Hull! The top local clubs could by now expect to command huge 'gates' for key matches. Ingrow reported around 2000 spectators for a game against Manningham Rangers in February 1889, while Shamrocks claimed 1500 for their home game against Ingrow the following season. Ironically, Shamrocks had just moved to a ground on West Lane, recently vacated by the first ever Keighley soccer team, who had struggled to entice any spectators at all to their games. Shamrocks seemed to move all over town in the 1890's - Holycroft, Dalton Lane, West Lane, Highfield, back to West Lane, etc.

EARLY SCORING SYSTEMS

Prior to the 1886-87 season the way to win a rugby match was to score more goals than your opponents. This meant that teams who were quite simply outclassed by their opponents could achieve quite often lucky victories. A team might dominate a game, score a hatful of tries yet lose to a lucky goal. Minor touchdowns, when a defending team was forced to touch down behind their own goal-line, were an irrelevance, although they helped the reader to gauge the dominant team when reading the local sports results in newspapers such as the Keighley News and Keighley Herald. The Yorkshire Cup, inaugurated in December 1877, actually used minor touchdowns to separate teams in tied matches, but in the main, goals and tries were the means of scoring.

In October 1886 the Rugby Football Union decided that three tries would equal a goal, in September 1891 modifying this slightly to make three tries superior to one goal. This only slightly redressed the problem. The 1889-90 season was the first in which 'points' were used – a goal counted as three points and a try as one (as above), a try going up in value to two points in 1891.

KEIGHLEY F.C.

First Team.	A Team.
Oct. 6 Halifax St. Joseph's, h	Halifax St. Joseph's away
13 Bradford Trinity, away	Bradford Trinity, home
20 Hull Southcoates, home	Leeds East End, away
27 Skipton, away	Skipton, home
Nov. 3 Bradford Rangers, h	Bradford Rangers, away
10 Bingley, away	Kirkstall St. Stephen's h
17 Holbeck, away	Holbeck, home
24 Otley, home	Otley, away
Dec. 1 Shipley, away	Shipley, home
8 Harrogate, home	Harrogate, away
15 Castleford, away	Keighley Juniors, home
22 Halifax St. Joseph's, away	Halifax St. Joseph's, home
29 Dudley Hill, away	Dudley Hill, home
Jan. 5 Hull Southcoates, away	Leeds East End, home
12 Skipton, home	Skipton away
19 Bradford Rangers, away	Bradford Rangers, home
26 Shipley, home	Shipley, away
Feb. 2 Harrogate, away	Harrogate, home
9 Holbeck, home	Holbeck, away
16 Otley, away	Otley, home
23 Bingley, home	Kirkstall St. Stephen's a
Mar. 1 (Cup Tie), Hipperholme & Lightcliffe, away	
15 Bradford Trinity, home	Bradford Trinity, away
22 Castleford, home	Keighley Juniors, away
29 Dudley Hill, home	Dudley Hill, away

Hon. Secs.—Mr. H. Wall, Wellington Buildings, and Mr. H. B. Summerscales

Captains—1st, Mr. W. Yiend ; 2nd, Mr. F. Rennie

Head-quarters and Dressing-room—Victoria Hotel

Ground—Dalton Lane, 5 minutes' walk from Keighley Station (Mid.)

Club Colours—Navy Blue and White Jersey, and Navy Blue Knickers and Hose

68

KEIGHLEY JUNIORS F.C.

Oct. 6	Opening Match, home
13	Bradford Rangers 2nd, away
20	Manningham Hornets, home
27	Leeds St. Andrew's, away
Nov. 3	Bradford St. Joseph's, away
10	Greengates, home
17	Otley 2nd, home
24	Great Horton 2nd, away
Dec. 1	Dewsbury Clarence, away
8	Leeds St. Andrew's, home
15	Keighley 2nd, away
22	Bingley (A team), away
29	Bradford Rangers 2nd, home
Jan. 5	Otley 2nd, away
12	Great Horton 2nd, home
19	Bradford St. Joseph's, home
26	Greengates, away
Feb. 2	Denholme, away
9	Bingley (A team), home
16	Manningham Hornets, away
23	Denholme, home
Mar. 1	
8	Skipton 2nd, away
15	Dewsbury Clarence, home
22	Keighley 2nd, home
29	Skipton 2nd, home

Hon. Sec.—Mr. Geo. Newhill, 23, Lustre Street

Captain—Mr. R. Wilkinson

Head-quarters and Dressing-room—King's Head Hotel

Ground—Adjoining Holy Croft Board School, half-mile from Keighley Station (Mid.)

Club Colours—Black

69

Keighley and Keighley Juniors fixtures for the 1883-84 season.

10

THE KEIGHLEY CHARITY CUP

The 1889-90 season saw the Keighley Charity Cup inaugurated, the first time that local clubs had silverware to compete for. The cup was offered by the Keighley Friendly Society Gala Committee, and all proceeds from the competition would be donated to the Keighley Cottage Hospital. The hospital had been established in 1876, before that local residents had been forced into making the long haul to the Bradford Infirmary for their medical treatment. The need for funds for the new institution was readily apparent – the hospital at first renting a house in Highfield Lane and using a kitchen table for operations. Originally there were only eight beds, most of which were unused. Extensively enlarged during the 1890's, in no small way due to the immense fundraising efforts amongst local people and their sporting institutions, the hospital was renamed the Victoria Hospital before the turn of the century.

The Keighley Charity Cup competition was therefore held open to all clubs within a five-mile radius of Keighley, presumably from the town centre, and the following sides were the inaugural contestants:
Aireworth Alexandra, Cross Roads, Keighley Shamrocks, Beechcliffe, Keighley Parish Church, Ingrow, Silsden, Haworth, Keighley 'A', Keighley Zingari, Keighley Amateurs, Keighley Hornets, Bingley Free Wanderers, Bingley 'A', Hainworth & Keighley Holy Trinity.

Those teams that took part were a mixture of village/community based sides (such as Cross Roads & Beechcliffe), as well as those from religious denominations (Holy Trinity & Parish Church), and of course the second strings of the Keighley and Bingley clubs. . The draw for the competition had actually been made the previous season at the Black Horse Hotel, with a Mr.C.Smith of 9 Moss Street, Keighley being given the role of competition secretary.

With no set date for early ties, the first match in the new competition was played on September 21st 1889, Keighley Shamrocks not exactly surprising anyone with their one-sided victory over Beechcliffe - the score being 6 goals, 5 tries & 12 minors to 1 goal and two minors. The competition certainly caught the imagination of the public, with 2000 spectators packing the Keighley Zingari enclosure at Stockbridge early in 1890 to see Ingrow book their place in the final at the expense of Bingley Free Wanderers.

Ingrow's rivals in the first ever Keighley Charity Cup final were Silsden. On February 8th 1890 between five and six thousand spectators crammed into Lawkholme Lane to see the cobbydalers win their first silverware with victory by 3 tries and 2 minors to nil. Unfortunately, the local mayor, who was called away on business in London, was not available to present the prizes, so Joseph Summerscales - president of Keighley Rugby Club - did the honours by presenting the trophy to the winners instead. The victorious Silsden team were treat to dinner at the Red Lion in the village the following Wednesday, and were said to have received a 'right royal reception' on their return to the village on the evening of their victory. The organising committee can certainly have taken heart from the fact that some £70 was donated to the Keighley Cottage Hospital following the final, fully justifying the decision to run the competition.

The sides for the first ever Keighley Charity Cup final were as follows:
Silsden: Dixon (back), W.Wilkinson, Wilson, John Moore (captain) (three-quarter backs), Green, R.Wilkinson (half-backs), Lee, Lambert, Tunnicliffe, Hargreaves, Slater, Cooper, Watson, Driver & Stephenson (forwards),
Ingrow: Mitchell (back), Weatherall, Bailey, Milner (three-quarter backs), Hudson, Taylor (half-backs), Ayrton, Jowett, Wigglesworth, Whitley, Heaton, Rookes, Sharp, Jones & Terry (forwards)

KEIGHLEY CHARITY CUP RESULTS - 1889-90 (winners listed first)

2ND ROUND	G	T	M		G	T	M
Silsden	0	4	3	Keighley Zingari	0	2	5
Ingrow	5	0	4	Keighley Shamrocks	0	0	1
Keighley Hornets	3	7	14	Hainworth	0	0	0
Bingley Free Wdrs	0	2	13	Cross Roads	0	0	13
SEMI-FINALS							
Silsden	1	0	2	Keighley Hornets	0	1	4
Ingrow	3	4	4	Bingley Free Wdrs	0	1	3
FINAL							
Silsden	0	3	2	Ingrow	0	0	0

Silsden defended their title successfully the following season - 1890-91. This time there were between eight and nine spectators present at Lawkholme, no doubt partly due to the fine weather that February day. Defeated finalists this time were Keighley Zingari, who could only muster two minor points compared to Silsden's three goals, 2 tries and 4 minors. Silver medals were awarded to each member of the victorious Silsden team on this occasion, their captain Lee receiving a silver medal inlaid with gold as well as the trophy. As losers, Zingari were presented with a consolation match ball.

There would be a new name on the trophy in the 1891-92 season, as Silsden chose not to defend the cup. Although Keighley's 'A' team were among the favourites to win, the finalists this time were Ingrow and Keighley Shamrocks, the former having edged out Haworth in the semi-final, with the latter having seen off Keighley 'A' at Bingley's ground. Despite losing Charles Hudson with a broken collar bone early in the game (no substitutes allowed in those days), Ingrow won a tight game in front of 5000 paying spectators through a first half Rookes try. The score was 2pts to nil, reflecting the new scoring system now in place in the world of rugby. In place of the previous complicated and ambiguous system, a goal kicked from a try counted as five points, a dropped goal or a goal kicked from a rolling ball four points, a penalty goal three points and a try two points. This made it much easier to determine the outcome of games and did away with the concepts of 'minor points'.

Shamrocks were missing from the following year's competition, no doubt still aggrieved at not being able to field their full strength team in the previous final - two players having being deemed ineligible to play in the tie (There were a plethora of reasons why players were ineligible, it is possible that the players in question had turned out for another side at some time during the season). Silsden returned, but only with their second string. Ingrow became the first side to reach three finals, but it was Keighley Zingari, nicknamed *'the gypsies'* , in their second final, who defeated the holders by three tries (6 points) to nil. There was no doubt that the better team won, their success as much due to their perseverance and determination as their skill according to the local press. Zingari had actually needed two games to dispose of Bingley Grammar School Old Boys in the semi-final. Despite winning the initial tie 13-5 they were forced to replay the game, having fielded an ineligible player. Luckily for them a 19-0 whitewash resulted in the replayed game at neutral Ingrow. Unfortunately only £19 was made available for division among the local charities from this, the 1892-93 competition, running costs having increased and gate receipts evidently falling.

In the mean time, the rugby scene had been continuing to develop in Keighley. There were fewer teams. Keighley still flew the flag for the town in senior terms, Shamrocks, Zingari, Ingrow and Silsden emerged as top dogs on the junior scene, entering the Yorkshire Cup competition alongside Keighley, albeit relatively unsuccessfully, with other sides such as Haworth, Hornets, Oxenhope, Cross Roads and Oakworth among the smaller clubs around, of which there were still quite a few. Scratch sides had virtually all disappeared, those based in villages had by now organised themselves on a more formal footing.

The first Airedale-v-Craven representative fixture was played at Manningham in November 1890, the return at Skipton the following season. Craven was represented by several players from the Shamrocks, Zingari, Silsden and Ingrow clubs. In fact, on November 5th 1891 the Craven & District Rugby Football Union was formed, consisting of all clubs in the Craven district and affiliating to the Yorkshire Rugby Union.

Among the low points of this era was the demise of the Keighley Hornets team. They had an awful 1891-92 campaign, but soldiered on to the end of the season despite losing the large majority of their fixtures. The new season saw the Hornets emerge again at their Dalton Lane enclosure, the players having *'struggled hard to keep the side together'* according to the local press. However, defeat by Keighley 'A' on 3rd September 1892 proved to be their final game. The club had £5 in the bank, but was said to be in desperate need of a new set of jerseys. A this point several players refused to play for the club again unless a new set was bought, at which point it was decided to close the club. A sad end to a respected local club.

Shamrocks meanwhile had problems of their own in the 1892-93 season. The nomadic club, were refused permission from the water board to collect balls that had accidentally gone into the reservoir adjacent to their West Lane ground! Ground problems aside, Shammies put out holders Idle in the Wharfedale Cup this season, the first time they, along with Ingrow and Silsden had entered the competition. Silsden KO'd Shamrocks in the following round, before they themselves fell to losing finalists Bankfoot (Bradford). Silsden actually tackled Keighley in the qualifying rounds of the Yorkshire Challenge Cup, going down 0-10 to their Lawkholme rivals.

The 1892-93 campaign was the first in which there were organised league competitions for Yorkshire's top club sides, in effect one of many factors that lead to the formation of the northern union (rugby league) in 1895. In addition to the Yorkshire Senior competition was a Yorkshire No.2 Competition, although neither Keighley nor the top junior sides in the town were involved yet.

CROWD PROBLEMS

There was a growing problem in the latter years of the 19th Century of crowd problems. Both soccer and rugby codes, even at a fairly minor level, were finding the control of unruly supporters difficult. This was not a problem endemic to Keighley, it was a nationwide concern. On many occasions it was the referee who bore the brunt of the frustrations of the home fans, with many many examples of the games' officials seeking protection in the dressing rooms of the away team or having to be escorted by the uniformed brigade from the ground. On other occasions, a victorious side playing away from home would be hounded from the ground in fear of their lives, and it was not uncommon for players to receive a far more severe punishment from members of an irate crowd than they had from the opposing players during the match. As a result, home teams would often be forced to put up notices warning their supporters of the implications of future unacceptable conduct around their enclosures. In other cases, a ground could be shut for a fixed period of time. This is exactly what happened to the Ingrow on two occasions in the early 1890's. In March 1890, a referee at the Fell Lane ground was said to have been subjected to 'ill treatment' by the locals - the result, a 2 week closure of the ground forced upon the club by the Yorkshire Union. Presumably, by October 1892 this had all been forgotten because the referee was attacked by irate Ingrow supporters following another game, leading this time to a ground closure of just one week.

The 1893-94 season did see local sides make that plunge into league competition. There was a new Yorkshire No.3 competition, divided into two groups, in which Silsden and Ingrow played in 'group A'. Keighley, following what had been their most successful playing season on record, found their competition in the Yorkshire Intermediate Competition, which was actually, in strength, located between leagues No.2 & No.3. Strangely, the first set of league tables in the local press showed winners of league matches receive one point, with one point deducted for a defeat. This was soon changed to the usual 2 points for a win, one for a draw system. There was no early success for the locals - although nearby Bingley won the No.3 competition title after a play off against 'group B' champions Hebden Bridge. Ingrow fared worse, following a 24-0 opening defeat of Tadcaster, their form deteriorated and eventually finished at the foot of their league. Disheartened, they failed to reappear the following season, this only twelve months after an appearance in the Charity Cup final.

This season's Charity Cup was won, for the second year in succession by Keighley Zingari, who had chosen not to play in league competition. Following a narrow victory over Haworth in their semi final (the third time Haworth had gone out of the competition at this stage), they went on to defeat Keighley's 'A' team 7-0 in the final; a drop goal and second half try, both by Johnson the difference between the teams, in front of what was described as a disappointing attendance.

Keighley Shamrocks almost had their name on silverware, losing to Farsley in the Wharfedale Cup final, played at Bowling Old Lane early on in the 1893-94 season. However, better things would follow. The side entered a new West Yorkshire League in 1894-95, and of course changed grounds again - now based further up West Lane at Calversyke Hill. Their season started well when they defeated Brownroyd Rec. (Bradford) 9-5 in the Wharfedale Cup final at Farsley at the end of October. Proof of the Irish community's regard for the club was the fact that the team was greeted at Keighley station that evening by St.Annes Catholic Band, who played a rendition of 'see the conquering hero come'. Things got better for the Shammies when Keighley Trinity, (who gave Keighley the fright of their lives in the Yorkshire Cup this season, narrowly going down 5-8) were defeated 11-0 in the Charity Cup final, in glorious weather and in front of some 2000 spectators. The competition actually yielded a profit of £40 for the local hospital, mainly due to the fact that it needed three games for Shammies to dispose of holders Zingari. The first game, in December ended pointless, the second, played some three months later due to the inclement weather and an inability to arrange a date for the replay, ended the exactly the same way. The second replay, early in April saw the West Lane side victorious by 5 points, a penalty and a try, no nil. In a fourth game between the teams, a Yorkshire Cup tie, Zingari had actually won 8-5, facing Keighley in the following round.

One week after their Charity Cup success, Shamrock's season was concluded with a league championship decider against Dewsbury St.Paulinus. The teams had already

15

defeated each other once, and a play off was deemed necessary to separate them - the Keighley side again winning, 6-3 through second half tries from McShee & Cullen. It was Shamrock's third silverware of the season, their best ever. It had actually been three seasons since Shamrocks had been defeated at home, and they looked ahead to Yorkshire League Competitions in coming seasons.

In a season when inclement weather wiped out most fixtures in the new year, Keighley and Silsden found themselves in the same level of competition - but not in name - the Intermediate Competition had become Yorkshire No.3, and Yorkshire No.3 had become Yorkshire No.4! Silsden's highlight was a resounding 43-0 success against struggling Haworth in the Yorkshire Cup.

The main talking point of the 1895-96 was the non-appearance of the Charity Cup competition. The trophy itself had been withdrawn 'sine die' by the cup committee due to the lack of interest now being shown towards the competition by local clubs. Keighley Hospital kept hold of the trophy, although there were continuous calls for a re-commencement of the competition at a later date in the local press. The summer had seen the breakaway from their county unions of the top clubs in Yorkshire & Lancashire - and the formation of the Northern Union, today's Rugby League. The town of Keighley was unaffected by the situation, neither the Keighley Rugby Club nor the junior sides in town were of a high enough standard to have been involved in the process.

However, with the Yorkshire No.1 competition in effect going over to the new Northern Union, then Keighley's No.3 competition became No.2, and Silsden were therefore elevated from No.4 to No.3! However, joining the cobbydalers at this level were local rivals Shamrocks and Zingari. Meanwhile, Keighley Trinity and Sutton were now ready for league action, in the newly formed Bradford & District League.

1893-94
YORKSHIRE INTERMEDIATE COMPETITION: KEIGHLEY, Alverthorpe, Buttershaw *(withdrew before end of season)*, Hull K.R, Pudsey, Goole, Bowling Old Lane, Armley, Ossett, Sowerby Bridge, Shipley, Mirfield, Normanton, West Riding,
YORKSHIRE NO.3 COMP - GROUP A: SILSDEN, INGROW, Saltaire, Bingley, Guiseley, Newtown, Idle, Tadcaster, Skipton, Horsforth, Stanningley, Windhill

1894-95
WEST YORKSHIRE LEAGUE: KEIGHLEY SHAMROCKS, Dewsbury St.Paulinus, Thornhill Lees Trinity, Garforth, Ripon, Leeds Institute, Burley & Normanton St.Johns *(the latter of whom failed to fulfil 2 fixtures)*

1895-96
BRADFORD & DISTRICT LEAGUE: KEIGHLEY TRINITY, SUTTON, Eccleshill Parish Church, Thackley, Thornton Rangers, Allerton, Great Horton Church, *Halifax West Mount (withdrew during the season)*
YORKSHIRE NO.3 COMPETITION: KEIGHLEY ZINGARI, KEIGHLEY SHAMROCKS, SILSDEN, Bingley, Skipton, Idle, Farsley, Guiseley, Saltaire, Windhill, Harrogate, Horsforth

The season saw league success come to Keighley for the first time. Silsden were narrowly pipped to their divisional title by Idle. The deciding league match between the two had actually been stopped five minutes before time due to the rough play shown by both sides (Silsden later appealed unsuccessfully against the result, which ended in a 3-0 victory for the Bradford-based team). Both Shamrocks, surprisingly, and Zingari found themselves at the wrong side of the table early in the season. Shamrocks recovered to climb the table in the New Year, and actually had a promising run through to the third stage of the Yorkshire Cup following a surprise defeat of Silsden. Zingari managed to recover late on in the season, but it was not enough to lift them off the foot of the table. Surprisingly, like Ingrow before them, Zingari were not around the following season, despite a late attempt to reform for a Yorkshire Cup tie, an idea that was thrown out by the competition's organising committee. It seems that league competition was the death knell of many well-established junior sides of the time.

Sutton meanwhile were going great guns in the Bradford League, this after almost disbanding during the summer of 1895. At the season's end they had finished joint top of the league with Thornton Rangers, prompting a play-off at the Keighley Trinity ground. The sides had drawn 0-0 in their final league game of the season, and again a goal-less draw resulted (shades of Shamrocks-v-Zingari the previous season). The league committee declared that both Sutton and Thornton would be declared joint champions, BUT another game would have to be played to decide who would play a 'rest of the league select'. Thornton won 3-0...but Sutton were still joint champions!

1895-96
BRADFORD & DISTRICT LEAGUE - Final Table

	P	W	L	D	Pts	
SUTTON	12	9	1	2	20)	joint
Thornton	12	9	1	2	20)	champions
Great Horton Church	12	7	5	0	14	
KEIGHLEY TRINITY	12	6	5	1	13	
Eccleshill Parish Church	12	3	8	1	7	
Thackley	12	2	8	2	6	
Allerton	12	2	10	0	4	

The Keighley Charity Cup was still not organised in 1896-97. However, Silsden were now in the Yorkshire No.2 competition along with Keighley. Sutton, who had moved to a new ground in the village close to the cricket field, joined Shamrocks in Yorkshire No.3, while Worth Village and Riddlesden, who had played friendlies the previous season, were accepted, strangely, into a Bradford based Horton & District League (the Bradford & District League having been wound up). Why they were not in the more locally based Shipley & District league is anyone's guess! Keighley Trinity had hoped to join Yorkshire No.3, but were refused entry.

The step up proved unsuccessful for both Silsden and Sutton, the latter finishing close to the bottom of their league. Shamrocks finished third in their competition, and reached the fourth round of the Yorkshire Challenge Cup - their best ever performance in this competition - while Keighley gained promotion to Yorkshire No.1, a win at Mytholmroyd sealing their first ever league title. The two local representatives in the Horton League were pipped at the post in a tight competition by Little Horton Athletic.

Towards the end of the 1896-97 season, the much sought after Harry Myers made his debut for Keighley. On the 10th April 1897 he took to the field against Shamrocks, before scoring one of five tries against Silsden on the final day of the season, seven days later. Myers had previously played for the Bramley club, but as they chose to join the new Northern Union, Myers opted to stay with the old code.

1896-97
HORTON & DISTRICT LEAGUE (almost final table)

	P	W	L	D	Pts
Little Horton Athletic	18	13	4	1	27
Bowling Rangers	17	10	3	4	24
WORTH VILLAGE	17	10	3	4	24
Undercliffe	17	9	4	4	22
RIDDLESDEN	17	9	4	4	22
Bradford Trinity	18	7	9	2	16
Bingley Juniors	18	4	9	6	13
Whetley Clarence	18	6	11	1	13
Bowling Rovers 'A'	18	2	13	3	7

Victoria Rangers, Bradford Victoria (withdrew during the season),
Tyersal Rovers (withdrew pre-season)

The Charity Cup was reconstituted for the 1897-98 season, but as a league competition for junior sides within a twelve (as opposed to the previous five) mile radius of Keighley. Sutton chose to move down from the Yorkshire competition, and Worth Village & Riddlesden moved across from the Horton League along with Bingley Juniors. Sutton looked likely to win the title all season, but they were pipped at the post by Keighley Trinity, who defeated them in an all-important decider late in the season. Unfortunately the competition was not deemed financially successful, a Trinity-v-Rest of League game raised only £2 at the season's end, and so the cup was again withdrawn....and with it went Keighley's first ever league competition.

Keighley finished runners-up behind Featherstone in the Yorkshire No.1 competition that season, but Silsden finished at the foot of No.2, with Shamrocks way down in No.3.

1897-98

KEIGHLEY CHARITY CUP LEAGUE COMPETITION: KEIGHLEY ATHLETIC, KEIGHLEY TRINITY, SUTTON, WORTH VILLAGE, RIDDLESDEN, KEIGHLEY PARISH CHURCH (withdrew early season), KEIGHLEY SHAMROCKS 'A' (withdrew early season), Gargrave, Shipley Clarence (withdrew late in season), Bingley Juniors, Giggleswick, Skipton

Despite the many new leagues coming and going, it was becoming harder and harder to run a financially successful rugby club, even at junior level. As the 1898-99 season began, both Silsden and Shamrocks, who had been included in the original line-up were missing from a reconstituted Yorkshire No.2 competition (Bradford section). Silsden chose to play friendly fixtures only, this just two seasons after competing at the same level as the Keighley club, while Shamrocks were missing completely from the fixture lists. Arguably the town's most successful junior club in the mid 1890's, they too had gone to the wall.

Worse was to follow. Keighley Trinity's championship success the previous season had been enough to see them elected to the same Yorkshire No.2 competition. However, by January 1899, bottom of the league and having seen a benefit match in their name against Keighley cancelled due to the weather, they withdrew from all competitions - citing financial problems. By now the only other competitive sides in the town alongside Keighley- who finished third in Yorkshire No.1 (this time behind Shipley and Sowerby Bridge) - were Worth Village and Riddlesden, in a reformed Bradford & District League. The latter of the two finished runner-up to Greenfield in the final reckoning.

Lawkholme Lane was actually the venue for the final of the Yorkshire Challenge Cup this season. On April 15th 1899 Alverthorpe and Sowerby Bridge played out a pointless-draw in front of over 3000 spectators, the replay at the same ground resulting in a 4-0 victory for Sowerby Bridge.

19

THE KEIGHLEY CHARITY CUP

The Keighley Charity Cup was competed for under rugby rules from 1899-1904, before being revived as a soccer competition between 1904 and 1940. After the Second World War it had become a dominoes trophy before being passed on to the Craven Cricket League, who duly awarded it to the league's runner-up club. The local Football Association tracked down and duly reclaimed the trophy in the late 1970's when the Keighley Charity Cup soccer competition was briefly revived.

The 'footballer' statuette in the photograph, which was itself found in a box of dominoes trophies in 1980, is obviously of a younger age than the main trophy.

(photo: Rob Grillo)

KEIGHLEY CHARITY CUP MEDALS

Above: awarded to J.Wigglesworth (Ingrow) 1891-92
Below: awarded to R.Smith (Keighley Zingari) 1892-93

NORTHERN UNION COMES TO KEIGHLEY

The great defection from the Rugby Football Union actually began in Keighley in the summer of 1899, some four years after the original meeting at the George Hotel, Huddersfield that had split the rugby world for good. Worth Village, Riddlesden, Sutton and Silsden went over to Northern Union, along with all other sides in the Bradford & District (Junior) League that season. The senior Keighley club initially remained loyal to the decimated Yorkshire Union, where only eight sides contested the county's No.1 competition, while a few minor clubs such as Keighley All Saints also adhered to the old code. All Saints actually pulled out of a fixture with Keighley Parish Church as their opponents played on the ground of Worth Village northern union club, such was the gravity of the situation.

There were several reasons behind the 'great split'. Firstly, the notion of broken time payments, inasmuch as the top clubs in the north were prevented from making such payments to their players, who could not otherwise the time off work as could the purely amateur, and better off 'gentlemen' players in the south of the country. Additionally, amongst several other reasons, the Rugby Union was dominated by the south. Although Yorkshire provided the union with over 40% of its clubs, and was easily the strongest county in playing terms, it - and Lancashire - had too little say in the running of the sport. The top clubs in Yorkshire & Lancashire therefore wanted much more say in the running of their sport.

Keighley was not represented among the original northern *elite* who broke away, however, within years all junior rugby clubs in the town had turned to the new 'northern union', and the situation was likewise in most other towns and cities in the north, leaving only a handful of rugby union clubs in existence in the counties affected. There had been no reason for the junior clubs to have made this conversion themselves though. None of the reasons behind the breakaway of the top clubs affected the junior organisations. However, the juniors did wish to show their allegiance to the cause, and others were left with the possibility of losing attractive - and money spinning - fixtures against the top sides around, even if the games were only against their 'A' (second) strings. The top clubs needed junior clubs around in order to tap the local talent and as a means of cementing their new union, so did nothing to prohibit the smaller clubs from turning their backs on the rugby union too, even if they had not always supported them when members of the old union.

Keighley won the Rugby Union's Yorkshire No.1 title in 1900, finishing ahead of Castleford, who defeated them in the semi-final of the Yorkshire Challenge Cup. Yet by the end of the season they too had moved over to the northern union, playing Manningham at home on April 14th 1900 in their inaugural match under the new rules, in front of some 2000 spectators (result: 2-5) Ironically their captain, Harry Myers, was presented with the Yorkshire No.1 competition match after the game by club president James Woodrow!

1899-1900
YORKSHIRE NO.1 COMPETITION - Final Table

	P	W	L	D	F	A	Pts
KEIGHLEY	14	9	2	3	203	34	21
Castleford	14	8	4	2	111	70	18
Skipton	14	7	3	4	151	42	18
Morley	14	6	4	4	103	92	16
Bottomboat	14	6	6	2	80	158	14
Otley St.Josephs	14	3	6	5	42	85	11
Cleckheaton	14	2	8	4	30	168	8
Bingley	14	2	9	3	22	96	7

KEIGHLEY'S RECORD IN YORKSHIRE LEAGUE COMPETITIONS PRIOR TO MOVING TO THE NORTHERN UNION

SEASON	League	P	W	L	D	F	A	Pts	Pos
1893-94	Intermediate	26	13	11	2	194	84	28	6/14
1894-95	No.3	26	8	13	5	93	159	21	10/16
1895-96	No.2	26	14	7	5	178	79	33	5/14
1896-97	No.2	24	20	2	2	272	56	42	1/13
1897-98	No.1	28	19	6	3	310	69	41	2/15
1898-99	No.1	26	16	6	4	230	109	36	3/14
1899-1900	No.1	14	9	2	3	203	34	21	1/8

Although Greenfield again won the Bradford & District league title, Worth Village managed to get their hands on some silverware. They were 1899-1900 Bradford & District Cup winners, beating Morley in a replay at Greenfield, Bradford on May 5th, following a 0-0 draw at Park Avenue the previous week, when Village had played the better rugby. Two Morley players were sent off in the replay for a foul tackle on Village's Frank Smith when he was about to score a try 8 minutes from time. The referee then ordered both teams off and awarded the game to Worth Village. The locals were leading through a W.Rundle penalty at the time. The referee sought protection from the Village players after the game. With substitutes not permitted at this time, Village's Tom Smith broke a collarbone during the game but bravely soldiered on. Village attracted a good crowd of 600 for their league encounter earlier in the season, the main disappointment of the campaign being the folding up of the Sutton club after only a few fixtures under the new code.

The introduction of northern union in the town created the impetus for more new clubs to spring up, and also for defunct sides such as Zingari and Shamrocks to play informal or benefit games using their old players. Keighley were admitted to the Yorkshire 2nd Competition (Western Section), where they finished as runners-up to Heckmondwike, thus gaining elevation to the Yorkshire Senior Competition for 1901-02, where they again had a fine season, finishing third. The switch of codes had not been in vain at Lawkholme Lane!

A new Keighley Junior League was formed for the 1900-01 season, five teams from the town being joined by two Bingley based sides and Gargrave. A deciding match was necessary to separate St.Annes and Bingley Trinity at the season's end, the former, said to be stronger and faster than their opponents, winning 3-2. There were only four sides in the Bradford League - Worth Village finishing runners-up behind defending champions Greenfield, with Silsden also included in the fixtures, although Riddlesden appear to have become defunct over the summer of 1900.

1901-02 saw another play-off for the Keighley League title, this time Bingley Clarence got the better of their Keighley namesake's second string, to the tune of 6-0 in front of 500 spectators at Haworth. The Bradford League was much stronger, with Worth Village again the bridesmaids, Bradford's Victoria Rangers pipping them for the title at the death. It is ironic that the death of Victoria herself was fresh in the minds of the local populace at the time, as Edward VII began his reign as King of England during 1901. During this time, Silsden had become defunct, but they were replaced by Keighley St.Annes (Keighley League champions, who had established themselves as the town's second 'Catholic' club after Shamrocks), Cross Roads, Keighley Clarence and one season wonders Steeton in the local association.

Steeton were surprise winners of a reconstituted Keighley Charity Cup, played towards the close of the 1901-02 season. Eight clubs entered a competition marred by poor conduct on the field of play. In the seven games played, there were 17 players sent off ! Gilstead actually walked off 12 minutes from time during their semi-final tie with Steeton after having a second player dismissed, and beaten finalists St.Annes finished one man short following their 0-2 defeat against Steeton, who won the cup through a Rundle penalty.

Having lost the use of their ground, Steeton were not around the following season, although there were now many sides in and around Keighley playing 'ordinary' or 'informal' fixtures again, this time under the new code. However, things quickly changed, as within two years the junior game had almost died out in Keighley!

The 1902-03 Charity Cup competition was actually deemed a great success - at long last . St.Annes disposed of Haworth - who else - in their semi final, and went on to narrowly defeat the Clarence club 5-4 in 'a capital game' in the final, on a fine pitch and in front of 3000 Lawkholme spectators basking in fine weather ! Both sides were described as being a credit upon themselves.

This is in marked contrast to what happened to be the last ever Keighley Charity Cup played under the rugby code in 1903-04. The final tie was described *as 'a wretched game, not only rough but scrappy and devoid of any interest'*. Losing finalists

24

were Keighley Olicana, in their first season, but what was at least heartening from the competition was that the eventual winners were, at least, Haworth. They broke their semi-final jinx, defeating Bradford side Idle Recreation 3-0, before recording a similar scoreline in the final, again in front of 3000 spectators. It was at first thought that the competition would be withheld the following season, but in the event it was re-established - successfully - as a 'soccer' competition as the round ball game, after several false starts, at last took off in the region. Keighley was swept along with the tide. Now young men wanted to play the 'new' game, easier to play, with less rules and much less chance of serious injury (although the 'association' game was still very rudimentary, and did result in fatalities). They turned their back on rugby, and Keighley - along with other towns in the West Riding- has never returned to the days when the local player had a myriad of rugby teams to choose from.

KEIGHLEY
1899-1900

Photograph taken of Keighley rugby club following their 'defection' to the Northern Union in 1900, almost five years after the original breakaway of 1895. The side is photographed with the 'Yorkshire R.U No.1 Competition Trophy'. Within days of securing the title close to the end of the season, the locals had defected to the new code.

Back: W.R.Elgie, R.Wooler, E.H.Jacobson, T.Mitchell, Harry Myers, J.Wigglesworth, A.Slater, A.Tillotson, J.W.Pearson, G.Newhill,
Middle: C.Kilbey, R.Jennison, J.Jacques, J.Cullen, A.Whittingham, R.Blades,
Front: P.O'Donnell, J.Routh, C.H.Caine, C.F.Saunders

A STRUGGLE FOR SURVIVAL

Keighley's rugby sides were finding little success in the Bradford & District League, and one by one they fell by the wayside. Cross Roads were wound up in the summer of 1903, selling their effects on to Ingrow. Ingrow themselves were defunct twelve months later, having spent just one season in the Bradford League stable. St.Annes, league runners up in 1903, survived just one more season after that. Both the Clarence and the previously successful Worth Village clubs failed to see out the 1903-04 season, and the Keighley Herald described the local junior scene as '*in a parlous state*'. Even the Keighley League was suffering, both Utley and Morton fell by the wayside during the 1903-04 season, leaving just five clubs in contention. It is also possible that Bingley Clarence and Ingrow were, for some unexplained reason, removed from the competition right at the death - leaving a final table consisting of just St.Annes Guild (who would have won the league anyway) and struggling Stockbridge and Haworth Rangers. The league died a quiet death, while St.Annes went on to compete, with disastrous consequences, in the Bradford League's second division the following season. Meanwhile, further up the aire valley, Skipton rugby club had decided to stick with the Yorkshire Union rather than switch codes, winning the Yorkshire Cup in 1903 after their opponents controversially scratched from a second replay. It is interesting to consider what success a Keighley side might have had in a drastically reduced Yorkshire Rugby Union at that time.

From the long list of local clubs in the first few years of the 20th century in Keighley, only Haworth survived, and they were joined by Keighley Olicana as the only junior rugby sides in town. The worth valley side had led the Bradford League early in the 1903-04 season, but had suffered a dire run around Christmas and finished the campaign well out of the reckoning. The following season Olicana had commenced playing 'ordinary' matches at Hard-Ings Road. They defeated several Bradford League sides and reached the Charity Cup final, before making the bold decision to join the Yorkshire Senior Competition prior to the 1904-05 campaign. Although they didn't exactly set the league alight, they more than held their own against more established sides.

Olicana were by now established enough to run a 'Workshops Competition' at the season's end for informal, scratch teams in and around town - Brunswick Arms (Keighley) defeating Bingley's Midland Hotel in the final. Competition rules generally debarred experienced rugby players from competing - '*no teams to have more than two players who have played for a recognised rugby club more than six times this season, and no two backs of the Keighley club will be permitted to play on the same side.*' (*Not that there were many 'recognised' teams left in the area*) Interestingly, many of the

26

sides in these workshops competitions adopted the names of teams of the past - thus the names of Keighley Athletic, Utley, Silsden Rangers and the like were briefly revived. There were also a number of teams representing local manufacturing firms springing up in workshops competitions, Hattersleys being representative of this number. The loom makers of George Hattersley & Sons could trace their origins back to 1789. Initially based at Stubbings Mill, Aireworth, manufacturing nuts & bolts, the firm expanded and diversified into manufacturing spindles and rollers, moving into new premises in 1900 closer to the centre of town in South Street. There had been a Hattersleys Fitters-v-Turners challenge match way back in 1885, and possibly since, while a works team had played informal fixtures during the mid 1880's. A new side representing the works appeared during the 1903-04 campaign, although it was to soccer that the workers turned to after that, enjoying a good degree of success in the Keighley & District soccer league during the 1920's & 30's.

It is interesting to note at this point that the Northern Union, which had until now continued with the old practice of 15-a-side teams, was in the process of reviewing its rules. Although the senior competitions, including the Yorkshire Senior Competition of which Olicana were members, continued with the 15 a side games, local competitions such as the Bradford League were by 1904 operating as 14-a-side competitions. It was not until 1906 when the Northern union finally made the decision to revert to the recognised 13-a-side game. At the same time, another profound change was that of the introduction of 'playing the ball', whereby a tackled player would pass the ball with his feet back to a team-mate rather than a 'scrummage' being formed. It was only now that the Northern Union game could be seen as being truly different from the long established rugby union game. From this time on, the 'new' game was much more open and the average number of points scored in matches rose considerably.

Keighley Olicana, meanwhile, made the decision to join the Bradford League for the 1905-06 campaign, and they were duly accepted into the top division. Now based at Lawkholme Lane, playing home fixtures while the senior Keighley club was away from home, they made a bright start to the season, lying in second place behind Buttershaw at Christmas Haworth, meanwhile, were struggling somewhat at the other end of the table, and it was no surprise when they tendered their resignation from the league in March 1906. Their West Lane ground became the first 'association' field in the village within months as the locals turned to the round ball to fulfil their sporting needs instead. Olicana did survive the season, despite falling off the pace in the new year, and although they again promoted a workshops competition at the season's end - assisted this time by the senior club in town - they too fell by the wayside during the summer.

This left no junior rugby clubs remaining in the Keighley area. As 'association' football took off in big style, and the formation of a Keighley soccer league in 1905, it was obvious that the northern union game was struggling to survive at grass roots level. Only the senior Keighley club remained, although it is possible that a number of 'scratch' sides - such as one at Ingrow – again began to operate around the early months of 1908. It is surprising that there was such a fall off in the number of local teams in the light of the fact that the town's professional club were enjoying a good deal of success at the time. This included a run through to the semi-final of the Challenge Cup competition in 1906, and qualification for the top 4 championship play-off's the following season, this despite the untimely death of favourite Harry Myers as a result of an accident in a league fixture against Dewsbury on 3rd November 1906.

The loss of half-back Myers was a major blow. Seen as a local hero, the highly skilled half-back had spent ten of his eleven seasons at Lawkholme Lane as captain, during which time the club had won both Yorkshire No.1 and No.2 competitions. He remains the Keighley club's only rugby union international, having played against Ireland at Twickenham in 1898, as well as being 'capped' 13 times for Yorkshire before the 'great split'.

An accidental collision with Dewsbury's Fred Richardson led to Myers sustaining serious spinal injuries in his final game at Crown Flatt. Despite regaining consciousness and absolving Richardson of all blame, he passed away at Keighley's Victoria Hospital on 19th December 1906, after having previously been treated at Dewsbury Infirmary. At the time of his death he was landlord at the Worth Valley Inn at Ingrow, having previously been in charge at the Fleece Tap and Brunswick Arms hostelries. Myers' death was felt all around town. Around the time of his death a musical production at the Queens Theatre included the following lyrics:

> ' If I could play half-back like Harry Myers
> Then I think I'd be satisfied with life'

Not surprisingly, these lyrics brought rapturous applause each night.

Faced with the prospect of their code dying a death at grassroots level, the professional northern union clubs soon realised that if they, and indeed the sport, were to survive, then something had to be done to introduce more young men to the sport. In turn they would benefit from signing-on the best of the new faces. Therefore the Keighley club were instrumental in the formation of the Keighley Intermediate League prior to the beginning of the 1908-09 campaign. A meeting in the August of 1908 at the Victoria Hotel, the club's headquarters, the new league was formally set in place. Other professional clubs were also instrumental in setting up such 'nursery' competitions for their townsfolk.

Eight clubs hoped to start the campaign in the new Keighley League, of which six, upon securing suitable fields, did so successfully: Keighley Clarence, Keighley Rangers, Ingrow, Steeton, Oakworth & Haworth. League rules stipulated that all players had to be 23 years of age or under, the reasoning behind this being that a grant from the County Committee would not be forthcoming for an 'open age' league.

Ingrow actually secured a ground at Cross Roads, which they hoped to share with a new Cross Roads club. Unfortunately the proposed new club never materialised and so Ingrow had sole use of the field instead. It was nice to see a reformed Steeton side, the previous incarnation having disbanded soon after winning the old Keighley Charity Cup competition, while there were great thing expected of the reformed Haworth, who for their first season in the new league were unfortunately unable to return to the old West Lane rugby ground. This field was being used by two local soccer teams, although by September 1909 the move back there was finally completed as one of the soccer clubs disbanded. With only six clubs in the league, it was decided that each should play the other four times - twice home, twice away - giving a total of 20 league fixtures each.

The impetus for the new league created was furthered when, in September 1908, Keighley Zingari was reborn. Wilfred Naylor was appointed club president, with T.W.Smith secretary and Arthur Slater as treasurer. They were hastily admitted to the Bradford & District League, and were allowed the use of Lawkholme Lane when Keighley were away, acquiring the services of former Bradford and Wigan professional Gomer Gunn. Thus they were the only 'open age' junior club in town. Unfortunately the side struggled throughout their campaign, and it wasn't until the end of February when they secured their first league points - a shock 11-3 defeat of high flying Stanningley. At the season's end, they had only Gomersal below them in the final standings.

Oakworth's league campaign was even more dire. Having lost their first 16 fixtures, a 0-0 draw in March against Ingrow saw them break their duck at last in the Keighley League, where crowds of up to 500 were being realised. Here there was a two horse race for the title, with Haworth pipping Keighley Clarence at the death. Steeton, who made no impression on the league leaders, at least made the semi final of the Bradford Intermediate Cup. In a season when Keighley's professional outfit drew 8-8 with the touring Australian national side, it was hoped that the 1908-09 season would see the rebirth of grassroots rugby in the town. Despite the promise shown in this season, there was a marked downturn in interest again the following season.

Prior to the 1909-10 campaign it was announced that of the local league clubs, Oakworth had decided to try their hand at soccer and that two others - Clarence and Steeton had disbanded. Steeton had in fact also abandoned rugby in favour of soccer. Therefore there were only four teams in the Keighley Intermediate League this season - Shamrocks joining the existing Ingrow, Haworth & Rangers clubs.

Following their return to West Lane, Haworth declared that they had enough players interested to form three teams - if only there were enough local leagues to field all three ! The side had a successful cup campaign, reaching the semi-final of the Bradford Intermediate Cup and then going one stage further in the Bradford Challenge Cup, where they met Caddy Field at Southowram. In the days when match reports usually came via the winning team only, there are no local reports of this cup final and therefore it can only be assumed that it was therefore lost by the locals.

What became of the local league however is unclear. Keighley Rangers swept all before them before Christmas, but the new year saw very few results appear in the local press for the competition. Keighley Zingari beat a Keighley League side 23-0 in the new year, although this representative team consisted of only Keighley Rangers and Ingrow players. With Haworth regularly on cup duty, it is likely that Shamrocks may have failed to complete the season (so much for their brief revival) and the league could have remained undecided. Press coverage of the Keighley Intermediate League was sparse to say the least.

Zingari were by now playing in either one or both of the Yorkshire Combination and Bradford & District Leagues. These competitions may have been one and the same but due to a lack of league tables and conflicting press make things unclear. It had actually been announced prior to the 1909-10 season that the side were no more, but they appear to have reformed - effectively as Keighley's 'A' string - in the early weeks of the campaign.

Not surprisingly there was no Keighley Intermediate League for the 1910-11 season as only Keighley and Keighley Zingari flew the flag in the town. Zingari themselves played friendly fixtures only this season.

BRADFORD & DISTRICT (JUNIOR) LEAGUE - Keighley sides
1898-99 - WORTH VILLAGE, RIDDLESDEN,
LEAGUE RECONSTITUTED AS A NORTHERN UNION LEAGUE
1899-1900 - WORTH VILLAGE, RIDDLESDEN, SILSDEN, *Withdrawn: SUTTON*
1900-01 - WORTH VILLAGE, SILSDEN,
1901-02 - WORTH VILLAGE, KEIGHLEY ST.ANNES, CROSS ROADS, KEIGHLEY CLARENCE, STEETON,
1902-03 - (division 1) WORTH VILLAGE, KEIGHLEY ST.ANNES, KEIGHLEY CLARENCE, CROSS ROADS, HAWORTH,
1903-04 - (division 1) HAWORTH, INGROW, *withdrawn: KEIGHLEY CLARENCE, WORTH VILLAGE*
(division 2) : *withdrawn: ST.ANNES GUILD*
1904-05 - HAWORTH *(KEIGHLEY OLICANA in YORKSHIRE SENIOR COMPETITION)*
1905-06 - HAWORTH, KEIGHLEY OLICANA
1908-10 - KEIGHLEY ZINGARI

1902-03 BRADFORD & DISTRICT (JUNIOR) LEAGUE

Final Table - division 1	P	W	L	D	Pts
Victoria Rangers	26	21	3	2	44
KEIGHLEY ST.ANNES	26	20	4	2	42
WORTH VILLAGE	26	16	4	6	38
Victoria United	26	17	5	4	38
Allerton	26	15	10	1	31
Pudsey Clarence	26	12	11	3	27
KEIGHLEY CLARENCE	26	12	11	3	27
Buttershaw	26	10	14	2	22
HAWORTH	26	9	14	3	21
CROSS ROADS	26	6	16	4	16
Greenfield	26	5	17	4	14
Croft & Perkins	26	5	17	4	14
Greengates	26	5	17	4	14
Lidget Green	26	4	16	6	14

1904-05 YORKSHIRE SENIOR COMPETITION

Final Table	P	W	D	L	Pts
Featherstone Rovers	20	16	1	3	33
Outwood Church	18	14	0	4	28
Saville Green	20	13	2	5	28
Ossett	14	10	1	3	21
Castleford Half Acre	19	9	0	10	18
Salterhebble	18	8	1	9	17
KLY OLICANA	18	8	0	10	16
Thrum Hall	18	6	1	11	13
Victoria United	15	3	1	11	7
Underbank Rangers	17	3	0	14	6
Kinsley	10	2	1	7	5
York Celtic	7	1	0	6	2

KEIGHLEY & DISTRICT JUNIOR LGE COMPOSITIONS (NORTHERN UNION)
1900-01: ST.ANNES, WORTH VILLAGE JUNIORS, CROSS ROADS, KEIGHLEY CLARENCE, SUTTON, Gilstead, Bingley Trinity, Gargrave
1901-02: PARK LANE ALBION, INGROW TRINITY, KEIGHLEY CLARENCE 'A', UTLEY, ST.ANNES GUILD, STEETON 'A', Ilkley, Denholme Juniors, Bingley Clarence,
1902-03: INGROW, ST.ANNES GUILD, STOCKBRIDGE, HAWORTH RANGERS, Bingley Clarence. *Withdrawn: UTLEY. MORTON*

KEIGHLEY INTERMEDIATE LEAGUE COMPOSITIONS (NORTHERN UNION)
1908-09: HAWORTH, KEIGHLEY CLARENCE, KEIGHLEY RANGERS, INGROW, STEETON, OAKWORTH. *Failed to start season: CROSS ROADS, Bingley,*
1909-10: KEIGHLEY RANGERS, HAWORTH, KEIGHLEY SHAMROCKS, INGROW

Note: 'Intermediate' status applied at that time to 'youths' who had left school

ZINGARI FLY THE FLAG

Following a year of playing friendly fixtures, Zingari made the decision to join the Leeds & District League in the summer of 1911. This league contained a mixture of junior clubs and 'A' teams of professional clubs. The competition was organised in the same way as the Northern Union Championship of the time, whereas clubs had to fulfil a certain number of fixtures to qualify for end-of-season play offs, rather than having to meet all other clubs home and away. The local club actually considered withdrawing from the competition prior to the start of the season when they encountered difficulties in arranging fixtures with their opponents, and a switch to the Halifax & District League considered.

Once they had managed to arrange - and indeed play - fixtures in their preferred league, things went well on the field. They won the majority of league fixtures, finishing just outside the play-offs, but had their biggest success in the Halifax Charity Cup. Following a defeat of a strong Halifax Campbells side in the semi final, they met Rastrick in the deciding tie at Thrum Hall.

Rastrick were completely overwhelmed by Zingari, who scored three tries through Rhodes, Taylor and Hewson (the first two of which were converted by Bateson, who also scored a penalty later on). Rhodes, along with two Rastrick players, was sent from the field for fighting late in the game, but this did not detract from the side's first ever success in local cup competition (although the previous Zingari club did win the Keighley Charity Cup), and they later dined at the Kings Arms Hotel to celebrate. This in a season when the senior Keighley club encountered a poor campaign.

The successful Keighley Zingari team in the 1911-12 Halifax Charity Cup final was: *Watmough (back), Smith, Hey, Rhodes, Hewson (three-quarter backs), Bateson, Taylor (half-backs), J.Feather, Pickles, Wilkinson, Martin, Brooksbank & Mountain (forwards).*

There was less success for Zingari in the Leeds & District Cup that season, losing to Hunslet in a replayed match after the first game had been abandoned due to the poor behaviour of the players from each side. Meanwhile there were three other sides operating in Keighley this season - Ingrow, Haworth and Exley Head playing friendly fixtures against each other. It is unclear whether they were around the following season although it is unclear whether the former two were related to earlier sides of the same name.

Following such a successful campaign, Zingari opted to play in both Leeds and Halifax Leagues for the 1912-13 campaign. Unfortunately the high hopes that went with it were not realised. Only one Leeds League fixture was won all season, and it wasn't until after Christmas that they managed to string together a reasonable run of results in the Halifax competition. Understandably, only one league was entered for the 1913-14 season - the Halifax & District competition. Things turned out much better this time around, and by Christmas they were challenging for the title along with Rastrick (on whose ground Zingari opened their campaign with an excellent victory) and Todmorden. At the season's end they were third in the table, thus qualifying for the top-four championship play-offs, but were unfortunately defeated by Rastrick in their semi-final tie.

There was better luck in the Halifax Charity Cup, where Zingari won the trophy for the second time in three seasons. Following a 13-0 defeat of Catherine Slack in front of 2000 at Lawkholme in the semi, Halifax Territorials were then defeated 3-2 in a tight final at Thrum Hall. There was also a useful run in the Northern Rugby Junior Cup, where Bradford Northern Juniors were defeated en route to a fourth round tie, which was lost, against Dewsbury's junior side.

A revived Keighley Junior League was again mooted at the end of the 1913-14 season, but this failed to materialise due a lack of clubs in the area and the obvious onset of war. Zingari did continue in the first war-time season, but made no impact in the Halifax League and were wound up during 1915. From 1915 there was a ban on competitive rugby, and like the association game, professional clubs were forced into hibernation or the playing of 'friendly' fixtures only. The amateur game disappeared completely and the local mensfolk took to new battlefields of far more importance than the playing fields of Keighley.

WORTH VILLAGE JUNIORS, 1920-21 Keighley Workshops competition winners

THE 1920'S

The senior Keighley club, along with Huddersfield, returned to competitive action twelve months after the rest of the professional northern union clubs. Due to the re-laying of the Lawkholme pitch and other improvements being made to the ground, the club were forced to use a ground at Stockbridge early season 1919-20. With over 50 players signed on, an 'A' team was entered in the Halifax Junior League, which consisted of several 'A' teams of professional clubs as well as junior clubs from the Halifax, Huddersfield and Bradford areas.

Unfortunately there was no reformation of Keighley Zingari after the war, the first junior club to reappear in the town being a revived Shamrocks prior to the 1920-21 season. They played alongside Keighley 'A' in the Halifax League (Keighley 'A' also played in the Northern Combination, a league for professional club's 'A' teams) but spent the campaign in the lower reaches of the division. Keighley 'A' meanwhile lost a play-off for the title to the all-conquering Wyke team.

Shamrocks played at Calversyke Hill, their first match at home to Bradford Northern 'A', which was lost 3-6 but played in front of around 1000 spectators. The Shamrocks team on that day was: *Meegan, B.Cummings, Holme, W.Cummings, Watson, McCormack, Bailey, Corbey, Golding, Humphries, Green, Gerrard, Darcy.*
Although finishing near the foot of the table they enjoyed some fine victories, their first in October at home to Oakenshaw (24-3) and their best, 29-0 against Idle.

Keighley held a workshops competition at the end of the 1920-21 season, Worth Village Juniors defeating Silsden 17-0 in the final. The workshops competitions of this time created a massive impetus to forming new or revived clubs in the town, and in fact within months the same Silsden side had officially reformed. Village went on the win the following season's workshop competition organised by the new Silsden club and were runners up to Bingley in the second Keighley club competition, before themselves forming a new junior side to play in the local league in 1922.

In December 1920, several 'old boys' of the Keighley Trade & Grammar School saw fit to form a new *rugby union* side in the town. Not since the formation of northern union (rugby league) had the old code been played in Keighley, but the new club was promised substantial financial backing by it's patrons. In true Grammar School style, the current head of the school, T.P.Watson became the first president of the new club and several fixtures were organised before the season's end, home fixtures played on a ground at Utley. By the start of the 1921-22 season a ground at Stockbridge, previously used by Keighley Town AFC, had been procured, and the Keighlians, as they were called, were well and truly up and running ! An opening

34

25-0 defeat of Baildon opened the season, the services of C.F.K Watson, (a Cambridge 'blue' and Scottish international) having been obtained for the season.

Following the war, there was a 'boom' in local rugby and association football. The number of clubs in the Keighley & District soccer league went through the roof, but there was still a dearth of rugby clubs in the Keighley and Bradford areas. However, a Bradford League was reborn, with six clubs forming a junior division - Keighley Shamrocks and Silsden included, with a seven strong Intermediate Division also running. This division actually contained four new Keighley clubs - 6th Duke of Wellington Regiment, Lawkholme Clarence, Utley St.Marks & Silsden 'A'. The sport was in fact now officially *'rugby league'*, having changed 'titles' in June 1922.

Reformed Silsden had secured a ground on Hainsworth Road, owned by the Hanson family, who were to become influential in the running of the club. Their first game was a friendly at home to Keighley 'A', which they lost 3-7. It was kicked off by Dr John Purcell, who had been instrumental in the formation of the original club back in 1883. Silsden had more than enough young men interested in playing for them, hence the introduction of a second team in the Intermediate League. Unfortunately their Bradford League campaign ended in chaos when league leaders Bradford Northern 'A' (due to dissention among their players) and Birstall Celtic (through a loss of players and financial problems) both withdrew from the league after Christmas ! As no other side could hope to overtake Northern's points total the championship was declared null & void, although a four team subsidiary competition between the four remaining teams was originally mooted. Silsden and Shamrocks had enjoyed some close encounters, Silsden winning by just one point on two occasions - 10-9 in the league and 3-2 in a qualifying round of the Northern Union Cup.

There was much better news in the Intermediate league however. Utley St.Marks won the title, defeating Silsden in a play-off at Lawkholme 2-0, a first half goal by Wilkinson being the only difference between the sides. Silsden did win some silverware in their inaugural season however, winning the league cup final 11-2 against Sticker Lane 'A' in front of 1500 at Birch Lane, Bradford. The league cup had been played in two groups - the four Keighley sides in a 'Keighley division' and the three Bradford clubs inn their own section, the winners playing off for the cup.

Professional Keighley, meanwhile, had endured three dire seasons in the Northern Union, so success at junior level at least gave rugby lovers in the town some satisfaction. Further good news for the local game came when a local league was at last reformed. A meeting at the end of the 1921-22 season was attended by 11 interested clubs, and with Utley St.Marks interested but not present, it was hoped that a combination consisting of 12 clubs could be formed for the 1922-23 season.

In the event, the Keighley & District League was reborn with eight clubs. Six from the meeting - Silsden (who entered their 'A' team), Knowle Park, Lawkholme Clarence, Keighley Low Street, Worth Village and Keighley Shamrocks (who had stepped down from the Bradford League), were joined by Keighley Hornets and Keighley Temperance Club. This led to a league with a number of newly formed clubs joining some established names.

Of the five clubs who had attended the original meeting - the 6th Duke of Wellington club appear to have disbanded, while Steeton, Fell Lane, St.Annes and Eastwood Rangers also failed to start the season. Utley St.Marks meanwhile elected to remain in the Bradford League, alongside Silsden in the single junior division, although by the start of the 1923-24 season they had jumped on the bandwagon and joined the Keighley soccer league instead !

The new Keighley Northern Union league was junior in status, and was titled 'Keighley & District Intermediate League', but it opted not to have an age limit. Each club was allowed to have no more than two first class northern union players in their side, and professionals on their books had to have played less than six times with their professional club.

There were a number of one sided matches in the local league in the first season 1922-23. Silsden achieved several high scoring victories, not least a 78-2 rout of the short lived Hornets club, but they were defeated 2-5 in a championship play-off by Worth Village in front of 800 spectators at Lawkholme at the season's end. The cobbydalers first team did win the Bradford League title though, a 2-0 success against Wyke in March 1923 sealing it.

Silsden had a disappointing campaign in the Bradford League the following year, and at times struggled to raise a competitive side. The local team of the season this season - 1923-24 - were Keighley Low Street, who had just stepped up from the Keighley League. They made the semi-final of both Halifax Charity and Bradford District cup competitions, but went on to defeat Windhill 12-0 in the Bradford League championship play-off at Birch Lane to lift the 'Yorkshire Sports Shield'.

Parkwood Hornets won the Keighley League, which also ran two youth sections this season (17-20 years & 14-17 years), and despite having problems finding committee men and finance the local league ran a team in the Yorkshire League's Intermediate Cup competition. Unfortunately the Keighley League were subsequently hammered 3-63 in their first round tie at Featherstone against a Wakefield League select, their only score being a try awarded for obstruction against Helliwell.

Despite poor attendances and overall support, which would lead to the demise of several local clubs over the following years, the Keighley Intermediate League managed at last to attract enough teams to make it viable, even though the better clubs in the town looked towards other competition.

One of these, Silsden, made the brave decision to join the Yorkshire Senior Competition for the 1924-25 campaign. In the light of recent problems this was indeed a strange development, and even more surprisingly they were accepted into the competition. They, along with Wyke and Elland, were the only first teams in a competition that was in essence a second team tournament for professional clubs. They opened with a 19-8 victory at home to Elland, but not surprisingly Silsden struggled in this grade of competition. A second league win, in February, was expunged from the table when their opponents on this occasion, Wyke, withdrew from the league. The locals suffered some heavy defeats, although at times the Hainsworth Road outfit did themselves no favours though, turning up at Huddersfield with only 9 men, and going down 0-94 in a 12-a-side game, after the homesters lent them 3 players ! Not surprisingly then, Silsden too resigned from the league following this debacle, in March 1925, citing an inability to raise a team.

Low Street meanwhile won their second successive 'Yorkshire Sports Shield' when Hipperholme were defeated 15-2 in the Bradford League championship decider. In a game marred by the 'overkeenness' of both sets of players, Low Street scored two tries, through Slater and former Keighley player J.Gamble. It was unfortunate then that the side folded up during the summer of 1925.

Worth Village, Silsden 'A' and Keighley Supporters went on to win the next three Keighley league titles. Village, winners in 1924-25 were defunct by the summer of 1926, while Keighley Supporters beat their own second team in a play-off at the end of the 1926-27 season after second placed title holders Silsden' A' had been expelled for non-fulfilment of fixtures.

Local sides were out of the honours in the Bradford League for a few seasons until Silsden's 13-0 victory against Bradford Northern Supporters in the 1926-27 league cup final. It was a credit to those in charge of the club that the team was able to recover from the trials and tribulations of the previous campaign. A league championship play-off against Windhill was unfortunately lost however (2-5).

1926-27 saw Keighley Highfield replace Worth Village in the Bradford League, and they proved an instant hit in their first season. The newcomers were formed by rugby league stalwart Ayrton Anderton, who had previously been in charge at Village, and they would have finished as runner-up in the league, but had two points deducted for playing an ineligible player in a game against Bradford Northern Supporters. As a result they finished level on points - joint second - with Silsden, and lost to their local rivals in a play-off to decide who played Windhill in the championship decider. Highfield did defeat Silsden 5-0 in the semi final of the Bradford Cup, but went down to a redoubtable Lindley team in the final at Birch Lane.

The remaining years of the 1920's saw Silsden, Keighley Highfield and Keighley Supporters fly the flag for the town in the Bradford League, which operated with an open age (junior) section and Intermediate section. The three local teams ran teams in both divisions, and were joined from 1928-29 by a new club, Keighley Northern Juniors, who had been formed at the beginning of that season by a Mr.R.Thomas, one of the driving forces behind junior rugby in the town. Bradford's Intermediate section, with the exception of Bradford Northern Supporters Club, was made up entirely of Keighley sides, who also made up the numbers in a reduced Keighley & District League.

Keighley Supporters enjoyed a successful 1927-28 season when they lifted a revived 'Charity Cup' competition in aid of the town's Victoria Hospital. A different trophy had to be used though, as the old one was still being used by local soccer sides. The first final saw the 34-strong Bradford Kilties Band march through the town prior to the match before parading round the Lawkholme Lane field accompanied by bagpipes & bugles! Following that, the Supporters Club accounted for Sowerby Bridge West End (who had been defeated by Silsden in their semi-final but won on appeal) 9-5.

Supporters and Highfield drew 3-3 in a decider for the Bradford Intermediate title this season, the result of the replay has been lost in the midst of time, but it is likely that it was Highfield who won the game, as well as the Keighley League title.

Silsden, who could depend at times on the services of Bradford Northern's Jack Thornber, a product of the Hainsworth Road club, returned to form in the 1928-29 season. Their final two seasons in the Bradford League saw them contest a total of EIGHT cup finals !

1928-29 –*(1) Keighley Hospitals Cup - lost 8-21 to Eastmoor (Wakefield) at Lawkholme Lane, attendance: 2000, (lost to Stainland in semi but won on appeal)*
(2) Keighley Intermediate League championship play-off : Silsden were losing 6-10 to Keighley Supporters until the tie was abandoned due to fighting, Supporters awarded the title. The Keighley League season did not begin until November of this campaign !
(3) Bradford Intermediate Division championship play-off for the 'Wilson Shield': lost 3-4 to Keighley Supporters at Keighley Highfield's ground. Supporters won through two Hodgson penalties, following an earlier Stacey try for the cobbydalers. Silsden & Keighley Highfield made no impression on the leaders in a very strong Open-age division.
(4) Bradford Northern Workshops Competition Final: beat Baildon Woodbottom 3-0, at Birch Lane, Bradford,
1929-30 – *(5) Keighley League play-off: beat Keighley Northern Juniors 8-5 at Lawkholme Lane, 1200 spectators,*
(6) Bradford & District u/21's decider: beat Keighley Northern Juniors 3-2 (after 5-5 draw)
(7) Halifax Cup: lost 5-35 to Calder Valley at Thrum Hall. Silsden were missing Summerscales, Watson, Sykes & Cryer who were all on duty for Bradford Northern

(8) Bradford League Final play off: beat Keighley Highfield 9-4 at Lawkholme Lane (despite complaints that Silsden had played ineligible players)

A benefit match was played towards the end of the 1928-29 season between a Keighley League select and Keighley 'A', for league official Ayrton Anderton, who had been burned by molten metal at work. Workshop competitions were also organised again at the season's end, by the Keighley club, and for the first time by Keighley Highfield, who had a cup presented by Montague Burton Ltd.

Silsden also made the semi-final of the Yorkshire Intermediate Cup during the 1929-30 campaign. After defeating a strong Siddal outfit in the quarter-final, they went out at the penultimate stage 0-8 against Huddersfield outfit Leeds Road, who were almost enjoying advantage - the tie played at the Huddersfield club's Fartown ground. Despite this, there was still a huge gulf between Keighley & Bradford junior sides and those from elsewhere in the county. This fact was made painfully obvious in the 1929-30 Charity Cup final, when Eastmoor won the second of their three successive victories in the competition with an emphatic 38-0 victory over Keighley Highfield, despite the local team having home advantage at Lawkholme Lane.

BRADFORD & DISTRICT (JUNIOR) LEAGUE COMPOSITIONS
(Keighley sides only)
1919-20 - KEIGHLEY 'A'
1920-21 - KEIGHLEY 'A', KEIGHLEY SHAMROCKS
1921-22 - Junior (Open-age) Division: SILSDEN, KEIGHLEY SHAMROCKS, Intermediate Division: SILSDEN A', UTLEY ST.MARKS, LAWKHOLME CLARENCE, DUKE OF WELLINGTON REGIMENT,
1922-23 - SILSDEN, UTLEY ST.MARKS
1923-24 - SILSDEN, KEIGHLEY LOW STREET, WORTH VILLAGE,
1924-25 - KEIGHLEY LOW STREET, MALTONIANS, WORTH VILLAGE *(SILSDEN in YORKSHIRE SENIOR COMPETITION this season)*
1925-26 - SILSDEN, WORTH VILLAGE
1926-27 - SILSDEN, KEIGHLEY HIGHFIELD
1927-28 - Junior (Open-age) Division: SILSDEN, KEIGHLEY HIGHFIELD, Intermediate Division: SILSDEN, KEIGHLEY HIGHFIELD, KEIGHLEY SUPPORTERS
1928-29 - Junior (Open-age) Division: SILSDEN, KEIGHLEY HIGHFIELD, Intermediate Division: SILSDEN, KEIGHLEY HIGHFIELD, KEIGHLEY SUPPORTERS, KEIGHLEY NORTHERN JUNIORS,
1929-30 - Junior (open-age) Division: SILSDEN, KEIGHLEY HIGHFIELD, Intermediate Division: SILSDEN, KEIGHLEY HIGHFIELD, KEIGHLEY NORTHERN JUNIORS,

KEIGHLEY & DISTRICT INTERMEDIATE LEAGUE COMPOSITIONS
1922-23 - SILSDEN 'A', KNOWLE PARK, LAWKHOLME CLARENCE, KEIGHLEY LOW STREET, WORTH VILLAGE, KEIGHLEY SHAMROCKS, KEIGHLEY HORNETS, KEIGHLEY TEMPERANCE CLUB,
1923-24 - KEIGHLEY LOW STREET, PARKWOOD HORNETS, MALTONIANS, KEIGHLEY NELSON, KNOWLE PARK, WORTH VILLAGE, SILSDEN 'A', KEIGHLEY SHAMROCKS (youth divisions only), Windhill, *withdrawn: SILSDEN 'A',*

1924-25 - PARKWOOD HORNETS, WORTH VILLAGE, SILSDEN RANGERS ('A'), THWAITES ROVERS, Windhill Rangers,
1925-26 - SILSDEN 'A'. PARKWOOD HORNETS, BEECHCLIFFE CELTIC, GREENGATE CELTIC, KNOWLE PARK, OAKWORTH ROAD HORNETS,
1926-27 - KEIGHLEY SUPPORTERS 'A', KEIGHLEY SUPPORTERS 'B', OAKWORTH ROAD HORNETS, DALTON SWIFTS, GREENGATE CELTIC, expelled: SILSDEN 'A', *(Addingham & Keighley Highfield also played a full series of fixtures against Keighley League teams)*
1927-28 - SILSDEN, KEIGHLEY SUPPORTERS 'A', KEIGHLEY SUPPORTERS 'B', SPRINGFIELD HORNETS/ROVERS, KEIGHLEY HIGHFIELD,
1928-29 - SILSDEN, KEIGHLEY SUPPORTERS, KEIGHLEY HIGHFIELD, KEIGHLEY NORTHERN JUNIORS,
1929-30 - SILSDEN, KEIGHLEY HIGHFIELD, KEIGHLEY NORTHERN JUNIORS,

A photograph that, it was thought, contained the successful Worth Village team of 1927-28. Village were actually defunct by this time and it is more likely to be **KEIGHLEY HIGHFIELD**, *who were formed by Ayrton Anderton, who left Village in 1926. The shields are likely to have been the Bradford & Keighley Intermediate League trophies. Back: the Middleton brothers, Maiden, McGowan, Anderton, Mitchell, Middle: Stansfield, Riley, Whittaker, Robinson, Meekin, Jackson, Anderton (ballboy). Front: Coupland, Calvert, Holmes, Moore,*

KEIGHLEY RLFC BOYS 1925-26

This was their first season, and they played in the West Yorkshire Supporters League before moving on, successfully to the Bradford and Keighley Intermediate Leagues

OAKWORTH ROAD HORNETS 1925-26

The side played in the Keighley Intermediate League in this, and the following season Back: Mr.Whtran, J.Meegan, B.Cone, H.Middleton, J.Hugill, unknown, L.McIntyre, A.Frith, Middle: G.Middleton, unknown, E.Farrah, T.Halligan, F.Longley, D.Pinder, Front: H.Green, Ickringill,

41

THE 1930'S - THE FALL AND RISE OF RUGBY LEAGUE

The 1930's opened with only two remaining junior rugby clubs in the district, following the demise of both Keighley Supporters and Northern clubs over the previous two summers. As a result there was no more Keighley League, and the Charity Cup ran for only two more seasons - Eastmoor beating Leeds team Buslingthorpe Vale 11-0 in 1930-31 and Keighley Highfield defeating Silsden 7-3 the following year, when it is likely that the two were the only teams invited to take part.

Silsden took part in a second successive Halifax Cup final. Rochdale League leaders and cup holders Calder Valley failed to turn up for their semi-final tie at Hainsworth Road, so Silsden met old rivals Rastrick in the deciding match - unfortunately going down 3-10. The same season they reached the top-four play-offs in the Leeds League but went down to Lindley in their semi-final tie. Silsden had joined this league in order to boost gates- and ultimately finances, although they did keep teams in the Bradford League alongside Keighley Highfield, who enjoyed a fine season and lifted the league title with some ease.

Silsden and Highfield both experienced life in the Leeds League, neither team continuously, as well as in the Bradford League, where junior (open-age) and Intermediate divisions (average age 21) were still run. Highfield spent the 1933-34 season playing as Haworth Highfield, although a return to the town was made the following year. Keighley Rangers appeared briefly in the early stages of the 1931-32 season, failing to last beyond the new year, while Keighley Temperance club also reformed a team which played friendly fixtures between 1932-34. Marshall Roe, who had previously been at the Keighley Supporters and Keighley RL club was 'employed' as club trainer but the side never aspired to playing in league competition.

Keighley rugby league club organised the 'Montague Burton Cup' competition for workshop teams - amongst the winners were Guardhouse in 1931 and 'Twelve Apostles' a year later. The West Yorkshire Road Car Company won in 1936, when the game was held up due to the guest appearance of the German 'Hindenburg' airship. The massive 804 feet long flying machine, en route from the USA to Frankfurt, dropped a parcel over Keighley High Street containing, amongst other things, a bunch of carnations, a small silver and jet crucifix and a message, written on Hindenburg notepaper. The finder of the parcel was asked, via this message, to deposit the goods on the grave of one Lieutenant Franz Schulte. It transpired that the brother of the said German officer, a prisoner of war who had died of influenza at Morton Banks Hospital in 1919, was on board the 'Hindenburg' at the time, the event arousing much national as well as local interest. However, the seemingly erratic course of the German airship suggested a much darker explanation for this, one of two local visits made prior to the Second World War. Spying mission or not, the local rugby scene would soon be affected by Hitler.

Local press coverage of the sport was at this time at an all-time low, the Highfield club did not send in reports of their games to the Keighley News, so there was no coverage of their Bradford League final in 1936, or of their final season, played out in the Leeds League. However, things were to dramatically change in 1937. The town suddenly endured a 'rugby-frenzy' when, for the first and only time, Keighley Rugby League club reached the Challenge Cup final. The local press ensured that the tie received maximum coverage, both before and afterwards, and although the locals were lost at Wembley to Widnes, there was a renewed enthusiasm for the sport again.

It was not immediately obvious that the local junior scene was to benefit. The 1937-38 season opened with Silsden playing 'friendly' fixtures only, although a number of newer sides such as Woodhouse Rovers were known to have started playing informal games too. However, behind the scenes things were very different. By January 1938 it was announced that another new Keighley & District League was to be formed. The representatives of 15 potential clubs attended a meeting at the Irish National Club in town that month, while Silsden agreed to lend aspiring teams their ground when they were playing away from home. Not all of these clubs actually appeared in the league, although it is possible that they were eventually formed with different titles.

Furthermore, there was enough interest in the game to form two sections - a Junior (Open-age) and Intermediate (average age 21), although with the new organisation starting so late it was decided to initially play 'friendly' fixtures, with a knock-out cup being organised for each section. The well established Silsden side were not surprisingly the strongest junior outfit, enjoying some large victories before a 14-5 defeat of Keighley Juniors in the Keighley League Junior Cup final. Victoria Park proved the outstanding Intermediate team, enjoying an easy 26-8 success against Aireworth Swifts in the Intermediate Cup final.

The only non-Keighley team in the league was Bingley. It was reported that this was the first rugby league / northern union club in the town since 1903, and was formed from the employees of the Parkland Manufacturing Company. Former Keighley and Silsden player N.Summerscales was said to be instrumental in their formation , which began the season playing at 'The Oval', Park Road (also known as the Oakwood Hall ground) before moving to Manor Park at Gilstead.

The new league was a resounding success, and the 1938-39 season saw many of the new clubs re-appear for the first full season of fixtures. A regular league programme was organised for the first half of the season, followed by a Charity

Cup league programme for Junior Section teams, and a 'Sam Slater' Cup, again on a league basis, for Intermediate clubs over the second half of the season. The season was concluded with play-offs from the first half of the season and final ties for the second competitions. League president this season was Sam Slater himself, with J.R.Wilson chairman, and P.Pullan secretary.

Dudley Hill won all of their Junior League fixtures to finish well clear of Silsden and Shamrocks (who had by now adopted the familiar title of 'Keighley Shamrocks'). However, owing to fixture clashes, they withdrew from the Charity Cup league and were replaced by Halifax side Luddendenfoot who promptly finished top of the group. The end of season play-offs did not go as planned though. The league championship final between Shamrocks (10-3 victors over Silsden in the semi-final) and Dudley Hill (resounding 40-2 victors over Keighley Rangers) went the way of the Keighley club. They scored three tries - through Unsworth, Foster & Moore, the latter of which was successfully converted by Foy - to win 11-4. The Charity Cup final ended in a 6-6 draw, after extra-time, between New Road Side, who were based at Hermit Hole, and Luddendenfoot. The trophy was therefore shared.

The Intermediate finals both resulted in expected victories for Victoria Park however. Ingrow were the unlucky finals in both League and 'Sam Slater' competitions, going down 3-19 and 0-19 respectively to the favourites. Victoria Park enjoyed a fine run in the Yorkshire Intermediate Cup this season, making it through to the semi-final where they met the holders, Hunslet Carr. Despite leading through a Roe penalty at half time they were eventually defeated 2-19 by the strong Leeds outfit.

The season however, was marred by the death of 19-year-old Silsden player Philip Royston, who received an accidental blow to the head in a game against Keighley Caledonians in April 1939. A benefit match at Lawkholme Lane for his widow raised £90, and despite an inquest returning a verdict of accidental death all of Silsden's remaining games were cancelled as a mark of respect.

There was no doubt at all that the new Keighley League had been a resounding success. Unfortunately the spectre of more local deaths was imminent - in the shape of the Second World War. The local league had been approached by the Halifax League with a view to a merger between the two, but in the event, a Keighley Junior League was forced to start late due to the onset of hostilities. Even then, several teams, including Silsden, had already decided to withdraw due to problems in raising enough men to field a competitive team. The league was only a few weeks old when the four remaining Keighley clubs - Rangers, Shamrocks, Caledonians and New Road Side agreed to a merger as they were all suffering from a lack of players. The league, as planned, was therefore abandoned as the four clubs became two. 'Lawkholme' and 'Worth Village' combination sides were thus formed to play against other sides in the league - Bingley, Luddendenfoot, Queensbury &

Dudley Hill, the latter of whom joined just in time. In the event, the league was not finished, and it is more than likely that the only team to complete the season, which was also hampered by a poor winter, were Ingrow, who competed with a good degree of success in the Bradford Intermediate League.

1937-38 KEIGHLEY & DISTRICT LEAGUE:
JUNIOR (OPEN-AGE) TEAMS: SILSDEN, ST.ANNES, HIGHFIELD SHAMROCKS, KEIGHLEY CALEDONIANS, KEIGHLEY RANGERS, HOLME MILLS, KEIGHLEY JUNIORS, NEW ROAD SIDE, WOODHOUSE RANGERS, Bingley,
INTERMEDIATE TEAMS (AVERAGE 21): WORTH VILLAGE, PARKWOOD, AIREWORTH ATHLETIC, HAWORTH, VICTORIA PARK, INGROW, OAKWORTH,
JOINED LEAGUE BUT DID NOT PLAY ANY FIXTURES: DEAN SMITH & GRACE, WARD, HAGGAS & SMITH,
AT ORIGINAL MEETING BUT DID NOT JOIN LEAGUE: SHOWFIELD, CO-OPERATIVE IRONWORKS, BROOMHILL, DEVONSHIRE WORKS,

1938-39 KEIGHLEY & DISTRICT LEAGUE:
JUNIOR (OPEN-AGE) DIVISION: SILSDEN, ST.ANNES, NEW ROAD SIDE, KEIGHLEY RANGERS, KEIGHLEY (GUARDHOUSE/HIGHFIELD) SHAMROCKS, KEIGHLEY JUNIORS, KEIGHLEY CALEDONIANS, Bingley, Queensbury, Dudley Hill, (Dudley Hill did not compete in the Charity Cup, but were replaced by Luddendenfoot) Keighley Juniors folded in December 1938
INTERMEDIATE DIVISION: NEW ROAD SIDE, OAKWORTH, INGROW, HAWORTH, VICTORIA PARK, WORTH VILLAGE, Queensbury, *(Haworth and Oakworth withdrew from Slater Cup late in the season)*

1939-40 KEIGHLEY & DISTRICT LEAGUE:
JUNIOR DIVISION: KEIGHLEY SHAMROCKS, KEIGHLEY RANGERS, KEIGHLEY CALEDONIANS, NEW ROAD SIDE, Bingley, Queensbury, Luddendenfoot - league abandoned & reorganised. The 4 Keighley clubs merged to form 2 new combinations.
REORGANISED LEAGUE: LAWKHOLME, WORTH VILLAGE, Queensbury, Bingley, Luddendenfoot, Dudley Hill - league not completed.
INGROW played in the Bradford Intermediate League this season.

RECOVERY, ALBION TO THE FORE

Rugby League did not shut down completely during World War 2. Keighley rugby league club played in wartime competition, while at grassroots level, Ingrow and Keighley Boys played in the Bradford & District League during the 1940-41 season, although only the latter were around for the following two campaigns. 1943-44 saw a Keighley Workshops Junior Rugby League formed with 4 teams. Three - Prince Smiths, Dean Smith & Grace and John Lunds - were works teams comprising those too young, old, or incapacitated, to fight. Keighley Juniors (formerly Keighley Boys) were the other team. The competition proved successful, with Dean Smiths defeating Prince Smiths in the final in front of 1000 spectators at Lawkholme (a Foy penalty and two tries the difference between the sides). Hargreaves Company and Riddlesden were also affiliated to the workshop competition, but did not take part in regular league fixtures. There was also, seemingly, a separate Keighley League this season, the Keighley News carrying a report of Prince Smith's defeat of Hunslet in the final, which they won through a last minute penalty goal from Inman after trailing by 11 points at one stage in the game.

Of all local manufacturing firms in the Keighley district to have fielded sports teams over the years, the name of Prince Smith & Stells must surely stand out ahead of the rest. The company developed its own sports club for employees, and with some of the best facilities in town were the envy of many in local cricket, soccer and rugby league circles. The company, formed through the merger of machine makers Hall & Stells and Prince Smith & Sons during the depression of the 1930's was instrumental in the country's war effort. With the introduction of female workers as part of the war effort, over one million spike bayonets were produced in its factories during the war years. The Prince Smith's name finally disappeared when the company was swallowed up by the larger, out of town Platt International in 1970.

Dean Smith & Grace was another company of machine tool makers who sponsored their own works team. Although their rugby team was only around for a few years, DSG became better known in local circles for their highly successful Sunday soccer league team.

Keighley Juniors renamed themselves Keighley Athletic for the 1944-45 season, joining the Huddersfield & District League alongside Prince Smith's & Dean Smith's. Strangely, Athletic played a four-legged Huddersfield Cup-tie against Netherton this season, losing 39-32 on aggregate! There was more success in the Bradford Cup however, Bradford Northern Juniors thrashed over two legs in the final, the second leg being played at Lawkholme Lane when Athletic had to lend Northern three players.

The following season saw only Athletic operating in league competition, but they were joined in the Halifax League late in the 1946-47 season by a revived Silsden, who took over the fixtures of Hunslet Engineering Company in February. Silsden had been reformed around October 1946, although the not inconsiderable sum of £150 was needed to re-equip the club for league competition. It was clearly going to take time before normality was to return to local sport, rationing continued for some time after the cessation of hostilities and reviving Keighley's junior rugby clubs was not high on the agenda. However, a revived Keighley & District League for the 1947-48 season was clearly an intention. Unfortunately only Silsden and Athletic were again playing competitive fixtures that season, this time in the Bradford League.

1947-48 was the season when rugby union made a comeback as Keighlians not only secured a new field at Thwaites, but achieved a fantastic Yorkshire Shield and Cup double. The Shield competition was organised to run concurrently with the early rounds of the more prestigious County Cup, prior to the entry of the seeded teams. After a 14-3 semi-final defeat of Old Leodiensians at Cleckheaton, Keighlians first ever Shield final saw them pitted against Sheffield, at Otley. Their 17-0 success, in front of 1000 spectators, including the Mayor & Mayoress of Keighley (Mr. & Mrs. J.H.Wright). This achievement in itself was a high enough honour, but the Keighlians were on a roll and were soon in their second final!

3000 spectators saw the locals defeat Huddersfield at Ovenden Park, Halifax, in the semi-final, the first time the Keighley side had been this far in the competition since 1924. Their 9-3 victory not only saw a final against Otley, but it was played at neutral Skipton, just up the road from Keighley. The 14-9 victory for Keighlians has never been repeated, but they went down in history as the first side ever to do the 'cup double' in Yorkshire rugby union circles. The following team represented Keighlians in the Yorkshire Cup final against Otley: *J.S.Smith, E.Clapham, L.Buckley (vice-captain), J.Ramsden, C.Shackleton, H.Fennerty, T.Fletcher, F.Spencer, K.Pickles, A.Hirst, H.L.Handley, C.Fearnside, G.S.Swift (captain), F.Kidd, K.Paver.* The same team beat Sheffield in the earlier Yorkshire Shield final, except that D.Pritchard had played in place of F.Spencer.

KEIGHLIANS - YORKSHIRE RUGBY UNION CUP TIES 1947-48
Rounds 1 & 2 - byes

Round 3 - Duke of Wellingtons		(a)	18-10
Round 4 - Baildon		(a)	16-0
Round 5 - Scarborough		(a)	12-3
Round 6 - Old Roundhegians		(h)	3-0
Q-F -	Old Hymerians	(h)	14-6
S-F -	Huddersfield	(at Halifax)	9-3
FINAL - Otley		(at Skipton)	14-9

While all this was happening, a Keighley League - of sorts - was formed in rugby league circles for the 1948-49 season. With only five clubs entered - Silsden and Keighley Athletic joined by 'new-boys' Keighley Co-op, Riddlesden, and Prince Smith & Stells, it was decided to combine with the Bradford League - thus the Bradford/Keighley League was formed. Keighley teams still played for points in a Keighley championship (Bradford clubs did likewise), so matches between Keighley teams were included in both competitions but matches between Keighley and Bradford clubs counted only for Bradford/Keighley League points. Devonshire Street ran a team in the under 18 section of the Bradford League for this season too, but do not appear to have been around the following year. It was Keighley Athletic who dominated local proceedings however. The club had officially closed down at the end of the previous season, but had been reformed, playing close to the Lawkholme Lane ground at Threaproyd. They won the Keighley League title before going on to beat the Co-op team 14-9 in the Keighley Charity Cup final.

Athletic changed their name the following season. As they had their base at Keighley Albion cycling club then it made sense to revert to Keighley Albion, a name that obviously continues today. It was not the first time the title had been used by a footballing side however - an Albion soccer club had existed in the town in the 1905-06 season (and were founder members of the Keighley & District Football League). Their first game under the new title was nothing short of disastrous - a 3-67 rout at the hands of Bradford based Laisterdyke ! However, the Keighley League title was retained, although a surprise 7-9 defeat at the hands of Silsden in the Keighley Charity Cup final meant that Albion took home only cigarette cases from this game, as opposed to the trophy and tankards awarded to the winners. The cobbydalers won in dramatic circumstances, a late late Harold Bancroft penalty seeing them through.

The Threaproyd pitch was the venue for a Keighley League-v-Bradford League challenge match during the 1949-50 season. The match had originally been switched to Lawkholme Lane from Odsal, but the state of the pitch there meant that the Albion were needed to rescue the situation. The locals lost 0-27 to their much stronger opponents, but were represented by the following players:
Kelly, Gallagher (both Co-op), Bailey, Atkinson, L.Inman, Bird, Sharpe, Brookes (all Albion), Barrett, J.Meegan, R.Bancroft, H.Bancroft (all Silsden), Bradley (Prince Smith's)
Local representative fixtures were also played against Keighley's Hull counterparts around this time, allowing the better local players the chance of further representative fixtures.

Eastwood Tavern were the new faces for the 1950-51 campaign. Licensees of the local hostelry, Mr. & Mrs. Faly were the first chairman and treasurer of the new club. They joined the other five local sides in the Keighley/Bradford League, but it was Albion who again lifted the Keighley title when they defeated Tavern 17-9 in the final. The winners, having reached the fourth round of the Yorkshire Junior Cup for the third year in succession were favourites to lift the Charity Cup too, but were again subject to a surprise defeat when Riddlesden came from behind to win the final 9-7. Also this season, Albion ran a youth team in the Bradford League's Intermediate section for the first time.

Silsden were by now becoming a force again, losing the 1951-52 Bradford/Keighley championship final to Queensbury. Prince Smith & Stells had undoubtedly their greatest season to date when they reached the final of the Bradford Cup the same season, meeting Queensbury, but despite Thurling and Baldwin playing exceptionally well, they went the same way as Silsden had done to their Bradford rivals. Meanwhile Silsden won a one sided Keighley Cup final 25-6 against Riddlesden. Keighley League champions were Eastwood Tavern, who beat Keighley Albion 13-6 in the final, despite losing 2 men with injury during the game. A feature of the Keighley League season had been the closeness of the league table, either one of the five teams could easily have made the final. Albion made the headlines earlier in the season when every member of their tram scored in a 115-8 rout of Bradford side Jack & Jill. Their 'intermediate' team enjoyed a thoroughly successful season, winning the Halifax Junior Cup (9-5 v Sedbergh YC) and Halifax League Cup (5-2 v Ovenden), both finals played at Thrum Hall.

Silsden won the 1952-53 Keighley League title, the first championship to be decided under the reign of Elizabeth II, although they were narrowly defeated by Bradford side Clayton in the local cup final at Lawkholme. A good run in the Yorkshire Cup included an excellent 52-0 win at Huddersfield outfit David Brown's in the second round. Meanwhile, Albion, in October 1952, became a nursery club for the professional Halifax club, their juniors continuing their fine run of success when Jack & Jill were thrashed 28-0 in the Bradford Under-18 League Cup final. The mid-1950's signalled the emergence of the Keighley Albion club as a major force in amateur rugby league circles. With many of their successful juniors breaking through to the senior set-up, the club embarked on an amazing run of success.

There was a concerted attempt to make the Keighley League independent of the Bradford League for the 1953-54 season, with a number of new sides hoping to take the to field as a consequence. The line up of the new league was: Silsden, Keighley Albion, Keighley Shamrocks, Eastwood Tavern, Riddlesden, Victoria Park Rangers (tenants at the Greyhound Stadium), and Prince Smith & Stells. The take up of additional new clubs never materialised though, especially when the proposed Denholme and Addingham YC clubs never actually made it to the starting line, the new names (Shamrocks and Victoria Park) were familiar ones, in effect reformed sides. Silsden won the league's Medal Competition final with a 13-8 victory over Albion. Albion also lost the Keighley Charity Cup final this season, Bradford's West Bowling defeating them 5-3, but it was the following season when the Theaproyd club dominated proceedings.

In an amazing end to the 1954-55 season they won four trophies. A convincing 18-5 defeat of Victoria Park in front of 1000 spectators in the Keighley Cup final; an astounding 28-0 runaway victory at Odsal against Queensbury in the Bradford Cup; victory the Halifax Cup, defeating Ovenden 12-8, following a 7-7 draw, at Thrum Hall (the first team from outside Halifax to win the competition since Keighley Zingari in the early years of the century); and Silsden defeated 13-10 in a Keighley League decider at Strong Close. The latter game saw Albion's resources stretched to the full, as due to injuries they were forced to field several reserves in their line-up. By now they were again independent of any professional club, although that did not stop them from churning out a long list of players for the professional game.

Although Albion and Silsden continued to take the field, the former with a good degree of success, several other local teams had brief existences around this time. The Co-op team disappeared at the same time as the Eastwood Tavern side emerged, many of their players going on to play for the new club. Tavern themselves shared the town's Greyhound Stadium with newcomers Victoria Park Rangers during the 1953-54 season before they too became defunct. By the summer of 1955, both Riddlesden and Prince Smiths had also withdrawn from league competition, while Shamrocks disbanded during the 1956-57 season. It was not long before Victoria Park had vanished too, although Silsden themselves almost went to the wall due to a lack of players.

In 1955-56, a season when Albion product Terry Hollindrake represented Great Britain at international level for the first time, against New Zealand, the Keighley League was, due to a lack of numbers, again forced into a merger with an outside competition - in this case with the Dewsbury & Batley League ! Thus the short-lived Keighley/Dewsbury League was born. Silsden, Keighley Albion and Victoria Park were joined by Thornhill Lees, Dewsbury Celtic, Heath Rangers, Overthorpe Rangers, Heckmondwike, and Hanging Heaton. Albion continued their winning ways, defeating Silsden 22-7 to win the Halifax Cup for a second successive season, although it was the cobbydalers who won the Keighley League final with a narrow 14-13 victory against Victoria Park at Shamrock's ground. Late in the season, Albion went down 10-13 to Dewsbury Celtic in the Dewsbury League's Oldroyd Trophy.

Local clubs decided not to stick together for the 1956-57 season. Only Silsden stayed in the Dewsbury competition, and for them it proved a struggle from the start. In November they resigned from the league due to the lack of players, playing friendly fixtures only for the rest of the season while they regrouped. However, their junior side still played competitive fixtures. Victoria Park and Shamrocks moved to the Halifax League, the former enjoying a relatively successful campaign, while Shamrocks failed to see out the season!

Keighley Albion opted for the Bradford League where they would go on to achieve two trebles in four years. The local clubs still played fixtures in a Keighley League competition to supplement their league fixtures - also because they had to do so due to rugby league rules at the time - and this is the just about the only local competition that Albion did not dominate. They thrashed Victoria Park in the 1957 final (although they were the only two amateur clubs left in the town at the time following the demise of Silsden & Shamrocks during the season), but the same opponents sprung a surprise 9-8 victory the following year, Albion's only defeat of the season. The 1958-59 final saw Albion win again, against the same opponents. Upon Victoria Park's demise over the summer of 1959, a new Worth Village emerged to defeat Silsden in the 1959-60 final. Village appeared in the Dewsbury League that season and contained many former Victoria Park players, including ace goalkicker Frank Moorby, in their line up but do not seem to have lasted longer than this single season.

Keighley Albion's 'trebles' refer to competitions they won three years on the trot. The Bradford League title was won in 1956-57 (Bradford's Victoria Rangers beaten 50-12 in the final), 1957-58 (Dudley Hill defeated 19-11) and again in 1958-59. In addition, the Bradford Cup was won in 1957-58 (Thornton defeated 43-5 in the final), 1958-59 (beat West Bowling 18-12) and 1959-60 (Wyke beaten 12-7). In amongst all of this, a weary Ovenden, playing their fourth game in eight days were routed 50-9 in the 1956-57 Keighley Cup final, and the following season Low Moor were defeated 16-5 in a Halifax League under 19's final. The Keighley Cup competition actually received very little press attention around this time. Winners in 1955-56 (finalists: Albion & Dewsbury Celtic) and 1958-59 (featuring Victoria Park Rangers) being untraced, Albion's defeated opponents in 1957-58 are also unknown.

There were a number of new clubs around towards the end of the 1950's. Keighley Central, Silsden, Holycroft and Cross Roads St.James Youth Clubs, and possibly Bracken Bank, all ran under 19 teams, although hopes to form a local league fell through. Albion's junior sides were still by far the top of the tree, as were their senior side. Albion's juniors actually played in a curtain raiser to the St.Helens - Hunslet league championship final at the conclusion of the 1958-59 campaign against a combined Bradford Junior side.

As the 1950's came to a close, there was no question as to who were top dogs in town. Keighley Albion had, since the war, brought the amateur game to a new level, never before or since matched. Their run of success lasted over 10 years, producing not only the international Terry Hollindrake but a host of other professional and top amateur players, many of whom feature in these pages. Unfortunately the local game as a whole was severely under reported in the local press, many clubs not bothering to inform the 'Keighley News' of their fixtures or results. This was in direct contrast to the local soccer scene, always well covered and in depth within the local newspapers sports pages.

EASTWOOD TAVERN
Photographed in the early 1950's.
Back: J.Lowe, J.Morley, E.Newton, G.Newton, unknown, H.Metcalfe, B.Emsley, R.Hinson, F.Fahy, J.McKie, T.Brooksbank,
Front: H.Slater, J.Midgeley, G.Brooksbank, B.Middleton, F.Moorby, J.Caine, unknown, Robinson, Buckley,

VICTORIA PARK RANGERS 1959

Two images of **RIDDLESDEN RUGBY CLUB.**
Top: The revived club in their first season, 1948-49
Bottom: 1950-51 team group proudly displaying the Keighley Cup, the clubs' only success in local league & cup competition

Clive Rees, Victoria Park's full-back.

Mr. K. I. Mason, manager, Keighley Lifts Rugby team.

John Bradley, Silsden's scrum half.

Barry Mitchell, Keighley Albion threequarter.

Harry East was a regular scribe for the Keighley News in the late 50's & early 60's. Local sport did not escape his attention, and neither did the individuals above.

THE 60'S & EARLY 70'S

The 1960-61 season proved to be the beginning of the end for the Silsden club, who were no longer the force they had been in the local game. Served with six months notice to quit their Hainsworth Road ground by the owner, Frank Hanson, with whom negotiations had deteriorated over the years, the search began for a new ground in the village. This was a great pity because Hanson was one of the prime movers behind the reformation of the club in the early 1920's and was in-fact it's first captain. Various possible locations were looked at, although none proved successful, and many of the players signed instead for Prince Smith's, reformed during the summer of 1961 and who did have a pitch and changing accommodation available. Despite Mr.Hanson's decision to remove the notice to quit later on, Silsden were then left short of players. Despite beginning the 1961-62 season at Hainsworth Road, several early-season games were postponed due to their inability to raise a side. When they did get around to playing, only eight men appeared for the home fixture with Wyke. Appeals for more players in the local press proved fruitless and it was no surprise that in November 1961 the club again disbanded their open-age side. Despite this, there was still money in the bank, but subsequent efforts to revive the club over the following seasons proved unsuccessful, including an effort to play rugby union, and the club was officially wound up in May 1963, with all assets - including their pavilion and equipment - sold off.

The Keighley Cup competition continued to be poorly reported in the press, although a lot of this had to do with the fact that Keighley teams were having problems winning it! Bradford sides, such as Wyke, West Bowling and Victoria Rangers dominated proceedings until Prince Smith & Stells took the trophy for the first time in 1963 when Keighley Albion were defeated. Likewise the Keighley League, where fixtures tended to be played early in the season. With neither the tiny Keighley nor larger Bradford Leagues publishing league tables of any sort, local progress was still reliant in the press on local clubs sending in their own reports. Winners of the Keighley League were never reported on in the early 1960's, and it is known that the Keighley & District Junior Rugby League, who administered the competition, was in dire financial straits in the early 60's. The association relied on the annual Lazenby Cup match between Keighley and Bradford Northern, but when this match was discontinued in 1961, the association found itself £100 worse off every season.

A Keighley League select did continue to play occasional challenge games against similar organisations. The local squad for a curtain raiser at Lawkholme Lane against a Leigh side in March 1962 was: *Blackwell, Smith, Ingham (all Prince Smith's), Taylor, Rochford, Caddy (Keighley Central), Browse, Cohen, Barker, Shelton, Uttley, Fryers, Jobbling, Sharpe, Shackleton, Bancroft, Adamson (all Keighley Albion)*

The reformed Prince Smiths works side, which had successful soccer and cricket sections with which to compete for glory, went straight into the Bradford League in their first season back and actually led the table by Christmas 1961. However a poor run after that scuppered any chances of silverware. Their Keighley Cup success in their second season was a surprise, not least following their 12-0 defeat of Yorkshire Junior Cup semi-finalists Ovenden. In the final, Carpenter, Clarke and Airey were outstanding in their 9-3 success against Albion.

The Keighley Cup did prove to be the springboard for local clubs Keighley Lifts and NSF. NSF Rangers were the works team of the National Switch Factory, which arrived in Keighley in 1940, after having been bombed out of their Croydon base. Lifts' first ever competitive fixture was a trip to cup holders Wyke early in 1962, and they went on to fulfil several more engagements that season before a brief flirtation with the Bradford League for the 1962-63 campaign. Unfortunately a poor winter that season meant that the side did not play a league fixture between the end of December and mid-March, and when they did finally have a fixture, could not raise a full team – an 11-a-side fixture with Prince Smiths played instead. Not surprisingly this works side did not reappear the following season. The NSF Rangers appear to have formed in time for the Keighley Cup in 1963. Their stay on the scene lasted much longer however, as we shall see, but the Keighley Cup was discontinued after Prince Smith's success, due in part to the debts the competition had accumulated.

Top dogs Keighley Albion turned to the Leeds League in the summer of 1961. They enjoyed quite a successful first season in the new surroundings, despite not lifting any silverware and despite suffering from several bouts of vandalism at Theaproyd, one such attack costing them in the region of £400 to rectify. No mean amount in the early 1960's. The 1962-63 season was a disaster, the side winning only two of 14 league fixtures before Christmas and enduring an unfamiliar position at the foot of the table. But how things change, and within months Albion were back at the top of the tree. They enjoyed a fine 1963-64 campaign, winning the league title in fine style, with scoring nearly 600 points during the campaign and defeating Oulton 16-8 in the league final in May.

A decision to revert to the Bradford League again for the 1964-65 season saw Keighley Albion line up in a ten strong division along with fellow Keighley sides NSF and Prince Smith & Stells, as well as West Bowling, Wyke, Dudley Hill, Victoria Rangers, Clayton and Thornton (several of whom are still going strong to this day). This marked the beginning of a decade of frustration for local sides as they became almost perennial bridesmaids in this company, although in this particular season all three Keighley sides struggled in the lower half of the table.

Playing temporarily at Marley, following the loss Threaproyd, Albion were surprisingly defeated by both Keighley rivals during the campaign, although they, along with NSF both improved after Christmas to finish 6th & 5th respectively . Both reached the semi-finals of the Bradford Cup, Albion going down 6-15 to league champions Wyke, while NSF who had former Albion players Don & Derek Kirkley in their ranks were defeated 4-10 by West Bowling. The two leading Keighley clubs then played out a 9-9 draw in a benefit game at Lawkholme Lane in aid of relieving the debts incurred by the former Keighley Rugby League, who had organised the now defunct Keighley Cup competition.

Albion, who were still heavily involved in the junior side of the game, with under 17 & 19 sides in the Halifax / Huddersfield and later Bradford Junior Leagues proved pioneers in the world of amateur rugby. They became the first amateur side to organise a 'sevens' competition as a curtain raiser to the 1965-66 season, one which would continue to run for a number of years.

KEIGHLEY ALBION 'SEVEN A SIDE' TOURNAMENT – early finals
1965-66 Wyke...11 Keighley Albion...3
1966-67 Clayton...13   Wyke...6 *(Albion thrown out following a brawl in their first round tie with St.Mary's, this in their own competition!)*
1967-68 Keighley Albion...8   Worth Village...7
1968-69 Clayton...21   West Bowling...6
1969-70 Illingworth...12   Worth Village...11

As Albion moved to a new base at Highfield prior to the 1965-66 campaign, Prince Smith's finally closed down the rugby league section of their sports club for good, leaving only two local sides in the Bradford League, which now operated with only nine teams. There was no mistaking the improved form displayed by the remaining Keighley sides though, with they and West Bowling battling for top spot throughout the season. NSF did the 'double' over Albion, beating their previously undefeated rivals 10-7 late in October and again 7-6 a month later. Both sides were again defeated in the semi-finals of the Bradford Cup again however – Albion 4-11 versus Victoria Rangers and NSF at 0-21 league champions Wyke (who also defeated them 0-29 in a league fixture). Despite this setback, the end of the regular league season saw both Keighley teams qualifying for the top four play-offs, NSF sitting proudly on top of the final ladder

BRADFORD LEAGUE – TOP 5 POSITIONS 1965-66

	P	W	D	L	Pts
NSF RANGERS	16	13	0	3	26
West Bowling	16	12	0	4	24
KEIGHLEY ALBION	16	12	0	4	24
Victoria Rangers	16	11	0	5	22
Wyke	16	10	0	6	20

Earning a home tie in their semi-final play-off, NSF reached their first final with a 20-7 success against Victoria Rangers, but hopes of an all-Keighley league championship final were dashed when Albion put up a woeful display at West Bowling in their semi-final, routed 0-42. The final itself proved a tight affair, Bowling racing into a 6 point lead by half time, with NSF unable to peg back the difference, despite a Feather try, converted by Hebden being not quite enough in a 5-6 defeat. To make matters worse for local teams, Albion's under 19 team went down 5-21 to Ovenden in their Halifax League final.

Undeterred, the locals approached the 1966-67 campaign with confidence. Breaking links with their parent company, NSF changed their name to Worth Village, electing former Hunslet player Alan Bancroft as captain. The first of many many Albion-v-Village local derbys therefore took place on October 15th 1966, Village winning 8-5 – 4 goals from ace-kicker Hartley proving the difference, with Albion scoring the game's only try through Blackwell. Hartley was proving a gem in the Village side, scoring a whopping 14 goals in their 52-0 rout of Thornton earlier in the season. The return, at Marley on November 19th saw Albion this time scrape home 8-4, with a McGlynn try early in the second half proving the decisive point.

With the league again operating with 10 clubs, newcomers being another works side with a multi purpose sports club, International Harvesters of Apperley Bridge, both Village and Albion (who inflicted Wyke's first home defeat for three years) again vied with West Bowling for top spot…..until January 30th 1967 that is.

Joint league leaders Worth Village had objected to the league's conduct during a disciplinary meeting in December, criticising them in a letter to rugby league secretary Bill Fallowfield. When Village refused to retract this criticism by January 30th the league controversially expelled them, and refused to acknowledge a belated apology offer the following month. The club were forced to play friendly fixtures only for the rest of the season, playing Leeds League sides as well as making a short tour to play several teams in a newly formed London Rugby League.

Albion meanwhile maintained their momentum in the Bradford League, and reached the finals of both competitions. Peel Park based Victoria Rangers were despatched in both semi-finals, 8-6 in the Bradford Cup and 10-4 in the league's top-four play-offs. Unfortunately, it proved to be another case of 'so near yet so far' as the locals lost both finals at Odsal – 8-13 to Wyke in the Cup and 3-10 to West Bowling in the league decider.

Despite relatively successful league campaigns, Keighley's amateur rugby league sides were making very little impression in the Yorkshire and national cup competitions, Albion's third round appearance in the county competition during the 1966-67 season being the furthest they had progressed for many years.

The 1967-68 season saw Worth Village playing in the Leeds League following their expulsion from the Bradford League. Despite being confident of reaching the high standards they had attained in recent seasons, the side struggled in their new surroundings. After losing a number of players, Village hit rock bottom and had to wait until December for their first victory, against Leeds University. Ironically this coincided with Albion's first dropped point of the season – a 5-5 draw with Clayton.

Albion were going well going into the new year, but five defeats in eight outings ruined any hopes of league success, although they again found themselves in the final of the Bradford Cup competition. Despite seeing their full back and captain Billy Walton voted the league's 'Sportsman of the Year' that season, another final defeat followed, Wyke retaining the trophy with an 11-2 success. In Bradford Junior League competition, Lawkholme Lane hosted a 'finals day' in May – Albion under 17's losing 7-16 to Bradford Juniors in their tie, and newly formed Keighley Junior Supporters Club defeated 6-11 by Clayton in their final. It looked as if the gods were against Keighley teams in local cup finals!

In retrospect, Village's expulsion from the Bradford League did neither side any favours, Village continued to struggle in the Leeds League, and were 'relegated' to a new second division for the 1968-69 season. The Bradford League replaced them with the Watsonians club, who proved nowhere near as strong as the Keighley side and thus led to a decline in overall strength of that league. Luckily, another new club came along in the summer of 1968 – with Keighley Shamrocks revived yet again! This time the new club was up to standard, surprising Keighley Albion with a 14-10 success (tries from Philbin & Spencer) late in October. However, this time Albion were not to be denied at the death and lifted their first Bradford League title in ten years.

Albion began the new season in fine form, this despite the shock defeat at Shamrocks, who themselves actually lost six of their first seven league fixtures. By early 1969 however, both Keighley sides were making light work of their opponents. Bert Woolley was scoring tries at will for the Shammies, with Terry Hollindrake doing the business with his boot. A measure of their strength were 73-0 and 44-0 victories over Pennine Rangers and Thornton. One problem faced by the team, also based at Highfield's Burgess Field was discipline – or a lack of it, a league fixture at International Harvesters abandoned due to constant fighting between the teams. Bobby Cryer was just as successful as Hollindrake, his penalties helping Albion to similar high scoring victories. In-fact, the same weekend Shamrocks defeated Harvesters in their rematch by 67-3, Albion routed Pennine Rangers to the tune of 79-4.

Shamrock's poor start to the season cost them a place in the top four play-offs at the season's end. Albion's third place earning them a tie at runners-up west Bowling in the semi final. They duly made amends for an earlier Bradford Cup semi-final defeat at the hand of Bowling (Shamrocks lost in the other semi to Wyke) by winning 16-9 to take them into yet another Bradford League final. This time it was their captain, Cryer, who made all the difference, his successful penalties and a try from Ashcroft crucial in a 13-2 victory for Coulton's boys at Thornton.

The winning Albion side was : *H.Ryder, R.Chapman, W.Walton, D.Sunderland, T.Caddy, B.Reynard, K.Hill, P.Ashcroft, J.Hodgson, R.Cryer (captain), A.Gordon, J.Riley, A.Rhodes & A.Coulton, coach: J.Coulton,*

In another busy end to the season, Albion's under 19 side lost to Siddal in their league final, while Keighley Junior Supporters under 20's also finished second behind West Bowling in their league. A second trophy did come Keighley's way however, as the Junior Supporters Club's under 18's won their league cup competition.

1969-70 proved to be a return to normal, as the season ended frustratingly for local sides. Worth Village missed out on honours in the Leeds League, while Albion lost their title when Wyke defeated them in the deciding play off 12-16 at Lawkholme Lane, the Keighley team finishing second in the final table. The 'Keighley News' reported that the game was *"marred by poor handling, over-robust tackling and a lack of fitness by both sides"*, and referring to the favourable weather conditions, *"undoubtedly the sun was the highlight of an unimpressive afternoon"*.

Albion's under 17 side also went down in the final of their league cup competition, 11-13 at Odsal to Bradford Police Boys, but at least the under 19's had something to cheer about when they lifted their divisional title. Shamrocks endured a disappointing campaign, another match being abandoned due to fighting during the season, this time against local rivals Albion who were leading 10-0 seven minutes from time. The side became defunct before the new season commenced, although the name 'Shamrocks' would continue successfully in local soccer.

The onset of the 1970's saw Albion retain their position as 'top dogs' in Keighley, although that was soon to change. The side failed to make the final of the league's top four play-offs in 1970-71, but did have the consolation of lifting the Bradford Cup for the first time since the 1959-60 season. Following a 10-2 semi-final at Highfield against Wyke, Dudley Hill were Albion's opponents in front of 1000 spectators at Odsal. In direct contrast to Albion's previous final, the game was a tremendous contest, the Keighley team building a early lead through a brace of tries from Hogarth (Shutt converting the second), and then sealing it when Shutt himself went over in the closing stages, 11-3 the final score. Their under 19 team contested top spot in their league with Keighley Junior Supporters, had, among others, three Plunketts and a Peter Roe in their ranks. It was the Junior Supporters who came out on top in their play-off tie, but they themselves failed to win the final of the league competition. Albion had the consolation of at least making the knock-out cup final, but Bradford Police Boys again proved superior with a 10-15 victory.

The top sides in Keighley were re-united when Worth Village were accepted back into the Bradford League for the 1971-72 season. The switch signalled a dramatic return to form for the Marley-based side and it took them no time at all take Albion's mantle of top team in town.

The first local derby since 1966 took place early in September 1971, Village winning a classic confrontation at Marley 26-24. Inspired by new player-coach Jack Coan they had John Inman to thank for his hat-trick of tries as well as a brace from Mick Coffey and one from Mick Wainwright. In addition, Ashcroft landed four conversions. The side then embarked on a long run of victories, their seventh consecutive win a 16-7 defeat of Albion in the return fixture. Victoria Rangers were the team of the season in the 12-strong Bradford League, with a 100% record they nevertheless hard to work hard for two narrow successes over Worth Village, who could not surpass Keighley Albion's feat of not quite being able to get past the 3rd round of the Yorkshire Cup (defeated by Castleford's Lock Lane at this stage).

The Keighley teams met for a third time this season in the quarter-finals of the Bradford Cup, with Village again on top with an even more resounding 22-3 victory. Unfortunately injuries to key players at a crucial time of the season cost Village any silverware, beaten by Queensbury in the semi-final of the cup and by Wyke in the top four play-off semis. Nevertheless, they had enjoyed a fine season and were fully justified in seeking to return to the league they had left so acrimoniously several years earlier. One piece of silverware that did come Keighley's way however, was the Bradford Sunday League's under 19's cup, which was won by Keighley Junior Supporters after a 10-4 defeat of Bradley Y.C. (Huddersfield) in the final, where Peter Roe and Peter Bibby each scored a try. The following season they would lose another final, this time in the 'Huddersfield Examiner' Cup to Huddersfield Juniors.

Village went one step better in the 1973-74 season when they reached the league final. Unfortunately luck deserted them again as Queensbury, who had disposed of Keighley Albion, won the deciding game 23-13, Village doing themselves no favours, particularly when key goal-kicker Inman was dismissed. Yet again, Keighley sides had dominated the Bradford League yet had nothing to show for their efforts. Worth Village also reached the semi-final of the Bradford Cup – a much improved Shipley defeating them 29-3 at Northcliffe Playing Fields, this after Village had beaten Keighley Albion 10-7 in the previous round through a late Steel try. There was bad luck for Keighley Rugby League Junior Supporters Club side who went down 7-19 to Castleford Juniors in the final of Yorkshire under 19's cup. Things could have been so different for them had Halligan not mistaken the field markings and touched down on the 10 yard line thinking he'd scored a try late in the game ! At least Keighley Albion managed to gain some silverware, both their open-age and under 19's winning their respective Bradford League 'seven-a-side' competitions.

KEIGHLEY SUPPORTERS CLUB *celebrate with the Halifax League's under 19's trophy in 1972. Holding the trophy are Peter Roe & Alan Hockey, the former of whom went on to greater things in the professional game, while the latter went on to greater things in local soccer.*

N.S.F. RANGERS 1964
Back: E.Cowling (president), C.Barrett, D.Kent, A.Bancroft, L.Latta, D.Browes, R.Lund, S.Kennedy, D.Williamson, D.Constantine (secretary), M.Sharp,
Front: D.Feather, C.Steele, R.Ramsbottom, S.Hebden, J.Hartley, A.Winterbottom, J.Horn,

Bradford Amateur Rugby League

Cup Final

Odsal Stadium

Keighley Albion

v

Wyke

Sunday April 9th 1967

Kick off 3 p.m.

Trophies Presented by

MR. J. PHILLIPS   (Bradford Northern Chairman)

MR. N. MITCHELL   (Keighley R. L. F. C. Chairman)

ADMISSION BY PROGRAMME 1/-

One of Keighley Albion's many league & cup finals.

A programme from the Bradford Amateur League's Cup Final. Albion unfortunately lost this, and the league championship decider at the end of the 1966-67 season.

.

(With thanks to Jack Riley)

KEIGHLEY ALBION		WYKE	
1	Walton W.	1	Kernall
2	Cockroft	2	Wilkinson
3	Coan	3	Clegg
4	Browes	4	Leek
5	Barrett	5	Flaherty
6	Child	6	Gledhill
7	Williamson	7	Rhodes
8	Haigh	8	McDermott
9	Walton. T.	9	Kilduff
10	Shaw or Caddy	10	Newton
11	Hill	11	Little
12	Ryder	12	Bennett
13	Jackson	13	Denton
Substitutes		Substitutes	
14	McGlynn	14	Strothers
15	Barker	15	Barraclough

Referee   J. SENIOR   Touch Judges   N. CLARK & W. MAY

PASTURES NEW

Local clubs said goodbye to the Bradford League for good in the summer of 1973. Both Worth Village and Keighley Albion opted for new competition for the 1973-74 season in an enlarged Huddersfield / Halifax Combined League. Unfortunately, as new members they were required to start at the bottom, and both teams found themselves in the competition's third division, playing alongside the reserve, or 'A', teams of leading clubs in the area. The Halifax district clubs, Village and Albion included, also ran their own competition, along the lines of the combined leagues of the past. 1973 proved pivotal in the interests of amateur code, with the formation of the British Amateur Rugby League Association (BARLA). This new association was in fact a breakaway from the professionally-dominated Rugby Football League which had deprived the amateur clubs of any voting rights or say in their own future. Albion and Village were very much part of this new set-up, and within years the number of amateur clubs, in the north of England particularly, was to explode.

There was no doubting the superiority of the locals in their new surroundings in the Halifax/Huddersfield League. Village had few problems with the majority of their opponents, losing their unbeaten record in February to Albion on a quagmire of a pitch at Marley. The match referee has earlier declared the ground unfit, but the game went ahead at the home team's insistence, amid pools of water and ankle-deep mud, and Albion, despite missing the influential Tony Westhuizen (serving a nine match ban) won 4-0 through a brace of penalties by Rooke. Undeterred, Village went on to win the divisional title, sealed with a 22-7 win against Salem Hornets, but their end-of-season form again let them down. Missing 8 regulars they were defeated by division one side Siddal in the semi-final of the Halifax Cup, and worse was to follow as they were defeated in the final of the top 4 play-off's – by their biggest rivals: Keighley Albion winning 13-0 in the deciding game at Lawkholme Lane.

Despite their lowly status in the combined league, both Worth Village and Keighley Albion qualified for the Halifax League's own play-off's. While Albion disposed of Ovenden 22-20 in a closely fought game, Siddal again proved too good for Village, winning 5-28. Unfortunately Albion could not hold their higher placed opponents, who went on to win the final 11-8.

The changing face of amateur rugby was illustrated when the Huddersfield / Halifax League, which already contained several sides from the other side of the county boundary from the Rochdale and Oldham areas, was re-created as the current 'Pennine League', a title which better reflected the amalgamation of clubs under it's auspices.

The Keighley teams were both 'promoted' to the second division of this competition, and in effect they began their Pennine League careers as they had finished their last – with a fair degree of success. The season actually began with a new curtain-raiser – the 'Tommy Holmes Trophy', in effect a new 'Keighley Cup' competition, but to be played for strictly by local teams only. A mark of the almost equal strength of Village and Albion were the results of the two games played between them in September 1974, a 9-9 draw in the new trophy game (each club holding the cup for six months) followed by a narrow 6-5 success for Village a couple of weeks later in the league. Village won again 13-3 and went on to lift the divisional title ahead of Huddersfield side Bradley, Albion just missing out on promotion in third place.

Under the auspices of BARLA, there was a renewed interest in rugby league at grass-roots level. With new regional leagues in operation, the number of new clubs around mushroomed. Keighley's Amateur Association was in effect reformed, and immediately set about promoting the game in the locality with their Schools and Youth team competition in 1975, attracting an incredible 35 teams, of which around 20 were school sides. Worth Village and Bracken Bank were founder members of a new Keighley & Bradford Youth League. Stuart Woolley, who had coached the successful Bracken Bank under 19's teamed up with Peter Roe, another former Keighley RLFC in 1976 to run a revived, albeit short-lived, Central Youth Club side in the same league.

Keighley's rugby league clubs found success much harder to come by in their 'new' league, with Lancashire clubs such as Rochdale's Mayfield and Saddleworth proving tough nuts to crack. For several years their success was limited to 'rugby sevens' – Albion making the BARLA finals and winning the St.Marys competition at Thrum Hall in the mid 70's, with Worth Village winning the Greetland sevens three years in succession – 1978-80 – their third success seeing them defeat Albion 11-8 in the final. Neither Albion or Village were able to break into the Pennine League's new premier division, but local derbies provided Keighley with tough, and controversial, cup ties – in which Village won the Tommy Holmes Trophy early in the 1978-79 season amid violent scenes on the field of play (spectators were also known to have their own pitched battles at times too!). An influential member of the Village team in their 30-17 victory was their former soccer star Peter Turbitt, a former England Youth International & Bradford City defender, who provided many points for the Marley side via his accurate goal-kicking. Later in the season Albion gained a revenge victory in the Halifax Cup, 14-12, although their opponents did have four tries disallowed!

Worth Village had at last managed to win a cup competition outside of Keighley when they won the Halifax (Infirmary) Cup – the very same competition that had provided success for Albion in the past. Their first success managed to elude the local press – being in 1977 or 1978, but their second success received much better coverage at the close of the 1979-80 season. The locals had Jack Plunkett, who played alongside his brothers Martin & Brian, to thank for his late try and conversion in a 12-10 victory over Ovenden in the semi-final. The final brought premier division Siddal to Thrum Hall, but Village rose to the challenge, their battered and bruised side scoring two tries in the final 15 minutes to win 8-0. Full-back Brian Plunkett scored the first, and with seconds remaining Fred Farrington went over, both converted by Jack Plunkett, to see Village regain the trophy. To cap a fine season Keighley Albion's under 17 side also won their Halifax Cup competition for a second successive year when they defeated Ovenden 12-5 at Thrum Hall. Tries, all unconverted ,were from Peter Kit (2), Paul Knapper and Gareth Jones.

The growth in amateur rugby did not pass Keighley by. With former Hull and Bramley professional Allan Bancroft now a member of the National Coaching Scheme, one of his aims was the running of coaching courses and ultimately in the formation of a teams. A member of the Silsden side that had closed down in the early 1960's, he set about trying to revive the village club. There were enough interested parties around to see this move successful in October 1978, with 23 committee members enlisted. The main problem faced by the new club however was the location of a suitable field. Away fixtures were not a problem, their first on December 16th at Garden Gate (Hunslet), which resulted in a 13-44 defeat for the inexperienced cobbydalers. Although the side ultimately managed to secure the use of 'the Arena' in Silsden park, although only after overcoming leasing and initial drainage problems, early homes games were played on a number of local fields – the club indebted to the owners of Low House and Old Hall Farms for the use of their enclosures in the first few weeks of the club's existence.

Silsden joined the expanding Pennine League for the 1979-80 season, elected to division six alongside Worth Village's second string. Their debut proved entirely successful. As Worth Village and Keighley Albion secured their Halifax Cup victories, Silsden were securing promotion at their first attempt, a 17-15 victory over St.Josephs 'A' sealing it. However, an internal dispute saw Bancroft, along with the influential Dave Ingham, leave the club and promptly set-about forming a new one! Silsden's policy at the time was to select players from the village first, irrespective of ability or form, with spare positions ten being offered to 'off-cum-dens'. This was not universally popular, which led to the dispute.

Thus Oakworth Wanderers' came into being. Initially based in Keighley, they were accepted at the last minute by the Pennine League to the new division seven for the 1980-81 season as 'The Wanderers'. The club subsequently secured the old football ground adjacent to Oakworth Cricket Club on Wide Lane, and despite initial objections from local residents began their first season there. Only a few players had actually followed Ingham and Bancroft from Silsden. In November 1980 the club registered with BARLA as 'Oakworth Wanderers'. Their first season saw them finish at the foot of division 7, with 3 wins and a draw from their 16 fixtures.

It was Worth Village who again stole the limelight this season, reaching the Halifax Infirmary Cup final again as well as retaining the Tommy Holmes Cup. The latter unfortunately ended in defeat, with Mixenden running out 13-6 winners, the locals not quite showing the form that got them to the final. Amends were made in the local final though, John Inman leading his side to a 14-7 success against a never-say-die Albion, although there were dark clouds ahead for Keighley's unofficial championship competition.

It was certainly a 'nearly' season for Albion's seniors, as they were narrowly pipped for promotion from Pennine's division two right at the death by Mayfield 'A' and Rochdale side East Ward. It was their recently revived under 17 side who gained silverware, defeating Furnace 16-2 to again retain the Halifax Cup. This was the season of their 'treble' as Bradford & Keighley Challenge and Supplementary Cups were also annexed.

OAKWORTH WANDERERS 1980-81
Back: D.Ingham (manager), B.Uttley (coach), N.Haley, P.Brierley, T.Kendrick, L.Robinson,
J.Spencer, M.Barr, N.Spencer, J.Dickinson, G.Bennett, G.Bairstow (chairman),
Front: K.Seaton, S.Hewitt, J.Ash, T.Coffey, G.Seward, J.Rall, M.Finn,

KEIGHLEY ALBION UNDER 17'S *proudly display their silverware for the 1980-81 season. Featured holding their trophies are captain P.Knapper (left) and S.Boocock (right) who missed all three finals with a broken wrist ! Also in the picture are, back: G.Tanner, G.Palmer, T.Williams, A.Preston, G.Smith, A.Karnasaukas, D.Nixon, P.Kit, J.Butterfield, S.Clarke, G.Gow, Front: A.McGuire, G.Kelly, A.Winterbottom, D.Williamson (coach), H.Packer, W.Rochford*

KEIGHLEY ALBION 1980-81

WORTH VILLAGE 1979-80

SILSDEN 1980-81

PENNINE LEAGUE YEARS

The 1981-82 campaign began with the formation of another new Keighley club. Keighley Star were formed following interest aroused when the pub of that name took on their Devonshire counterparts the previous season and the newcomers were immediately accepted into the Pennine League alongside Oakworth Wanderers in division seven. It was mooted that five clubs was one too many for the town, and that existing sides – particularly Worth Village who ran two open age teams – might struggle to attract sufficient players. Within twelve months Oakworth had resigned from the league, although this was not due to a player shortage but a lack of committee members. Their absence was at the time hoped to be temporary, but Wanderers were never revived and died a quiet death.

Star secured the use of Keighley RLFC's training ground and changing facilities at Lawkholme before their later move to Marley, their first competitive fixture an 11-9 success at Higginshaw 'A' thanks to tries from Whitton and Coulton. They were promoted at their first attempt. Oakworth would have joined them in division six the following season had they survived the summer.

Star's achievements were overshadowed by incidents surrounding Worth Village and the Tommy Holmes competition during the early months of 1982. Village suffered relegation from division one in the league, but this was nothing compared to the events that unfolded in the local competition. Following a 16-10 victory over Keighley Albion in the semi-final, the Villagers looked set to face Silsden in the deciding tie. Unfortunately things then got out of hand. Albion then appealed, successfully, against the result to BARLA, citing an ineligible player. Unfortunately Village were informed of the decision too late to prevent their players from also turning up to face Silsden in the final, resulting in three teams turning up to contest the game. Ugly scenes followed, which resulted in the tie being abandoned before a ball had been kicked and the cup being held over until things had been sorted out. The newly formed Keighley ARL was immediately mothballed as a result, and Village were barred from the competition for one year. Albion beat Silsden 11-3 in a game played at the beginning of the 1982-83 campaign, and with only three teams eligible to compete in the 1982-83 season the Halifax ARL, who had taken on the organisation of the competition, decided to temporarily wash their hands of it. In amongst all the chaos, Albion's juniors won the Halifax under 19 cup against Siddal (in a tie that was meant to be a curtain raiser to the Tommy Holmes fiasco), but it was not long before they too were involved in controversy.

1983-84 saw Albion's youth team in the West Riding Youth League, continuing their fine run with a resounding 64-12 demolition of Park Amateurs in the semi final of the West Riding Youth Cup. In all, thirteen tries were scored, including a first half hat-trick from Higgins. The final at Dudley Hill late in the season saw Apperley Bridge based opponents 'Touchdown' in opposition, but yet again another cup final ended in chaos. Albion trailed 10-18 with only four minutes to go when the referee abandoned the game due to fighting. What followed was worse that anyone could have imagined – the fighting continuing some ten minutes after abandonment, and three Albion teenagers returning to 'battle' even after they had been sent off! As a result the league banned the club for life, fined them £50 and banned the three who had returned to fight until the end of the following season. Although Albion appealed successfully against the severity of the measures, the West Riding Youth League continued to refuse to allow them to compete in the competition.

At least three Keighley open-age teams gained promotion this season, Albion from division 2, their second string from their division, and Star for the second successive campaign from division 6 despite being bottom of the division for much of the season, a late run seeing them rise to 6th of 11 teams.

Late in the 1983-84 season, Holy Family School's rugby league team formed the nucleus of a new Keighley Celtic Youth team which went on to compete successfully in the West Riding Youth League as Keighley's only junior club. Following a successful 1985-86 campaign the nucleus of what had previously been Celtic's under 19 side joined the Pennine League alongside the town's other open age sides (an under 17 side was still run in the Youth League). What followed was an amazing run of promotions which saw Celtic rise from division 8 to division 3 in successive seasons.

Within weeks of Celtic's formation as a youth side, another new club was formed in the area. This time the new club was formed through a split in the ranks of an existing one. Thus the nomadic existence of Silsden Rangers was begun, as the village now had two sides to support for the first time since 1888. Familiar names were behind the formation of the new club, Alan Bancroft among them, along with existing players Matthew Boothman and the hard working Les Scaife. The club joined the Pennine League for the 1984-85 season, gaining promotion from division 7 at the first attempt behind Birkenshaw 'A' and firmly establishing themselves as rivals to the older Silsden club in the process. Ironically the two village clubs were drawn together in the first round of the Pennine Cup in that first season, Rangers going down 10-13 in an exciting game at 'The Arena'. The 1985-86 season opened with the first 'Silsden Shield' game played – Silsden again defeating Rangers, this time by 18 points to 6.

Keighley sides found cup final success elusive during this era. Albion's 'A' string going down 8-22 to Boothtown in the Halifax Supplementary Cup at the end of the 1984-85 season, despite Neil Palmer and Simon Rix tries. The following season Worth Village again made the Halifax Cup final (defeating Albion in the semi final

16-2 when on-song Steve Boocock bagged two tries and two goals). Unfortunately the villagers were unable to overcome holders Elland in the Thrum Hall final although they put up a mighty performance in a 22-30 defeat, and at least had the satisfaction of taking Pennine's division two title to join Albion in the league's first division again. However, the club suffered fines from the Halifax RL for refusing to have drinks and refreshments with the Elland club at the conclusion of their cup final. The mid 80's saw Village continuing their good run of success in pre-season 7-a-side tournaments, winning the Keighley RLFC competition prior to the 1984-85 campaign with runners up placings at both Greetland and Pennine competitions around that time.

It was Keighley Albion's turn to get their hands on the Tommy Holmes Trophy again in the mid 80's, an 8-6 defeat of Village in the preliminary round of the 1984-85 season was followed by a heart stopping 33-24 semi final victory over a surprisingly resilient Silsden Rangers and an easier 30-14 final victory over Silsden in the final. A 70 yard Nixon try was the highlight, with other scores coming from Coffey, Moran, Rochford, Dunne and Higgins. The following year Village were beaten again, but this time in the final by 16 points to 10, Mark Ingham's try proving decisive. Albion struggled in the league that season, their first win not coming until January, although relegation was avoided at the season's end. However, the 1986-87 final saw the first real shock result in the history of the competition when for the first time a club other than Albion or Village lifted the trophy. Now coached by Paul Kelly, Silsden Rangers reached the final courtesy of victory over Keighley Star in the semi, but they were not expected to be a match for Albion, some five divisions higher in the league. At 14-6, Albion looked to be in control of the Lawkholme final ,but the underdogs hit back with tries from Steve Dawson and substitute Peter Millgate, and coupled with goals from John Sutcliffe it was they who turned the tables to win 20-14.

For a while it looked as if Keighley would have yet another amateur rugby league side when Green Gables were accepted into a new division 8 of the Pennine League for the 1986-87 season. However, despite having a coach (Harry Plunkett), ground and playing strip in place the venture failed before a ball had been kicked. A lack of players was the reason, Gables opting to resign from the league rather than poach from other local clubs. In a season when the town's professional club were again saved from the brink of folding, Village secured their second successive promotion behind Park Amateurs to take their place among Pennine's elite. There was a major upset when Silsden Rangers lifted their first – and only – Tommy Holmes title when they came from behind to defeat an ill disciplined Albion 18-14. They had John Sutcliffe to thank for his match-winning five goals in an exciting game at Lawkholme. Albion's under 17's, coached by Peter Adamson, had the satisfaction of a Halifax Cup final success against Ovenden at Thrum Hall (and were losing finalists twelve months later) late in the 1986-87 campaign, while Celtic saw their young under 13's defeat Oulton 18-6 at Odsal in their West Riding Cup final , again proving that junior rugby league was alive in the town. For Celtic's youngsters, coached by Dave Williamson, Diminski scored a brace of tries, while Dyson managed a try and three goals.

1987-88 proved to be Keighley Star's final full season. The side, by now based at the Great Northern, had a desperate start to the campaign, having to wait until February for their first points in a 32-7 victory over Stainland. Despite a late surge towards the latter end of the season the club finished way down the division five table, but were spared relegation due a league reorganisation at the season's end. They re-emerged as great Northern the following season, but again at the foot of the table, the team had disbanded before Christmas and were no more.

Worth Village celebrated mid table security in the Pennine League premier division with a convincing 30-3 rout of Silsden in the 1987-88 Tommy Holmes final – Steve Mears awarded man of the match – but they were defeated by Albion in the 1988-89 final. Stephen Hall scored a vital try, goaled by Simon Kelk, to give Albion the lead just before the interval and it was they who went on to win 27-14.

However, the 1988-89 Tommy Holmes competition was marred by the disgraceful scenes at Highfield in a semi-final tie between Albion and Village 'A'. The referee was forced to halt the original game just after half time with Albion leading 15-0 and a mass brawl breaking out between players. The crowd of over 400 were witness to some of the worst scenes seen in local rugby circles, and matters were made worse for those concerned when the 'Keighley News' printed photographs of the brawl the following Friday. Albion won a much tamer replay 32-4 but the damage had been done. Earlier in the season, seven players had been dismissed during an Albion 'A' v Celtic league match.

The local highlight of the 1988-89 campaign was Albion's success in the Halifax Cup competition, their first success in that particular competition since 1956 and the first time in nine years that a local side had lifted the trophy. Final opponents Illingworth led 10-6 at half time, but the Keighley side stormed to success thanks to four second half tries – two from Palmer – to win 28-10. The locals narrowly missed out on promotion to the Pennine League premier division under coach Peter Roe but it seemed only a matter of time before they joined Village in the top flight.

The 1989-90 Tommy Holmes final was a clean encounter between Worth Village and Keighley Celtic – the former winning against their emerging rivals 26-2. 1000 Lawkholme spectators saw former Albion man Simon Kelk (who would return to his former club the following season) score a hat-trick of tries in the match. By now Keighley had it's own representative side in the BARLA Inter-Town's competition but by now all was not well at Keighley Albion.

Albion struggled throughout the 1989-90 season after Peter Roe defected to Bradford's Dudley Hill club, taking several players with him. Under new coach Chris Ambler the side were forced to regroup and although they finished the campaign in a relegation place they were spared demotion at the season's end, although their 'A' team was a temporary casualty of the enforced changes at the club.

On a brighter note, a new 'Keighley & District Amateur Rugby league' was established in 1989, with the emphasis on giving local players the opportunity to play for the town in BARLA's 'Inter-Town' Cup competition and therefore to gain better recognition on the county stage. The main driving force behind the formation was David Ingham, who was, at the time, chairman of the Halifax & District ARL. The Halifax ARL were fully supportive of the move and actually made a substantial donation to the fledgling organisation, which saw the likes of Kevin Narey, Fred Farrington, Keith Bowen & Frank Moorby come on board. Despite the local team not making a great impression in the tournament (their first game was against Barrow ARL), in the following years Darren Walton became Keighley's first county representative for over 25 years when he played against Lancashire & Wayne McComb followed two years later when selected to play for Yorkshire against the Australian Aboriginal Tourists at Batley. Albion's Wayne Smith also earned county recognition during the 1990's.

KEIGHLEY STAR *photographed during their first season, 1981-82*

SILSDEN 1982-83

CHANGING TIMES

The start of the 1990's saw Keighley represented by five clubs – Keighley Albion, Worth Village, Keighley Star, Silsden and Silsden Rangers – yet by the end of the decade of these only Albion would still exist in their own right, without any of the others having actually fallen by the wayside! The decade would also see Albion's first team wave goodbye to Pennine League rugby as they took amateur rugby in Keighley to a new level, but they would have to move out of town to do this.

By the early 1990's the two Silsden clubs had put their original differences well behind them, and with some training sessions being joint ventures then the joining together of Silsden and Silsden Rangers was therefore not unexpected. At a meeting at the Bridge Inn in the town on August 2nd 1992 the merger was seen through – thus the new name of 'Silsden Park Rangers' was born. A new committee made up of members of both clubs was formed and Martin Plunkett, formerly of the Rangers club, became club coach. The 'new' club took the place of its forerunners in the Pennine league's third division .

The Pennine League was reorganised for the 1991-92 campaign, with 'A' teams forming their own short-lived three-division 'Alliance'. By now Keighley Celtic had risen from division 8 to division 3 in successive seasons. They suffered relegation back to division 4 this season, but at the time this was seen as a minor setback for a side that was beginning to challenge the dominance of Village and Albion in the town. However, 1994-95 proved a turning point for the club. Their successful annual '7's' tournament was switched from Lawkholme Lane to Keighley RUFC at the last minute due to reseeding at the professional club's ground. Ironically, the town's rugby union club had won the tournament 12 months previously, reflecting the newly created co-operation between the codes. Celtic's senior side was then forced into a 12 month sabbatical from the Pennine League due to a player shortage. Luckily history did not repeat itself, and unlike Oakworth Wanderers in the 1980's, the club proved true to its word and were back in division 5 of the league for the 1995-96 season. Their first game back was a 10-10 draw at Peel Park, Bradford against Shipley with tries from Steve Underwood and Phil Law, and by the end of the season they had made the Tommy Holmes final.

Major success in the Pennine League has continued to elude Keighley clubs, although the 1993-94 marked an upturn in the fortunes of local amateur rugby. Village took the division one title only 12 months after relegation from the premier division, while Albion followed them in the leagues elite with runners-up spot in the same division. It was a close run thing, with Halifax outfit Illingworth pipped for that vital second promotion spot on points difference. The 1994-95 campaign was therefore the first time two Keighley sides had appeared in the premier division at the same time, and although no honours came the locals' way that season both Village and Albion maintained their status. It was particularly pleasing for Village who lost their coach Dean Loynes at the beginning of the season due to work commitments. Gary Moorby, meanwhile, had successfully made the transition from player to successful coach while at Albion's helm. Keighley was in the grip of 'Cougarmania' – Cougars, 104-4 winners against Highfield, were in full flight but the professionals, who had worked so hard to evolve links with the community, were cruelly denied promotion to rugby league's elite when the introduction of 'Super League' made a mockery of the sport. Village meanwhile embarked on a tour to RAF Bruggen on the German/Dutch border and promptly won a competition against the RAF teams based in that region, and were actually involved in a rare 0-0 draw in a league match – against Keighley Albion of all teams in monsoon conditions at Marley. Albion themselves underlined their improvement when they inflicted on champions' Park Amateurs one of only two league defeats they suffered that season. Both local clubs were still in the premier division (Village finishing a fine third in 1995-96) when, in 1998, Keighley's local rugby scene began to dramatically change.

Late in the 1997-98 season, Keighley Albion made the bold bid of applying for election to the expanding National Conference League for the following season. Amateur rugby league's flagship competition was in the process of enlarging it's three divisions and it was recognised that the town of Keighley was not represented in its set-up ,and should be. Albion were duly elected, although it was recognised that their Highfield base would not be acceptable for their new league. An agreement was promptly reached with Crossflatts cricket club and the decision to move the first team to play on the adjoining field there was made, although it was with disappointment that a suitable ground within the boundaries of Keighley could not be used instead. As a result, Albion's junior section merged with the Bingley junior club, with 'Keighley Albion and Bingley' junior sides now operating in the west Riding Youth League. The necessary improvements to the new base were made in time for the opening of the 1998-99 campaign, when it was hoped that Albion would make an immediate impact in their new surroundings. Albion's 'A' team meanwhile, which had just won the division 5 title and divisional play-offs, continued in the Pennine League alongside Keighley's other clubs.

It proved to be a rude awakening for Albion. The Conference proved a much stronger undertaking than anything ever experienced before and that first season proved one long struggle – made worse when the division's other struggling club, Ovenden were thrown out of the league, leaving Albion stranded at the bottom with one league victory to their name. Luckily the club was re-elected at the end of the season at the following two seasons saw Albion attain mid-table safely in each (Albion's full National Conference record is listed later).

With Albion now established in the National Conference at Crossflatts, it was time for Keighley's other clubs to make the headlines twelve months on. In July 1999 it was announced that Worth Village and Keighley Celtic, two clubs who had always enjoyed a close relationship were to merge in order to create a 'super club' in town. With Albion moving outside the town boundaries it was hoped that the newly merged club could attract vital sponsorship and support from the town, with a long term goal of also making the National Conference. Initially the new club was known as 'Worth Village/Celtic' but within weeks had become the first rugby club to adopt the title 'Keighley Town' (the title had been used by several soccer teams over the years but had not been used since Keighley Town '79, which had disbanded it's senior team in 1988, dispensed with it's junior teams of the same name in the early 1990's). Both the Lord Rodney (Village) and St.Annes Centre (Celtic) were retained as joint bases and it was hoped that three teams could initially be maintained in the Pennine League – the first team taking Village's place in division one (having themselves just been relegated).

The Tommy Holmes competition remained as competitive as ever throughout the 1990's, although there was only one cup final shock. Inspired by man of the match Darren Walton, Village ran out 22-10 winners over Albion in the 1990-91 final, Albion regaining the trophy the following year when Silsden Park Rangers were denied another shock victory, five years after their previous success. Rangers led early on through a Stewart Johnson try but Albion hit back with tries from Roger Simpson (2), Paul Sin field and Steve Hunter (with Simon Kelk adding three conversions) to win 22-11. The following three finals saw Worth Village dominant over Albion – winning easily 36-4 in the 1992-93 final, they scored five second half tries the following year to set up an amazing treble over their rivals (having narrowly pipped them to Pennine's first division title and defeating them in the Jessop Marine trophy – see below), and again 25-4 in the 1994-95 final. On this occasion both teams had enjoyed their first season together in the premier division and despite an early brawl the holders won with tries from Morphed, Burkett, and McComb (2) and Rankin, with Hollingsworth adding the other points with his boot.

1995-96 saw Albion rout a revived Keighley Celtic 62-2 to set up the biggest ever winning margin in the final. An injury time Chris Kelly try in the semi-final had seen off Village 6-4 but the final at Keighley Rugby Union club proved no contest. Village retained the trophy 12 months later – Albion defeated 32-8 in a final that returned to Lawkholme Lane – or rather 'Cougar Park' as it is now known. This was to be the final time that the name of Worth Village would be engraved on the trophy.

1997-98 proved the year of the underdog as Silsden Park Rangers lifted their first silverware as a merged club. The 'Cobbydalers" some four divisions lower than their rivals, Village, secured a sensational 13-10 victory, although they were heavily defeated 10-42 by a rampant Albion one year on. Albion retained their title with a 19-10 victory over Keighley Town in the 1999-2000 final, and were again winners over Silsden Park Rangers in a final played prior to the opening of the 2001-2002 campaign.

With the merger of the Silsden clubs in 1992 there emerged a third 'A' team in the district, this being preceded by the ' Jessop Marine Trophy' which came into being for Keighley's second teams – donated by the local 'gold bullion' businessman Keith Jessop for the 1992-93 season. Rangers themselves made the first final following a 'round robin' group stage, but failed to make an impression as Village and Albion dominated the competition until the competition faded away in the early years of the new century.

The highly successful **LAWKHOLME LADIES** *side of 1985-86. Back: Karen Dunne, Victoria Hepworth, Heather Wilkinson, Julie Ellis, Helen Bailey, Senta Hepworth, Becky Vincent (manager), Middle: Mary Illingworth, Kathleen Peyton, Jayne Moses, Christine Hemsley, Jackie Spencer, Jane Thompson, Debbie Nixon, Front: Carolyn Armitage, Sarah Turner, Susan Thompson, Rhona Robinson, Angie Pickard, Michelle Redman,*

SILSDEN RANGERS
featured in the early 1990's

SILSDEN
photographed after defeating rivals Rangers to retain the Silsden Shield in November 1986

KEIGHLEY ALBION 1991-92 *Tommy Holmes Cup winners*
(photo : Trevor Smith)

WORTH VILLAGE 1992-93 *Tommy Holmes Cup winners*
(photo: Trevor Smith)

KEIGHLEY CELTIC 1992-93

Back: K.Tretton, S.Jowett, C.Hannah, S.Atkins, I.Anderson, C.Bell, S.Revak, M.Anderson, T.Walsh, G.Parker,
Front: D.Spencer, P.Young, G.Rankin, P.Bastow, mascot R.Spencer, P.Walsh, H.Parker, J.McComb, B.Shires,

KEIGHLEY CELTIC 1997-98
(photo: Trevor Smith)

WORTH VILLAGE 1996
(photo: Trevor Smith)
Village defeated the hosts, Keighley Rugby Union Club, to win Celtic's pre-season 7's competition. Team: J.Lister, C.Morphet, W.McComb, J.McComb, D.Birkett, J.Shaw, D.Walton, G.Baker, A.Feather,

WORTH VILLAGE 1997-98
back: C.Kelly, R.Curtain, J.Lister, D.Walton, R.Hellawell, J.McComb, D.Summerscales, D.Atkinson, R.Shaw, D.Cox,
front: M.Plunkett (coach), D.Birkett, J.Shaw, W.McComb, R.McNulty, J.Hollingsworth, B.Davey, A.Higgins, L.Steadman,
(photo: Trevor Smith)

... AND INTO THE 21ST CENTURY
(in brief)

2000-01 saw Silsden Park Rangers' first ever league title since the 'merger'. Following a voluntary demotion of two divisions the previous season in order to regroup, the side took division 4 by storm and secured the title with a 45-10 victory over Liversedge. However,f this was seen as a sign of things to come then nothing could have been further from the truth. With several players moving on and others retiring, the club struggled to raise a team the following season, and by Christmas 2001 it looked as if the club would be forced to disband. Following two unfulfilled fixtures- and therefore the deduction of four points – things remained on a knife edge as teams failing to fulfil a third league fixture were automatically expelled from the league. With only one win to their credit and a points total of minus two going into March one would expect Silsden to have been rock bottom of Pennine's division three – but Halifax side Boothtown Terriers had also had four points deducted, and with no wins to their credit they took the bottom spot with minus four ! Ovenden's second string failed to put in a late season appearance at Silsden, at least allowing the locals the ignominy of having less points at the start of the season than they had started with. Ironically, Silsden found themselves promoted only months later. Following a highly successful recruitment drive during the summer of 2002, the club was only too delighted to swap places with struggling Guiseley Rangers in division two for the 2002-2003 campaign !

The club fell from grace again as the rest of the decade proved to be a real struggle, dropping from division 2 to 5 in successive seasons, as player shortage problems raised their ugly head again. Luckily, things were again stabilised and unlike many other clubs in their situation they were able to survive. In the summer of 2010 the club once again became simply 'Silsden', dropping the 'Park Rangers' part of their title.

Two new clubs appeared – albeit briefly. South Craven Crushers unfortunately fell foul of the 'three failed appearances and your out' rule as the South Craven School based side failed to complete their only season – 2000-01. Later, Keighley Pumas were formed as an open-age team of the Keighley Cubs junior club. They played for just one season (2008-09) in the Yorkshire League, finishing bottom of division four (the bottom division), but this was harsh as several weaker teams dropped out during the season. In the summer of 2009 they moved from their Utley base to Bradford & Bingley RUFC – renamed themselves Bradford & Bingley Pumas in the process, and joined the Pennine League, where they played only a handful of games in division 7 before folding. Unlike Silsden, they could not survive a player shortage.

The 2001-2002 campaign was undoubtedly Keighley's least successful for many many years. With the town's three remaining clubs all struggling, local rugby league received a shock when the entire management committee of the Keighley & District Amateur Rugby League resigned due to a number of disagreements within the local game. Although the Inter-Town Cup had been discontinued in 1999, the local league still had the Tommy Holmes Trophy to organise and still had a seat on BARLA and Pennine League committees. This left Keighley in a position of having to resign its membership of BARLA, with local clubs forced to reapply for membership of the Halifax or Bradford ARL's and the Tommy Holmes Trophy therefore going into hibernation.

Keighley's Ladies side – under the banner of Keighley Albion Ladies since September 1998 and more recently as Keighley Wildcats – achieved Women's Premier League status, this following a flawless league record during the 1999-2000 campaign. They also reached the semi-final of the Challenge Cup in the 2001-02 season. Castleford were seen off by 28-14 in the last 8 through tries from Gemma Liddon, Jodie Billing, Jodee Loader and a brace from Saima Hussein (one of three Cats players in the England ladies development squad) with Laura Ackland adding points with her boot. The side were originally known as Lawkholme Ladies in the early 90's but are now firmly part of the Albion set-up. The Challenge Cup final was at least attained during the following year, but a disappointing defeat against arch rivals Bradford followed.

The recently formed Women's Conference saw Keighley crowned summer 2010 champions, after having won the Yorkshire section the previous season. The 2010 Grand Final saw them defeat Stanningley 18-14 in August, thanks to a 'golden-point' Saima Hussain try, bringing to the close a season during which they remained unbeaten. They had finished top of their section, and defeated Wigan in the semi-final en-route. This compensated somewhat for a 30-22 defeat to Bradford Thunderbirds in the Winter Challenge Cup final in April, a match which they led at the break.

Keighley's other successful club is that of the immensely successful Keighley Cougar Cubs, who continue to develop the town's young talent. Formed in 1991 the club has run teams at all age groups in the West Riding Youth League, and for a while the Yorkshire Combined League.

Keighley Albion have made use of Cougar Park/Lawkholme Lane in recent seasons, while initially maintaining their main base at Crossflatts. Despite being firmly established in the second division of the National Conference, their fourth campaign in the competition turned into an unexpected nightmare, with defeat after defeat the side trailed their rivals by some margin, although the club 'A' team pushed for promotion from the third division of the Pennine League. During the season it became clear that their Crossflatts base would no longer be available to them in future seasons, which along with their poor playing record threatened their existence in the Conference. A third blow was the death, during the season of the inspirational Jimmy Coulton, who had led the club to it's amazing run of success in the 1960's & 70's. A decision to revert back to Pennine League rugby for the 2002-03 campaign was therefore made, as the club looked for a new home. Being members of the Conference is hugely expensive and puts a lot of constraints on clubs, who have to match set criteria for membership such as having dug-outs, scoreboard, perimeter fencing and match-day programme. Albion were therefore in a position where they would have no home ground at which they could attempt to meet any of the Conference criteria. (The title 'National' Conference by now being a misnomer, as virtually all member clubs are now in that M62 corridor, those from farther afield such as Hemel Hempstead, Nottingham & London Skolars having left the league through a variety of reasons). Returning to the Pennine League at Highfield, Albion gained promotion to the premier division at the first attempt and then continued to hold their own until the 2009-10 season when they finished in a relegation spot – also earning themselves a points deduction for the following season due to an unfulfilled fixture (not something you are supposed to do in the top division).

Albion have battled through to the final of the Joseph Fee sponsored Halifax Cup several times in the last few seasons – without actually winning it on either of their appearances ! They went down fighting to favourites Illingworth at the end of the 2004-05 season, before two successive final defeats to Halifax Irish in 2007 and 2008, and again a to Siddal 'A', their victors in a close 2009 final.

Keighley Town initially failed to reach the standards expected from the merger of Village and Celtic, and they struggled near the foot of Pennine's division one during the 2001-02 & 2002-03 seasons. It was also a struggle at times to put out two teams at times, a problem which has also been experienced by Albion. They at last fulfilled their promise, joining Albion in the Pennine premier league for the 2005-06 campaign, but have since fallen back into the league's third tier.

A brighter spark has been the formation of the first rugby club in Cowling, the side joining the Pennine League for the 2002-03 season. They acquitted themselves well in division 6 of the Pennine League, although have not yet shows signs of rising beyond the bottom divisions in the league.

The formation of BARLA in 1973 saw the number of amateur clubs rise from less than 150 to over 1400 by the turn of the new century. The number of junior clubs had risen from around 30 to 900 or so in the same period. New clubs had been formed in Keighley since then, but many have since fallen by the wayside.

As other northern towns and cities boasted a huge increase in local clubs since the formation of BARLA, Keighley could not mirror that increase. The recent mergers between the Silsden clubs and Worth Village/Keighley Celtic enabled Keighley's current crop of clubs to survive in-tact, but in effect also helped to cushion the town from the staggering loss of amateur clubs seen in the county over the past five decade, particularly those from the more industrial areas of West Yorkshire.

The proposed move to summer rugby could have major implications for the amateur game. What this means to Keighley's amateur clubs remains to be seen.......

SELECTED PENNINE LEAGUE
TABLES (lower divisions where relevant & when available)

* = indicates points adjustments,
w/d = withdrawn

1974-75

DIVISION 2

	P	W	D	L	%
WORTH VILL.	24	20	0	4	83.33
Bradley	23	18	0	5	78.26
KEIGHLEY ALB.	24	18	0	6	75.00
St.Marys	24	15	0	9	62.50
Mayfield 'A'	23	14	0	9	60.86
Greetland A.R.	24	13	2	9	58.33
Fitton Hill	24	12	3	9	56.25
Clayton	22	9	2	11	45.45
Wyke	24	9	1	14	39.58
Int. Harvesters	24	8	1	15	35.41
Ferranti	24	7	1	16	31.25
Salem Hornets	24	2	0	22	8.33
Victoria Rangers	24	2	0	22	8.33

1975-76
Division 1: WORTH VILLAGE
Division 2: KEIGHLEY ALBION

1976-77, 1977-78, 1978-79
Division 2: WORTH VILLAGE
Division 3: KEIGHLEY ALBION

1979-80
Division 1: WORTH VILLAGE
Division 2: KEIGHLEY ALBION
Division 6: SILSDEN, WORTH VILL 'A'

1980-81
Division 1: WORTH VILLAGE
Division 2: KEIGHLEY ALBION
Division 5: SILSDEN
Division 6: WORTH VILLAGE 'A'
Division 7: OAKWORTH WANDERERS

1981-82
Division 1: WORTH VILLAGE
Division 2: KEIGHLEY ALBION

DIVISION 5

	P	W	D	L	Pts
Kirkholt WMC	16	13	1	2	27
SILSDEN	16	12	0	4	24
St.Josephs 'A'	16	9	2	5	20
Dudley Hill 'A'	16	9	1	6	19
Swan B's	16	8	2	6	18
Queen Anne	16	7	0	9	14
Spotland 'A'	16	5	1	10	11
Clayton 'A'	16	4	0	12	8
Greetland A.R. 'A'	16	1	1	14	3

Division 6: WORTH VILLAGE 'A'
Division 7: KEIGHLEY STAR, OAKWORTH WANDERERS

1982-83
Division 2: KEIGHLEY ALBION, WORTH VILLAGE
Division 4: SILSDEN
Division 6: KEIGHLEY STAR, WORTH VILLAGE 'A'
Division 7: KEIGHLEY ALBION 'A'

1983-84

DIVISION 2

	P	W	D	L	Pts
Shaw	18	16	0	2	32
KEIGHLEY ALB.	17	14	0	3	28
Illingworth	18	10	0	8	20
Greengates	17	9	1	7	19
WORTH VILL.	18	9	0	9	18
New Hey	18	6	3	9	15
Britannia Works	18	7	0	11	14
Greetland A.R.	18	7	0	11	14
Clayton	18	6	1	11	13
Wyke	18	2	1	15	5

Division 4: SILSDEN
Division 6: KEIGHLEY STAR, WORTH VILLAGE 'A'
Division 7: KEIGHLEY ALBION 'A'

1984-85
Division 1: KEIGHLEY ALBION
Division 2: WORTH VILLAGE
Division 4: SILSDEN
Division 5: KEIGHLEY STAR
Division 6: KEIGHLEY ALBION 'A', WORTH VILLAGE 'A'

DIVISION 7

	P	W	D	L	Pts
Birkenshaw 'A'	20	18	0	2	36
SILSDEN RGRS	20	14	0	6	28
Boothtown	20	13	2	5	28
Moldgreen 'A'	20	13	1	6	27
Bradley	20	12	1	7	25

Mixenden 'A'	20	9	1	10	19
Queensbury 'A'	20	8	1	11	17
Elland 'B'	20	8	1	11	17
Horton	20	5	2	13	12
Wyke 'A'	20	2	2	16	6
New Hey 'A'	20	1	1	18	3
Salem Hornets 'A'	*w/d*				

1985-86
Division 1: KEIGHLEY ALBION
Division 2: WORTH VILLAGE *(champions – no table available)*
Division 4: SILSDEN
Division 5: KEIGHLEY STAR
Division 6: SILSDEN RANGERS, WORTH VILLAGE 'A', *KEIGHLEY ALBION 'A' (w/d)*

1986-87
Division 1: WORTH VILLAGE, KEIGHLEY ALBION
Division 4: SILSDEN
Division 5: KEIGHLEY STAR
Division 6: SILSDEN RANGERS, WORTH VILLAGE 'A'
Division 8: KEIGHLEY CELTIC, KEIGHLEY ALBION 'A'

1987-88

PREMIER DIV.	P	W	D	L	Pts
Mayfield	14	12	0	2	24
St.Annes	14	7	2	5	16
Elland	14	8	0	8	16
Saddleworth	14	7	2	5	16
Park Amateurs	14	6	0	8	12
WORTH VILL.	14	5	2	7	12
Underbank Rgrs	14	3	0	11	6
Waterhead	14	3	0	11	6

Division 1: KEIGHLEY ALBION
Division 4: SILSDEN
Division 5: SILSDEN RANGERS, KEIGHLEY STAR, WORTH VILLAGE 'A'
Division 7: KEIGHLEY CELTIC, KEIGHLEY ALBION 'A'

1988-89
Premier Division: WORTH VILLAGE
Division 1: KEIGHLEY ALBION
Division 4: SILSDEN

Division 5: SILSDEN RANGERS, WORTH VILLAGE 'A', *GREAT NORTHERN (w/d)*
Division 6: KEIGHLEY CELTIC, KEIGHLEY ALBION 'A'

1989-90
Premier Division: WORTH VILLAGE
Division 1: KEIGHLEY ALBION
Division 4: SILSDEN, SILSDEN RNGRS
Division 5: KEIGHLEY CELTIC, WORTH VILLAGE 'A'

1990-91
Premier Division: WORTH VILLAGE
Division 1: KEIGHLEY ALBION
Division 3: SILSDEN RANGERS
Division 4: SILSDEN,KEIGHLEY CELTIC
Division 5: WORTH VILLAGE 'A'
Division 8: KEIGHLEY ALBION 'A'

1991-92
Premier Division: WORTH VILLAGE
Division 1: KEIGHLEY ALBION
Division 3: SILSDEN, SILSDEN RANGERS, KEIGHLEY CELTIC
Alliance 1: WORTH VILLAGE 'A'
Alliance 3: KEIGHLEY ALBION 'A'

1992-93

PREMIER DIV.	P	W	D	L	Pts
West Bowling	18	15	0	3	30
Park Amateurs	18	11	0	7	22
Elland	18	11	0	7	22
Ovenden	18	11	0	7	22
Clayton	18	10	0	8	20
Littleborough	18	9	0	9	18
Siddal	18	9	0	9	18
Birkenshaw	18	7	0	11	14
Illingworth	18	4	0	14	8
WORTH VILL.	18	3	0	15	6

Division 1: KEIGHLEY ALBION
Division 3: SILSDEN PARK RANGERS
Division 4: KEIGHLEY CELTIC
Alliance 2: KEIGHLEY ALBION 'A', WORTH VILLAGE 'A',
Alliance 3: SILSDEN PARK RNGRS 'A'

1993-94

DIVISION 1

	P	W	D	L	Pts
WORTH VILL.	18	16	0	2	32
KEIGHLEY ALB.	18	15	0	3	30
Illingworth	18	15	0	3	30
Odsal Sedbergh	18	11	0	7	22
Milnrow/ N.Hey	18	9	0	9	18
Salem Hornets	18	7	0	11	14
South Bradford	18	5	1	12	11
St.Josephs	18	5	0	13	10
Kirkholt	18	3	1	14	7
Paddock	18	3	0	15	6

Division 3: SILSDEN PARK RANGERS
Division 4: KEIGHLEY CELTIC
Alliance 2: KEIGHLEY ALBION 'A', WORTH VILLAGE 'A',
Alliance 3: *SILSDEN PK RNGRS 'A' (w/d)*

1994-95

PREMIER DIV.

	P	W	D	L	Pts
Park Amateurs	18	15	1	2	31
Ovenden	18	12	0	6	24
West Bowling	18	11	1	6	23
Siddal	18	11	0	7	22
Littleborough	18	10	0	8	20
WORTH VILL.	18	8	1	9	17
KEIGHLEY ALB.	18	7	2	9	16
Clayton	18	7	0	11	14
Underbank Rgrs	18	6	1	11	13
Elland	18	0	0	18	0

Division 3: SILSDEN PARK RANGERS
Alliance 1: WORTH VILLAGE 'A',
Alliance 2: KEIGHLEY ALBION 'A',
Alliance 3: SILSDEN PARK RNGRS 'A'

1995-96

PREMIER DIV.

	P	W	D	L	Pts
West Bowling	18	17	0	1	34
Park Amateurs	18	14	1	3	29
WORTH VILL.	18	12	1	5	25
Underbank Rgrs	18	10	2	6	22
Siddal	18	11	0	7	22
Clayton	18	9	2	7	20
KEIGHLEY ALB.	18	5	1	12	11
Birkenshaw	18	4	0	14	8
South Bradford	18	3	0	15	6
Littleborough	18	1	1	16	3

Division 4: SILSDEN PARK RANGERS
Division 5: KEIGHLEY CELTIC
Alliance 1: WORTH VILLAGE 'A',
Alliance 2: KEIGHLEY ALBION 'A',
Alliance 3: *SILSDEN PARK RGRS 'A' (w/d)*

1996-97

Premier Division: KEIGHLEY ALBION, WORTH VILLAGE
Division 4: SILSDEN PARK RANGERS
Division 5: KEIGHLEY CELTIC
Alliance 1: KEIGHLEY ALBION 'A', WORTH VILLAGE 'A',
Alliance 2: SILSDEN PARK RNGRS 'A'

1997-98

PREMIER DIV.

	P	W	D	L	Pts
Clayton	16	15	0	1	30
West Bowling	16	13	0	3	26
Park Amateurs	16	10	0	6	20
Lindley Swifts	16	9	0	7	18
Queensbury	16	9	0	7	18
Underbank Rgrs	16	5	0	11	10
KEIGHLEY ALB.	16	4	0	12	8
WORTH VILL.	16	3	0	13	6
Illingworth	16	3	0	13	6
Deighton Woolpack		*w/d*			

Division 4: SILSDEN PARK RANGERS, KEIGHLEY CELTIC
Division 5: KEIGHLEY ALBION 'A' *(champions)*
Alliance 1: WORTH VILLAGE 'A',
Alliance 2: *SILSDEN PK RNGRS 'A' (w/d)*

NATIONAL CONFERENCE & PENNINE LEAGUE TABLES

1998-99
NATIONAL CONFERENCE

DIVISION 2	P	W	D	L	Pts
Ideal Isberg	24	22	1	1	45
Eccles	24	20	0	4	40
Blackbrook	24	14	3	7	31
Eastmoor	24	15	1	8	31
Hull Dockers	24	14	0	10	28
Crosfields	24	13	1	10	27
London Skolars	24	11	0	13	22
Normanton	24	10	1	13	21
Dodworth	24	8	0	16	16
Dewsbury Moor	24	8	0	16	16
New Earswick	24	8	0	16	16
York Acorn	24	7	1	16	15
KEIGHLEY ALB.	24	1	0	23	2
Ovenden	w/d				

PENNINE LEAGUE

PREMIER DIV.	P	W	D	L	Pts
Park Amateurs	18	15	1	2	31
West Bowling	18	12	3	2	27
Queensbury	18	11	2	3	24
Elland	18	9	3	6	21
Clayton	18	10	0	8	20
Underbank Rgrs	18	10	0	8	20
Lindley Swifts	18	7	1	10	15
Undercliffe	18	4	0	13	8
Sowerby Br. Rob	18	3	0	15	6
WORTH VILL.	18	2	0	16	4

Division 3: SILSDEN PARK RANGERS
Division 4: KEIGHLEY CELTIC, KEIGHLEY ALBION 'A'
Division 6: WORTH VILLAGE 'A', KEIGHLEY CELTIC 'A', *SILSDEN PARK RANGERS 'A' (w/d)*

1999-2000
NATIONAL CONFERENCE

DIVISION 2	P	W	D	L	Pts
Eastmoor	26	24	0	2	48
West Bowling	26	22	0	4	44
Waterhead	26	18	1	7	37
Crosfields	26	16	0	10	32
Hull Dockers	26	14	1	11	29
Normanton Kn.	26	13	1	12	27
Dewsbury Moor	26	12	1	12	25
Milford Marlins	26	10	1	15	21
KEIGHLEY ALB.	26	10	1	15	21
New Earswick AB	26	10	0	16	20
Hillsborough H.	26	8	2	16	18
Castleford Panth.	26	6	5	15	17
York Acorn	26	7	0	19	14
London Skolars	26	5	1	20	11

PENNINE LEAGUE
Division 1: KEIGHLEY TOWN
Division 2: SILSDEN PARK RANGERS
Division 3: KEIGHLEY ALBION 'A', KEIGHLEY TOWN 'A'
Division 6: KEIGHLEY TOWN 'B' (w/d)

WOMEN'S FIRST DIVISION

	P	W	D	L	Pts
KEIGHLEY ALB	10	10	0	0	20
Milford/Hunslet	10	6	0	4	12
Birkenshaw	10	6	0	4	12
Hull Dockers	9	5	0	4	10
Rochdale	9	1	0	8	2
Halifax	10	1	0	9	2

2000-01
NATIONAL CONFERENCE

DIVISION 2	P	W	D	L	Pts
Thatto Heath	22	21	0	1	42
Hull Dockers	22	18	1	3	37
Crosfields	22	14	3	5	31
Sheff.Hillsboro' H	22	10	1	11	21
KEIGHLEY ALB.	22	10	1	11	21
Cottingham Tgrs	22	10	1	11	21
Normanton Kn.	22	8	2	12	18
York Acorn	22	8	1	13	17
Castleford Panth.	22	8	0	14	16
Milford Marlins	22	7	1	14	15
Dewsbury Moor	22	6	1	15	13
New Earswick AB	22	6	0	16	12
Blackbrook, London Skolars (w/d)					

PENNINE LEAGUE
Division 1: KEIGHLEY TOWN
Division 3: KEIGHLEY ALBION 'A'

DIVISION 4	P	W	D	L	Pts
SILSDEN P.R.	18	16	0	2	32
Stainland Stags	18	15	0	3	30
Greetland A.R.	18	13	0	5	26
Dodworth	18	10	1	7	21
Liversedge	18	9	1	8	19
Wetherby	18	6	0	12	8*

91

Clayton 'A'　　　18　4　2　12　8*
Hillsboro' H 'A'　18　5　1　12　7*
KEIGHLEY TN 'A'　18　5　0　13　6*
West Bowling 'B'　18　3　1　14　5*
Boothtown 'A', Lindley Swifts 'A' w/d

Division 6: S. CRAVEN CRUSHERS (w/d)

2001-02
NATIONAL CONFERENCE
DIVISION 2	P	W	D	L	Pts
Crosfields	22	20	0	2	40
Hunslet Warriors	22	20	0	2	40
Milford Marlins	22	17	0	5	34
York Acorn	22	14	0	8	28
Heworth	22	14	0	8	28
Normanton Kn.	22	12	0	10	24
Castleford Panth.	22	9	0	13	18
Sheff.Hillsboro' H	22	7	0	15	14
Millom	22	6	1	15	13
Dewsbury Moor	22	6	1	15	13
Cottingham Tigers	22	5	0	17	10
KEIGHLEY ALB.	22	1	0	21	2

PENNINE LEAGUE
Division 1: KEIGHLEY TOWN
Division 3: SILSDEN PARK RANGERS,
KEIGHLEY ALBION 'A'
Division 5: KEIGHLEY TOWN 'A'

2002-03
PENNINE LEAGUE
DIVISION 1	P	W	D	L	Pts
Westgate Red'bt	22	20	1	1	41
KEIGHLEY ALB.	22	18	0	4	36
Thornhill Tr 'A'	22	13	3	6	29
Victoria Rangers	22	13	2	7	28
Halifax Irish	22	13	2	7	28
West Bowling 'A'	22	11	3	8	25
Crigglestone AB	22	9	2	11	20
Clayton	22	9	2	11	20
Brighouse Rangers	22	7	3	12	17
KEIGHLEY TOWN	22	4	0	18	8
Emley Moor	22	4	1	16	7*
Rotherham	22	1	1	20	1*

Division 2: KEIGHLEY ALBION 'A'
SILSDEN PARK RANGERS *(moved from division 3 to division 2 at start of season)*
Division 5: KEIGHLEY TOWN 'A'
DIVISION 6	P	W	D	L	Pts
Bailiff Bridge	20	17	0	3	34

Thornton	20	16	0	4	32
Bank Top Harriers	20	12	0	8	24
COWLING HARL.	20	8	4	8	20
Clayton 'A'	20	10	1	9	19*
Rotherham 'A'	20	9	1	10	17*
Halifax Irish 'A'	20	10	1	9	17*
Underbank Rgr 'A'	20	9	1	10	15*
Greetland AR 'A'	20	7	0	11	14
Wyke 'A'	20	5	1	14	9
St.Josephs 'A'	20	3	1	16	7
Hoyland Vik 'A' w/d					

2003-04
PENNINE LEAGUE
PREMIER DIV	P	W	D	L	Pts
Elland	18	18	0	0	36
Ovenden	18	14	0	4	28
Westgate Redoubt	18	11	1	6	23
Siddal 'A'	18	9	0	9	18
Illingworth	18	9	0	9	18
Queensbury	18	9	0	9	18
Birkenshaw	18	7	0	11	14
KEIGHLEY ALB	18	6	1	11	13
Victoria Rangers	18	4	0	14	8
Park Amateurs	18	2	0	16	4

Division 1: KEIGHLEY TOWN
Division 2: SILSDEN PARK RANGERS
Division 4: KEIGHLEY ALBION 'A'
Division 5: KEIGHLEY TOWN 'A'
Division 6: COWLING HARLEQUINS

2004-05
PENNINE LEAGUE
PREMIER DIV	P	W	D	L	Pts
Drighlington	18	17	1	0	35
Illingworth	18	14	1	3	29
Elland	18	13	0	5	26
Clayton	18	11	0	7	22
Siddal 'A'	18	8	0	10	16
Queensbury	18	7	1	10	15
KEIGHLEY ALB	18	7	0	11	14
Westgate Redoubt	18	7	0	11	10*
Birkenshaw	18	3	1	14	7
Victoria Rangers	18	1	0	17	0

DIVISION 1	P	W	D	L	Pts
Brighouse Rangers	20	18	0	2	36
KEIGHLEY TOWN	20	14	0	6	28
Dodworth	20	13	0	7	26
Park Amateurs	20	12	0	8	24

92

Dudley Hill	20	12	0	8	22*
Halifax Irish	20	11	1	8	21
St.Josephs	20	9	1	10	20
Thornhill 'A'	20	9	0	11	14*
West Bowling 'A'	20	7	0	13	14
Calder Valley	20	3	0	17	4
Odsal Sedbergh	20	1	0	19	2

Division 2: SILSDEN PARK RANGERS
Division 4: COWLING HARLEQUINS,
KEIGHLEY ALBION 'A' w/d
Division 6: KEIGHLEY TOWN 'A'

2005-06
PENNINE LEAGUE

PREMIER DIV	P	W	D	L	Pts
Drighlington	22	18	0	2	36
Sharlston Rovers	22	16	0	4	32
Elland	22	14	1	5	29
KEIGHLEY ALB	22	14	0	6	28
Brighouse Rangers	22	11	0	9	22
Queensbury	22	9	0	11	18
Clayton	22	7	1	12	15
Westgate Redoubt	22	6	0	14	12
Siddal 'A'	22	6	0	14	12
Illingworth	22	5	1	14	11
KEIGHLEY TOWN	22	2	1	17	3

Division 2: SILSDEN PARK RANGERS
Division 6: COWLING HARLEQUINS
KEIGHLEY TOWN 'A'

2006-07
PENNINE LEAGUE

PREMIER DIV	P	W	D	L	Pts
Drighlington	18	15	0	3	30
Sharlston Rover	18	14	0	4	28
Halifax Irish	18	13	0	5	26
New Earswick AB	18	11	0	7	22
Queensbury	18	11	0	7	22
KEIGHLEY ALB	18	8	0	10	16
Elland	18	7	0	11	14
Clayton	18	7	0	11	14
KEIGHLEY TOWN	18	2	1	15	5
Siddal 'A'	18	1	1	16	1

Division 3: SILSDEN PARK RANGERS
Division 5: KEIGHLEY TOWN 'A'
Division 6: COWLING HARLEQUINS
KEIGHLEY ALBION 'A' (champions)

2007-08
PENNINE LEAGUE

PREMIER DIV	P	W	D	L	Pts
Halifax Irish	18	17	0	1	34
Sharlston Rovers	18	13	1	4	27
Drighlington	18	12	1	5	25
KEIGHLEY ALB	18	10	3	5	23
Clayton	18	8	0	10	16
New Earswick AB	18	8	0	10	16
St.Josephs	18	6	2	10	14
Queensbury	18	5	2	11	12
Kippax Welfare	18	5	0	13	10
Elland	18	1	1	16	3

Division 1: KEIGHLEY TOWN
Division 4: SILSDEN PARK RANGERS
Division 5: KEIGHLEY ALBION 'A'
KEIGHLEY TOWN 'A'
Division 6: COWLING HARLEQUINS

2008-09
PENNINE LEAGUE

PREMIER DIV	P	W	D	L	Pts
Sharlston Rovers	18	16	1	1	33
Drighlington	18	16	1	1	33
Halifax Irish	18	12	1	5	25
Siddal 'A'	18	12	0	6	24
KEIGHLEY ALB	18	8	1	9	17
St.Josephs	18	7	1	10	15
New Earswick AB	18	5	0	13	10
Crigglestone AB	18	4	1	13	9
Clayton	18	5	0	13	8*
Queensbury	18	2	0	16	4

Division 1: KEIGHLEY TOWN
Division 5: KEIGHLEY ALBION 'A'
KEIGHLEY TOWN 'A'
SILSDEN PARK RANGERS
Division 6: COWLING HARLEQUINS

YORKSHIRE LEAGUE

DIVISION 4	P	W	D	L	Pts
Heworth 'A'	14	13	0	1	26
Mirfield	14	10	0	4	20
Commercial Cgrs	14	8	0	6	16
Old Church Tav A	14	8	0	6	16
Eastmoor Drag 'A'	14	7	0	7	14
Upton 'A'	14	6	0	8	12
Heckmondwike	14	2	0	12	4
KEIGH. PUMAS	14	2	0	12	4

(several teams w/d during the season)

2009-10
PENNINE LEAGUE

PREMIER DIV	P	W	D	L	Pts
Drighlington	18	17	0	1	34
Sharlston Rovers	18	15	2	1	32
Siddal 'A'	18	11	0	7	22
Crigglestone AB	18	8	1	9	17
St.Josephs	18	6	3	9	15
Kippax Welfare	18	8	0	10	14*
Halifax Irish	18	5	3	10	13
Elland	18	6	0	12	12
New Earswick AB	18	5	1	12	11
KEIGHLEY ALB	18	4	0	14	6*

Division 1: KEIGHLEY TOWN
Division 4: KEIGHLEY ALBION 'A'
Division 5: KEIGHLEY TOWN 'A'
SILSDEN PARK RANGERS
Division 6: COWLING HARLEQUINS

2010-11
PENNINE LEAGUE
Division 1 West: KEIGHLEY ALBION
Division 2: KEIGHLEY TOWN
Division 4: SILSDEN
KEIGHLEY ALBION 'A' *(w/d pre-season)*
Division 6: KEIGHLEY TOWN 'A' *(w/d during season)*
COWLING HARLEQUINS

KEIGHLEY ALBION
NATIONAL CONFERENCE
RECORD 1998-2002
(Home fixtures in capitals, Albion score first)

1998-99

22/8/98	ECCLES	L	14-38
29/8/98	Normanton	L	24-30
5/9/98	OVENDEN	W	25-4
12/9/98	London Skolars	L	10-24
19/9/98	DODWORTH	L	20-32
26/9/98	Hull Dockers	L	0-52
3/10/98	NEW EARSWICK	L	10-15
10/10/98	IDEAL ISBERG	L	16-44
17/10/98	Eastmoor Dragons	L	8-24
24/10/98	DEWSBURY MOOR	L	8-14
7/11/98	BLACKBROOK	L	4-44
14/11/98	York Acorn	L	5-26
21/11/98	NORMANTON	W	16-14
28/11/98	Ovenden	L	4-38
12/12/98	LONDON SKOLARS	L	19-20
2/1/99	Dodworth	L	8-44
9/1/99	HULL DOCKERS	L	8-20
16/1/99	New Earswick	L	10-16
23/1/99	Ideal Isberg	L	10-30
20/2/99	Dewsbury Moor	L	0-25
27/2/99	CROSFIELDS	L	21-32
13/3/99	YORK ACORN	L	16-32
20/3/99	Eccles	L	0-56
27/3/99	Crosfields	L	10-54
3/4/99	EASTMOOR	L	20-26
14/4/99	Blackbrook	L	12-48

Matches v. Ovenden declared null & void due to Ovenden not completing the season

SILK CUT CHALLENGE CUP
5/12/98 rd1 DODWORTH L 6-42

BARLA NATIONAL CUP
30/1/99 rd 2 Pudsey D 17-17
(Albion won on tries scored)
13/2/99 rd 3 SKIRLAUGH L 14-54

1999-2000

28/8/99	York Acorn	L	18-27
4/9/99	WEST BOWLING	W	21-4
11/9/99	Dewsbury Moor	W	10-6
18/9/99	MILFORD	W	21-4
25/9/99	London Skolars	W	32-4
2/10/99	CROSFIELDS	L	12-15
9/10/99	New Earswick	W	30-16
16/10/99	CAS. PANTHERS	W	21-0
23/10/99	Eastmoor	L	6-28
30/9/99	Waterhead	L	6-14
6/11/99	HULL DOCKERS	W	23-14
13/11/99	Normanton	L	9-10
20/11/99	SHEFF. HILLSB' H	W	25-6
27/11/99	West Bowling	L	7-27
8/1/00	LONDON SKOLARS	W	15-13
15/1/00	Crosfields	W	24-14
22/1/00	NEW EARSWICK	L	15-16
5/2/00	Castleford Panthers	D	16-16
19/2/00	WATERHEAD	L	17-24
26/2/00	Hull Dockers	L	4-28
4/3/00	EASTMOOR	L	6-29
11/3/00	Sheff. Hillsboro' H	L	6-12
18/3/00	YORK ACORN	L	14-32
1/4/00	Milford	L	14-32
8/4/00	DEWSBURY MOOR	L	22-41
22/4/00	NORMANTON	L	0-24

SILK CUT CHALLENGE CUP
11/12/99 rd1 SIMMS CROSS W 17-10
3/01/00 rd2 STANLEY RGRS L 1-14

BARLA NATIONAL CUP
30/1/99 rd 2
      PILKINGTON RECS W 18-6
13/2/99 rd 3
      PARK AMATEURS L 18-26

2000-2001

26/8/00	SHEFF. HILLSB' H	W	8-6
2/9/00	Dewsbury Moor	L	13-16
9/9/00	NORMANTON	L	19-20
16/9/00	New Earswick	W	28-6
23/9/00	THATTO HEATH	L	4-48
30/9/00	YORK ACORN	L	10-17
7/10/00	London Skolars	L	3-6
14/10/00	MILFORD	W	16-12
29/10/00	HULL DOCKERS	L	6-18
11/11/00	CAS. PANTHERS	W	20-8
18/11/00	Cottingham	W	20-14
26/11/00	DEWSBURY MOOR	W	16-10
9/12/00	NEW EARSWICK	W	20-14
6/1/01	York Acorn	W	16-10
13/1/01	LONDON SKOLARS	W	36-14
3/2/01	Normanton	L	4-16
17/2/01	Blackbrook	W	52-4
24/2/01	Crosfields	L	10-40
10/3/01	Sheff.Hillsboro' H	L	16-17
17/3/01	Milford	W	32-14
24/3/01	BLACKBROOK	W	26-14
31/3/01	Castleford Panthers	L	6-26
14/4/01	CROSFIELDS	L	14-19
21/4/01	COTTINGHAM	W	39-12
25/4/01	Thatto Heath	L	4-42
5/5/01	Hull Dockers	L	6-44

Matches v. Blackbrook and London Skolars declared null & void due to these teams not completing the season

SILK CUT CHALLENGE CUP

2/12/99	rd1 Thatto Heath	L	22-24

BARLA CUP

27/1/99	rd 2 EMBASSY	W	30-4
13/2/99	rd 3 EGREMONT	L	4-14

2001-2002

25/8/01	Milford	L	6-32
1/9/01	Cottingham	L	4-23
8/9/01	DEWSBURY MOOR	L	13-18
15/9/01	Crosfields	L	7-48
22/9/01	YORK ACORN	L	16-26
29/9/01	Sheff.Hillsboro' H	L	18-20
6/10/01	Normanton	L	8-18
13/10/01	HUNSLET WARR.	L	4-22
20/10/01	Millom	L	10-30
27/10/01	CAS. PANTHERS	L	14-18
3/11/01	Heworth	L	10-16
10/11/01	COTTINGHAM	L	24-26
17/11/01	Dewsbury Moor	L	10-30
24/11/01	CROSFIELDS	L	16-58
15/12/01	Sheff. Hillsboro' H	L	10-36
19/1/02	Castleford Panthers	L	12-30
16/2/02	MILFORD	L	6-42
23/2/02	Hunslet Warriors	L	0-56
2/3/02	HEWORTH	L	14-23
9/3/02	NORMANTON	L	0-44
23/3/02	York Acorn	L	6-46
30/3/02	MILLOM	W	23-2

CHALLENGE CUP

1/12/01	EASTMOOR	L	10-44

BARLA NATIONAL CUP

12/1/02	Heysham Atoms	W	20-18
26/1/02	ROCH.MAYFIELD	L	14-18

ROLL OF HONOUR

A list of victorious Keighley Amateur clubs through the years.
Note: the results of some competitions are unknown.

KEIGHLEY CHARITY CUP FINALS
1889-90 Silsden, 3 tries & 2 minors, beat Ingrow, 0 points
1890-91 Silsden, 3 goals, 2 tries & 4 minors, beat Keighley Zingari, 2 minors
1891-92 Ingrow...2 Keighley Shamrocks...0
1892-93 Keighley Zingari...6 Ingrow...0
1893-94 Keighley Zingari...7 Keighley 'A'...0
1894-95 Keighley Shamrocks...11 Keighley Trinity...0
1897-98 Keighley Trinity (played on a league basis)
1900-01 Steeton...2 Keighley St.Annes...0
1902-03 Keighley St.Annes...5 Keighley Clarence...4
1903-04 Haworth...3 Keighley Olicana...0
Charity Cup discontinued as a rugby competition.
New Charity Cup:
1927-28 Keighley Supporters...9 Sowerby Bridge West End..5
1928-29 Eastmoor (Wakefield)...21 Silsden...8
1929-30 Eastmoor...38 Keighley Highfield...0
1930-31 Eastmoor...11 Buslingthorpe Vale (Leeds)...0
1931-32 Keighley Highfield...7 Silsden...3

KEIGHLEY & DISTRICT CUP FINALS
1947-48 winners unknown
1948-49 Keighley Athletic...14 Keighley Co-op...9
1949-50 Silsden...9 Keighley Albion...7
1950-51 Riddlesden...9 Keighley Albion...7
1951-52 Silsden...25 Riddlesden...6
1952-53 Clayton...15 Silsden...14
1953-54 West Bowling...5 Keighley Albion...3
1954-55 Keighley Albion...18 Victoria Park...5
1955-56 Keighley Albion v Dewsbury Celtic - result unknown
1956-57 Keighley Albion...50 Ovenden...9
1957-58 winners: Keighley Albion
1958-59 winners unknown
1959-60 Wyke (Bradford)...16 West Bowling (Bradford)...0
1960-61 winners unknown
1961-62 winners unknown
1962-63 Prince Smith & Stells...9 Keighley Albion...3

KEIGHLEY & DISTRICT LEAGUE winners & championship finals

1899-00 final: St.Annes...3 Bingley Trinity...2
1901-02 final: Bingley Clarence...6 Keighley Clarence 'A'..0
1902-03 champions: St.Annes Guild
1907-08 champions: Haworth
1908-09 champions: unknown
1922-23 final: Worth Village...5 Silsden...2
1923-24 champions: Parkwood Hornets
1924-25 final: Worth Village...12 Thwaites Rovers...0
1925-26 final: Silsden 'A'...5   Parkwood Hornets...0
1926-27 final: Keighley Supporters 'A' beat Keighley Supporters 'B'
1927-28 champions: Keighley Highfield
1928-29 final: Keighley Supporters...10 Silsden...6
1929-30 Silsden...8 Keighley Northern Juniors...5
1936-37 Junior Cup final: Silsden...14 Keighley Juniors...5
         Intermediate Cup final: Victoria Park...26 Aireworth Athletic...8
1938-39: Junior League final: Keighley Shamrocks...11 Dudley Hill (Bradford)...4,
         Intermediate League final: Victoria Park...19 Ingrow...3,
         Junior League Charity Cup final: New Road Side...6   Luddendenfoot
         (Halifax)...6 (shared),
         Intermediate League 'Sam Slater' Cup final: Victoria Park...19 Ingrow...0
1942-43 Workshops League final: Dean Smith & Grace beat Prince Smith & Stells
         Wartime League final: Prince Smith & Stells beat Hunslet
1947-48 champions: Keighley Athletic
1949-50 champions: Keighley Albion
1950-51 champions: Keighley Albion...17 Eastwood Tavern...9
1951-52 final: Eastwood Tavern...13 Keighley Albion...6
1952-53 champions: Silsden
1953-54 champions: Keighley Albion
         Medal Competition final: Silsden...11 Keighley Albion...3
1954-55 final: Keighley Albion...13 Silsden...10
1955-56 final: Silsden...14 Victoria Park Rangers...13
1956-57 final: Keighley Albion...33 Victoria Park Rangers...7
1957-58 final: Victoria Park Rangers...9 Keighley Albion...8
1958-59 final: Keighley Albion...12 Victoria Park Rangers...8
1959-60 final: Worth Village beat Silsden
1960-61 winners unknown

TOMMY HOLMES CUP FINALS
1973-74 Worth Village...9 Keighley Albion...9
1978-79 Worth Village...30 Keighley Albion...17
1979-80 Worth Village beat Keighley Albion
1980-81 Worth Village...14 Keighley Albion...7
1981-82 Keighley Albion...11 Silsden...3
1982-83 *no final, competition suspended for one year*
1983-84 Worth Village...13 Keighley Albion...12
1984-85 Keighley Albion...30 Silsden...14
1985-86 Keighley Albion...16 Worth Village...10
1986-87 Silsden Rangers...18 Keighley Albion...14
1987-88 Worth Village...30 Silsden...3
1988-89 Keighley Albion...27 Worth Village...14
1989-90 Worth Village...26 Keighley Celtic...2
1990-91 Worth Village...22 Keighley Albion...10
1991-92 Keighley Albion...22 Silsden Rangers...11
1992-93 Worth Village...36 Keighley Albion...4
1993-94 Worth Village beat Keighley Albion
1994-95 Worth Village...25 Keighley Albion...4
1995-96 Keighley Albion...62 Keighley Celtic...2
1996-97 Worth Village...32 Keighley Albion...8
1997-98 Silsden Park Rangers...13 Worth Village...10
1998-99 Keighley Albion...42 Silsden Park Rangers...10
1999-2000 Keighley Albion...19 Keighley Town...10
2000-01 Keighley Albion...30 Silsden Park Rangers...18 (played in August 2001)

JESSOP MARINE TROPHY FINALS
1991-92 Keighley Albion 'A'...14 Worth Village 'A'...12
1992-93 Keighley Albion 'A'...10 Silsden Park Rangers 'A'...6
1993-94 Worth Village 'A' beat Keighley Albion 'A'
1994-95 Keighley Albion 'A'...28 Worth Village 'A'...14
1995-96 Worth Village 'A'...24 Keighley Albion 'A'...4
1996-97 Keighley Albion 'A'...32 Worth Village 'A'...20
1997-98 Keighley Albion 'A'...20 Worth Village 'A'...0
1998-99 Worth Village 'A' beat Keighley Albion 'A'
1999-2000 Keighley Albion 'A'...25 Keighley Town 'A'...16

SILSDEN SHIELD
1985-86 Silsden...18 Silsden Rangers...6
1986-87 Silsden...16 Silsden Rangers...10
1987-88 Silsden Rangers...44 Silsden...4
1988-89 Silsden Rangers...16 Silsden...6

OTHER LEAGUE/CUP COMPETITIONS WON BY KEIGHLEY TEAMS

1894-95 WHARFEDALE CUP, WEST YORKSHIRE LEAGUE: Keighley Shamrocks

1895-96 BRADFORD & DIST. LEAGUE: Sutton (joint champions)

1899-1900 BRADFORD & DISTRICT CUP: Worth Village

1911-12 HALIFAX CHARITY CUP: Keighley Zingari

1913-14 HALIFAX CHARITY CUP: Keighley Zingari

1921-22 BRADFORD & DIST. LEAGUE: INTERMEDIATE DIVISION: champions: Utley St.Marks, Supplementary League Cup: Silsden 'A'

1923-24 BRADFORD & DIST. LEAGUE: Keighley Low Street

1924-25 BRADFORD & DIST. LEAGUE: Keighley Low Street

1926-27 BRADFORD & DIST. LEAGUE CUP: Silsden

1927-28 BRADFORD & DIST. LEAGUE: INTERMEDIATE DIV: Keighley Highfield

1928-29 BRADFORD & DIST. LEAGUE: INTERMEDIATE DIV: Kly Supporters
BRADFORD NORTHERN WORKSHOPS COMPETITION: Silsden

1929-30 BRADFORD & DIST. LEAGUE (Junior/Open Age Division): Silsden, (Intermediate/under 21 Div.): Silsden

1930-31 BRADFORD & DIST. LEAGUE: Keighley Highfield

1944-45 BRADFORD & DISTRICT CUP: Keighley Athletic

1951-52 HALIFAX UNDER 18 LEAGUE CUP, HALIFAX JUNIOR (U-18) CUP: Keighley Albion

1952-53 BRADFORD UNDER 18 LEAGUE CUP: Keighley Albion

1954-55 BRADFORD CUP, HALIFAX CHARITY CUP: Keighley Albion

1955-56 HALIFAX CHARITY CUP: Keighley Albion

1956-57 BRADFORD LEAGUE: Keighley Albion

1957-58 BRADFORD LEAGUE, BRADFORD CUP, HALIFAX UNDER 19 LEAGUE: Keighley Albion

1958-59 BRADFORD LEAGUE, BRADFORD CUP: Keighley Albion

1959-60 BRADFORD CUP: Keighley Albion

1963-64 LEEDS LEAGUE: Keighley Albion

1968-69 BRADFORD LEAGUE: Keighley Albion
BRADFORD SUNDAY JUNIOR LEAGUE CUP (UNDER 18'S): Keighley Junior Supporters Club

1969-70 BRADFORD SUNDAY JUNIOR LEAGUE (UNDER 19'S): Keighley Albion

1970-71 BRADFORD CUP: Keighley Albion

1971-72 BRADFORD SUNDAY JUNIOR LEAGUE CUP (UNDER 19'S): Keighley Junior Supporters Club

1973-74 HUDDERSFIELD / HALIFAX COMBINED LEAGUE: DIVISION THREE: Worth Village
HUDDERSFIELD / HALIFAX COMBINED LEAGUE: DIVISION THREE PLAY-OFFS: Keighley Albion

1974-75 PENNINE LEAGUE DIVISION 2: Worth Village

1976-77 HALIFAX CUP: Worth Village

1977-78 HALIFAX CUP: Worth Village

1978-79 HALIFAX UNDER 17'S CUP: Keighley Albion

1979-80 HALIFAX CUP: Worth Village
        HALIFAX UNDER 17'S CUP: Keighley Albion
1980-81 HALIFAX UNDER 17'S CUP, BRADFORD & KEIGHLEY CHALLENGE
        AND SUPPLEMENTARY CUPS: Keighley Albion
1981-82 HALIFAX UNDER 19'S CUP: Keighley Albion
1985-86 PENNINE LEAGUE: DIVISION 2: Worth Village
1986-87 HALIFAX UNDER 17'S CUP: Keighley Albion
        WEST RIDING UNDER 13'S CUP: Keighley Celtic
1988-89 HALIFAX CUP: Keighley Albion
1993-94 PENNINE LEAGUE: DIVISION 1: Worth Village
1997-98 PENNINE LEAGUE: DIVISION 5: Keighley Albion 'A'
1999-2000 NATIONAL WOMENS RUGBY LEAGUE: DIVISION 1
        (& WESTERN CONFERENCE): Keighley Cats
2000-01 PENNINE LEAGUE: DIVISION 4: Silsden Park Rangers
2006-07 PENNINE LEAGUE DIVISION 6: Keighley Albion 'A'

Since 1976-77 the Halifax Cup has been more commonly known as the 'Joseph Fee Memorial Trophy'.
Note: Keighley Cougar Cubs have achieved success at many age-group levels in the West Riding Youth League since 1991. Full list not available.

Looking at the above list, top level success has certainly eluded Keighley's open-age teams in recent years. Whereas many of the top sides in Halifax & Bradford – Siddal, Dudley Hill, etc - have become established, and successful at National Conference level, as well as continuing to pick up silverware in the higher echelons of the Pennine League, Keighley has not seen that progress made by any of its clubs in recent years.

KEIGHLEY'S RUGBY CLUBS

Note: up to 1899-1900, all clubs played 'Rugby' (Today's Rugby Union). From the 1899 local clubs went over to Northern Union (today's Rugby league), unless stated otherwise.
Does not include sides entered in various ' workshop competitions'.

Keighley's rugby clubs fall into several categories, listed below. There are obvious exceptions, but generally they have the following origins:

- Early church-based teams, reflecting 'Muscular Christianity' whereby the Church of England encouraged young men to partake in sporting pursuits as a means to achieving mental & spiritual fulfilment. Sponsoring their own rugby, cricket or soccer teams also helped local churches to encourage men into their congregation.
- Village sides, reflecting distinct communities. These include those teams from parts of Keighley, (eg. Ingrow) with their own identity.
- Teams reflecting local industry – local mills (eg. Acre & Sutton Mils) and engineering works (eg. NSF) in particular, the latter of which had faded from the scene by the 1960's as local firms went into decline.
- Club sides from Keighley itself. These clubs – Keighley Albion being a recent example – representing the whole town rather than distinct villages or communities.
- In recent times, 'pub' sides have been in existence in local rugby across the north of England. Local sides have always been based at local hostelries, but in recent years sponsorship from these public houses has led to these clubs adopting the title of their base. The Eastwood Tavern & Keighley Star clubs are examples of this.
- Junior clubs – formed specifically for the younger player. Whereas established clubs such as Albion, Silsden & Worth Village operated junior sides, others such as Aire Valley Bulldogs & Bracken Bank were formed as purely junior clubs, running sides at various age-groups.
- 'Supporters Clubs' – these being associated with the town's professional rugby league club. (eg. Keighley Supporters club)
- In the early years of the sport, several 'scratch' teams experiment with rugby. Some eventually becoming well organised clubs, others disappearing as quickly as they had at first appeared.

ACRE MILLS - Northern union club playing 'friendly' fixtures during 1902-03 season. Although unreported in the local press, other local mill sides, consisting of the local workforce, probably ran rugby teams around the same time, playing informal fixtures.

AIREDALE FREE WANDERERS - Based at Stockbridge. In the absence of organised 'leagues' at the time, they played 'friendly' fixtures from 1885-1888. Club colours were known to be blue & white.

AIREWORTH ALEXANDRA - Informal side operating between 1886-90. Played on a ground at Stockbridge, opposite the Bridge Inn.

AIREWORTH ATHLETIC – Played for a single season – in the 1937-38 Keighley & District League (Intermediate Division)

AIRE VALLEY BULLDOGS – This outfit was around in the 1990-91 season, a club catering for junior players and operating at under 12 & under 14 level. In order to forge closer links with the professional Keighley Cougars the club changed its name to **Keighley Cougar Cubs** at its AGM in July 1991, amalgamating with Keighley Albion's junior sides around the same time.

BARCROFT – Played at least one friendly fixture early in 1893, but were likely to have been an 'informal' side, no doubt formed by locals of the Barcroft area of Cross Roads.

BEECHCLIFFE - Based at Utley, played between 1887-91. Became defunct during around spring/ summer of 1891. A Beechcliffe side played a few friendly fixtures during the 1894-95 season.

BEECHCLIFFE CELTIC - A team that lasted only one season, playing in the Keighley & District League in the 1925-26 season.

BRACKEN BANK – (1) Appeared in the 1959-60 season, when they played fixtures against other local under 19 sides.
(2) Coached by Stuart Woolley, a new Bracken Bank Juniors competed in the Keighley & Bradford Youth League in the mid-1970's.

BROOMHILL - A club of this name hoped to play in a reformed Keighley & District League during the 1937-38 season, but did not take their place.

CO-OPERATIVE IRONWORKS – Reflecting the engineering presence in the town, a club of this name hoped to play in a reformed Keighley & District League during the 1937-38 season, but did not take their place in the new league.

COWLING HARLEQUINS – Throughout the years, Cowling had never had a rugby club, despite a well established cricket & soccer club. This all changed when Cowling Amateur Rugby League club joined the Pennine League for the 2002-03 campaign, playing initially at the village playing fields on Keighley Road.

CROSSHILLS – First opponents of the newly formed Keighley rugby club in 1877 – little else is known about this side, who may well have been an informal or 'scratch' team.

CROSSHILLS JUNIORS - Informal side operating during the 1886-87 season. It was well over 100 years before another club appeared in Cross Hills (South Craven Crushers) although nearby Sutton operated a successful side before 1900.

CROSS ROADS - (1) Formed late 1888/ early 1889. Did not compete in any league competition. Became defunct in the summer of 1894.
(2) Reformed as a northern union club, played in the Keighley & District Junior League in 1900-01, and the following two seasons in the Bradford & District League. Disbanded during the summer of 1903, selling their effects to Ingrow in August of that year.
(3) A new club hoped to play in the Keighley Intermediate League for the 1908-09 season, sharing a ground in the village with the Ingrow club. Unfortunately this never materialised and only Ingrow took the field that season.
(4) It was also hoped to revive the club for the 1921-22 season, again this proved unsuccessful, although a successful soccer team was formed instead.

CROSS ROADS ST.JAMES Y.C. - Appeared in the 1959-60 season, when they played fixtures against other local under 19 sides.

DALTON SWIFTS – Played only in the 1926-27 Keighley & District League. Were not in existence the following season.

DEAN SMITH & GRACE - Joined the Keighley & District League for the 1937-38 season but do not appear to have played any fixtures. However, during World War 2 this works-based team played in the 1943-44 Keighley Workshops Junior League and the 1944-45 Huddersfield & District League. In later years, the engineering works would sponsor a highly successful Sunday league soccer team.
Honours: Keighley Workshops League 1943-44,

DEVONSHIRE STREET SPORTS – This team played in the Intermediate (Under 18) section of the 1948-49 Bradford League. They appear not to have been around the following season.

DEVONSHIRE WORKS - A club of this name hoped to play in a reformed Keighley & District League during the 1937-38 season, but did not take their place in the new league.

6th DUKE OF WELLINGTON REGIMENT -
(1) Northern union club playing 'friendly' fixtures during the 1901-02 season.
(2) 1921-22 Bradford & District league (Intermediate Division) Were to have taken part in the 1922-23 Keighley & District League but seem to have disbanded during the summer of 1922.

EASTWOOD RANGERS - Hoped to compete in the 1922-23 Keighley & District League but this never materialised.

EASTWOOD TAVERN -Played at Utley, and then Parkwood Greyhound Stadium. Disbanded in 1954, with most of the club's players moving on to the Victoria Park Rangers club, who shared the same ground.
1950-53 Bradford/Keighley League
1953-54 Keighley & District League
Honours: Keighley League 1951-52

EXLEY HEAD - Played some 'friendly' fixtures along with Haworth and Ingrow during the 1911-12 season. Possibly linked to the local Methodist Church in the area.

FELL LANE - Hoped to compete in the 1922-23 Keighley & District League but this never materialised. Several local soccer teams played in the Fell Lane area both before and at this time, this club possibly being formed by soccer players looking for a fresh challenge.

GLUSBURN – see Sutton

GREAT NORTHERN – see **Keighley Star**

GREEN GABLES – Looked all set to join the Pennine League for the 1986-87 season, with a coach (Harry Plunkett), ground and playing strip all in place. Unfortunately this new club was unable to attract sufficient players, and rather than poaching those from other local clubs decided not to take it's place in division 8 that season. No serious attempts were made to 'revive' this pub-based club in subsequent seasons.

GREENGATE CELTIC – Played for two seasons only, in the Keighley & District League (1925-27).

GUARDHOUSE SHAMROCKS - see **Keighley Shamrocks**

HAGGAS & SMITH – Reflecting the engineering presence in town, this team joined the Keighley & District League for the 1937-38 season but do not appear to have played any fixtures.

HAINWORTH - Informal side operating between 1887-90. Their ground was described as a *'breezy eminence at the back of Hainworth Wood'*, which is likely to be that which was later used by Hainworth City AFC, and more recently used by Ingrow Cricket Club.

HARGREAVES CO. - During World War 2 they affiliated with the 1943-44 Keighley Workshops Rugby League, but played only 'friendly' fixtures.

HATTERSLEYS EMPLOYEES - A Hattersleys Fitters-v-Turners challenge match was played at the Worth Village ground in January 1885. A Hattersleys works side then played friendly fixtures at least during the 1886-87 season, and again during 1903-04. Hattersleys later operated a successful soccer team.

HAWORTH - (1) The first club in the village was formed prior to the 1884-85 season. It did not compete in any league competition and became defunct in the summer of 1895.
(2) Haworth were reformed around the summer of 1901, and played 'ordinary' fixtures during the 1901-02 season. Between 1902-06 they played in the Bradford & District Junior League. The club won the last Keighley Charity Cup to be played under rugby rules in 1903-04 season, but disbanded in March 1906, while bottom of the Bradford League. Their ground was at West Lane, which was used by local soccer teams for a number of years after that, and now by Haworth Cricket Club.
Honours: Keighley Charity Cup 1903-04,
(3) A revived club played in the Keighley Intermediate League between 1908-10. They played the 1909-10 campaign at the West Lane ground, and used the Black Bull as headquarters / dressing rooms. Appear not to have continued when the local league went into hibernation after the 1909-10 season, although a Haworth team is known to have played friendly fixtures only during the 1911-12 season.
Honours: Keighley Intermediate League 1908-09,
(4) The final club to bear the village name played between 1937-39 in the Keighley & District League (Intermediate Division). They withdrew due to a player shortage during their second season.

HAWORTH ALBION - (1) Informal side operating between 1885-87.
(2) A Haworth Albion side also played a few friendly games during the 1892-93 season.

HAWORTH HIGHFIELD - see **Keighley Highfield**

HAWORTH RANGERS - (1) Informal side operating during the 1886-87 season.
(2) A relatively minor side of this name played during the 1889-90 & 1890-91 seasons.
(3) Northern union side formed around 1902, playing in the 1902-03 Keighley & District Junior League.

HAWORTH ROVERS -Informal side operating in 1888-89 season. A Haworth Rovers side also played a few friendly games during the 1892-93 season.

HAWORTH TRINITY - Informal side operating in the 1885-86 season.

HAWORTH 1904-05 *(courtesy of Steven Wood)*

HAWORTH 1909

HIGHFIELD SHAMROCKS - see **Keighley Shamrocks**

HOLME MILLS - 1937-38 Keighley & District League (Junior Division). This appears to be their only competitive season although it is possible that other 'friendly' fixtures were played around this time.

HOLYCROFT – An early Northern union club playing 'friendly' fixtures during the 1902-03 season.

HOLYCROFT YOUTH CENTRE - Appeared in the 1959-60 season, when they played fixtures against other local under 19 sides.

INGROW - (1) First appeared in 1885-86 season, following a Keighley rugby club friendly against an **Ingrow & District select.** Their initial ground was at Knowle Spring Brewery, but by September 1889 they had moved to a new field on Fell Lane. The start of 1892-93 season saw them move to a new, larger field, also on Fell Lane. Played in the Yorkshire No.3 competition (group A) 1893-94, but disbanded after finishing bottom of the table.
Honours: Keighley Charity Cup 1891-92
(2) Northern Union club, possibly a continuance of the Ingrow Trinity team that was formed around 1900.
1902-03 Keighley & District League
1903-04 Bradford & District League.
Disbanded during the summer of 1904.
(3) Reformed club played a few 'friendly' fixtures during the 1907-08 season before playing in the Keighley Intermediate League between 1908-10. Seem to have become defunct, along with the local league during the summer of 1910. Played at Cross Roads. HQ at The New Inn, Barcroft. Colours: black & amber. An Ingrow team did play some friendly fixtures during the 1911-12 season and is possibly related in some way to this club.
(4) It was hoped to revive the Ingrow club prior to the 1921-22 season, but unfortunately this never came to fruition.
(5) The fifth and final club to bear the Ingrow name played competitive rugby between 1937 & 1941.
1937-39 Keighley & District League (Intermediate Division)
1939-40 Bradford Intermediate League
1940-41 Bradford & District Wartime League

INGROW RANGERS - Local side operating from 1885-88, playing friendly fixtures, in the absence of organised competition.

INGROW ST.JOHNS – A church-based northern union side that played friendly fixtures between 1900-04. Also took part in the Keighley Charity Cup competition during the 1903-04 season.

INGROW TRINITY – Another church-based northern union club formed prior to the 1900-01 season, in which they played 'ordinary' games only.
Played in the 1901-02 Keighley & District Junior League and it is likely that the **Ingrow** team of 1902-04 had its roots in the Trinity team.

JOHN LUNDS WORKS - During World War 2 they played in the 1943-44 Keighley Workshops Junior League.

KEIGHLEY - Formed as a rugby and association club on 17th October 1876, although the association section never took off and rugby was the principal interest from the onset. Playing at first on a field in the Lawkholme area of town (owned by one E.Holmes), then on Dalton Lane from 1878, they merged with Keighley Athletic & Football club in April 1881. Moved to Lawkholme Lane upon a further merger with the Keighley cricket club.
1893-94 Yorkshire Intermediate Competition (between No.2 & No.3 competitions)
1894-95 Yorkshire No.3 competition
1895-97 Yorkshire No.2 competition (renamed No.3 competition) - winners in second season
1897-98 Yorkshire No.1 competition (runners up in first two seasons). Towards the close of this season the club defected to the northern union and have since been the town's professional rugby league club. The subsequent history of the professional Keighley Rugby league Club is of course another tale.

KEIGHLEY ALBION - Formed prior to the 1948-49 season as a revived **Keighley Athletic**, renamed Keighley Albion from the 1949-50 season. Originally played at Theaproyd, close to the Lawkholme Lane ground, until 1964. Played temporarily at Marley (1964-65) before a permanent move to Highfield. Moved to Crossflatts Cricket Club in 1998 in order to meet National Conference requirements, although some home games were played at Lawkholme Lane / Cougar Park. Moved back to Highfield when they dropped out of the Conference, but returned to Crossflatts in 2010.

1949-53 Bradford / Keighley League
1953-55 Keighley & District League
1955-56 Keighley / Dewsbury League
1956-61 Bradford League
1961-64 Leeds League
1964-73 Bradford League
1973-74 Huddersfield / Halifax League
1974-98 Pennine League
1998-2002 National Conference ('A' team in the Pennine League)
2002- to date Pennine League

Honours: Keighley League 1949-50, 1950-51, 1953-54, 1954-55, 1956-57, 1958-59, Keighley Cup 1954-55, 1956-57, 1957-58, Halifax Charity Cup 1954-55, 1955-56, 1988-89 Bradford League 1956-57,1957-58,1958-59, 1968-69, Bradford Cup 1954-55,1957-58, 1958-59, 1959-60, 1970-71, Leeds League 1963-64, Huddersfield/Halifax League division three play-offs 1973-74, Tommy Holmes Cup: 1981-82, 1984-85, 1985-86, 1988-89, 1991-92, 1995-96, 1998-99, 1999-2000, 2000-01,
'A' team: Pennine League division 5 1997-98, division 6 2006-07, Jessop Marine /Keighley 'A' teams Trophy: 1992-93, 1994-95, 1996-97, 1997-98, 1999-2000,
Under 17's – Halifax U17 Cup 1979-80,
Under 18's - Halifax Junior Cup 1951-52, Halifax U18 League Cup 1951-52, Halifax U19 League 1957-58, Bradford U18 League Cup 1952-53
Under 19's –Bradford Sunday Junior League 1969-70,

KEIGHLEY ALEXANDRA - Formed as Keighley Shamrocks' third team at the start of the 1886-87 season, renaming themselves as Keighley Alexandra in December 1886. Did not reappear the following season.

KEIGHLEY ALL SAINTS - Played friendly fixtures during 1899-1900 season under old rugby union rules, despite most other clubs in Keighley playing northern union from this season. Reverted to northern union during 1900-01 season. Played on a field at Highfield. Still around 1902-03, still playing friendly fixtures only.

KEIGHLEY AMATEURS - Played between 1886-91. Ground at Springfield used early on, but by 1889 were playing home games at Stockbridge.

KEIGHLEY ANCHOR IRONWORKS C&FC - An informal side operating between 1886-88.

KEIGHLEY ATHLETIC - (1) Played in the Keighley Charity Cup League during the 1897-98 season, but appear to have become defunct during the summer of 1898. (2) During World War 2, **Keighley Boys** played in the Bradford & District wartime League between 1940-43. They were known as **Keighley Juniors** during 1943-44, when they played in the Keighley Workshops Junior League, and then became **Keighley Athletic** the following season.

1944-45 Huddersfield & District League

1945-47 Halifax & District League

1947-48 Bradford League

Reformed for the 1948-49 season, playing in the Bradford / Keighley League. Became **'Keighley Albion'** the following season.

Honours: Bradford & District Cup 1944-45, Keighley Charity Cup 1948-49, Keighley League 1948-49,

KEIGHLEY ATHLETIC & FOOTBALL CLUB - Formed in October 1879 as a football section of Keighley Cricket Club, they playing on a field adjacent to that of the cricket section on Lawkholme Lane. They merged with the better-established **Keighley** club (which was still based at Dalton Lane) in April 1881. The combined Keighley rugby club later merged with the cricket club in April 1885, the newly re-merged club taking up residence at Lawkholme Lane!

KEIGHLEY BOYS - see **Keighley Supporters Club** & **Keighley Athletic**

KEIGHLEY CALEDONIANS - 1937-39 Keighley & District League (Junior Division). (See also Keighley League Combinations)

KEIGHLEY CELTIC – The third 'catholic' club in the town after the long gone Shamrocks and St.Annes sides. Started out as an under 16 team early in 1984, centred around the Holy Family School rugby league side of that era. Played in the West Riding Youth League, forging close links with the Worth Village club, and running under 17's & under 19's sides until they became a senior outfit.

As a senior team, they played in the Pennine League between 1986-94 (rising from division 8 to division 3 in their first five seasons). Did not play during the 1994-95 season due to a player shortage, but returned to the Pennine League the following season. Merged with Worth Village prior to the 1999-2000 season, initially as **Worth Village Celtic** but renamed **Keighley Town** weeks later.

KEIGHLEY CENTRAL YOUTH CLUB – (1) Appeared in the 1959-60 season, when they played fixtures against other local under 19 sides. Played in the Leeds League (under 19 section) during the 1960-61 season. For the 1961-62 campaign they ran an open age team in the Leeds League, the under 19 side withdrawing before the end of the season from their league. It seems that the side disbanded completely during the summer of 1962, although a highly successful soccer team continued under the youth club banner.

(2) Rugby League was revived at the youth club for the 1976-77 season. Coached by Peter Roe & Stuart Woolley, they competed in the Bradford Youth League.

KEIGHLEY CLARENCE - (1) Played in the first Keighley & District Junior northern union League in 1900-01. Between 1901-04 they competed in the Bradford & District Junior League (their second string continuing in Keighley & District League during 1901-02) Disbanded in 1904 due to financial problems.
(2) A revived club played in the 1908-09 Keighley Intermediate League. Finished as runners-up to Haworth but surprisingly did not reappear the following season.

KEIGHLEY CONSERVATIVE CLUB JUNIORS - Played friendly fixtures during 1899-1900 season under old rugby union rules, despite most other clubs in Keighley playing northern union from this season.

KEIGHLEY CO-OP (also known as **KEIGHLEY I.C.S**)
Between 1948-50 this club played in the Bradford / Keighley League. Three of the club's players went on to play rugby league professionally: George Saxton & Ernest Redman (Keighley) and Stan Bottomley (Halifax). Apparently they were to have taken part in the 1950-51 campaign, but did not do so, many of the club's players turning out for the newly formed **Eastwood Tavern** club instead.

KEIGHLEY COUGAR CUBS - The Cougar Cubs have been around since 1991, coming into existence when Aire Valley Bulldogs changed their title in order to forge closer links with the town's professional club. An amalgamation with Keighley Albion's junior teams was also made around this time. Since then they have successfully run various age groups with in the West Riding Youth, and more recently, Yorkshire Combined Leagues. The club quickly outgrew their Lawkholme facilities and since the summer of 1993 have been based at Keighley RUFC, Utley, although Marley has also been used in the past. Several Cougar cubs since have gone on to sign for professional clubs, Karl Smith, Chris Hogg & Matthew Steele for Cougars, Richard Moore for Bradford Bulls, Simon Bissell for Wigan and Chris Feather & Tommy Haughey for Wakefield among them. Much of the Cubs success can be attributed to two men with almost identical names – Steve V.Kelly and Steve P.Kelly, whose energy and enthusiasm have clearly rubbed off on the town's youth.
(see also **Keighley Pumas**)

KEIGHLEY FREE WANDERERS - (1) An informal side that played at least one fixture during the 1884-85 season.
(2) Another club bearing this name played during the 1886-87 season at Worth Village. They were formerly known as **Keighley Juniors**. Disbanded during the summer of 1887.

KEIGHLEY HIGHFIELD – Formed by rugby league stalwart Ayrton Anderson, who had previously run the Worth Village club, Highfield initially played at Calversyke Hill, on a ground previously used by Keighley Shamrocks. From around 1931the club played home fixtures at Lawkholme Lane on a regular basis.
1926-32 Bradford & District League (open age/junior & intermediate sections), also
1928-30 Keighley & District League
1932-33 Leeds League
1933-36 Bradford & District League
1936-37 Leeds League
During the 1933-34 season the team played at Haworth as **Haworth Highfield**, reverting back to Keighley Highfield the following season.
Honours: Bradford & District League: (Champions) 1930-31, (Intermediate Division) 1927-28, Keighley Hospitals Charity Cup 1931-32, Keighley Intermediate League 1927-28,

KEIGHLEY HORNETS - (1) Formed prior to 1884-85 season, playing on a ground at Stockbridge. Moved to Dalton Lane the following season. Played at Thwaites 1887-88, again at Dalton Lane 1888-89. Possibly played at Bradford Road 1889-90, although back at Dalton Lane the following season until their demise late in 1892.
(2) The name was revived, briefly, in the 1922-23 season, playing in the Keighley & District League
(3) A new short lived Hornets played in the Leeds Junior League during the 1964-65 season.

KEIGHLEY HORNETS 1888-89

KEIGHLEY I.C.S - see **Keighley Co-op**

KEIGHLEY JUNIORS - (1) First appeared in October 1880, playing at Lawkholme Lane in place of the Athletic club side that had merged with Keighley rugby club. Played at Lawkholme Lane in their early years, then at a ground at Holycroft for 1883-84 campaign. Club colours at this time were black, with headquarters at the Kings Head Hotel. Moved to a new ground at Worth Village in 1884-85 season. Changed their name to **Keighley Free Wanderers** for 1886-87 season. Disbanded during the summer of 1887.

(2) A new Keighley Juniors played friendly fixtures between 1893-95. They did not compete in any league competition. Possibly played at a ground at 'Kester Wood Top'.

(3) 1937-39 Keighley & District League. Withdrew from the league mid-way through their second season.

(4) **Keighley Athletic (2),** who eventually became the current **Keighley Albion** ran under the banner of Keighley Juniors during the 1943-44 season.

Note clubs (1) to (4) above – the 'Juniors' tag reflected the status of the players, not their ages !

(5) **Keighley RLFC Juniors** - Keighley's professional side ran a junior teams, usually under 19's, from around 1956 up to the early 1960's . **Keighley RLFC Colts** also operated during the 1970's & 80's.

See also **Keighley Supporters, Keighley Cougar Cubs** & **Keighley Junior Supporters** Clubs

KEIGHLEY LADIES – Beginning as **Lawkholme Ladybirds** in the early 1990's, Keighley's ladies club has since re-emerged as **Keighley Cougar Cats** and, since September 1998, as **Keighley Albion Cats**. Their most successful season was in 1999-2000 when the side won the first division of the Women's League (as well as the 'Western Conference') with a 100% league record to gain promotion to the premier division. 2001-2002 saw them reach the semi-final of the Women's Challenge Cup. That season they had three players, including Saima Hussein, included in the England ladies development squad.

KEIGHLEY LEAGUE COMBINATIONS - Due to problems in fielding sufficient players during the 1939-40 season, four Keighley clubs amalgamated in order to form two teams to play in the Keighley League for the remainder of the season. **Keighley Shamrocks, Keighley Rangers, Keighley Caledonians** and **New Road Side** thus joined forces to form **'Lawkholme'** & **'Worth Village',** titles that presumably reflected the grounds they played on.

KEIGHLEY LIFTS - Lifts' first competitive match was a Keighley Cup tie early in 1962. For the 1962-63 season they played in the Bradford League but they failed to reappear the following season. Played home fixtures at Marley.

KEIGHLEY LOW STREET - A successful side that started out in the 1922-23 Keighley & District League. Between 1923-25 they operated in the Bradford & District League. Champions in both of their Bradford League seasons, but disbanded in the summer of 1925 due to poor support!
Honours: Bradford & District League 1923-24, 1924-25,

KEIGHLEY MASHERS – A strangely-titled side that played at least one informal fixture during the 1891-92 season.

KEIGHLEY NELSON – A short-lived club that played in the 1923-24 Keighley & District League but failed to reappear the following season.

KEIGHLEY NORTHERN JUNIORS - Formed at the beginning of the 1928-29 season by a Mr.R.Thomas. Played in the Bradford & District League (Intermediate Division) & Keighley & District League between 1928-30.

KEIGHLEY OLICANA - First appeared during 1903-04 season, playing 'ordinary' fixtures as well as reaching final of the last Keighley Charity Cup to be played as a rugby competition.
1904-05 Yorkshire Senior Competition
1905-06 Bradford & District League
Also ran a workshops competition at end of the 1904-05 season. Disbanded at the end of the 1905-06 season.

KEIGHLEY OLYMPIC - Informal side operating during the 1886-87 season.

KEIGHLEY ORLEANS – Another informal side operating in the 1886-87 season.

KEIGHLEY PARISH CHURCH - (1) First referred to when the local press made reference to a forthcoming fixture with Bingley Grammar School 'A' in November 1881. Played series of fixtures at Dalton Lane during 1882-83 (see also **Keighley Zingari**). Also playing fixtures between 1887-90. **Keighley Parish Church Choir** played occasional fixtures from early 1889, against **Holy Trinity Choir**, and then against **Holy Trinity 'A'**.
(2) Keighley Parish Church Athletic Club (who also ran a harriers section) commenced the 1896-97 season playing on Dalton Lane. Played in the Keighley Charity Cup League during the 1897-98 season, but withdrew early in the campaign. Played friendly fixtures during the 1899-1900 season under old rugby union rules, despite most other clubs in Keighley playing northern union from this season. Also around 1902-03, again playing friendlies only.

KEIGHLEY PUMAS – Formed as an open-age team of the Keighley Cubs, they played for one season (2008-09) in the Yorkshire League. They finished bottom of division four (the bottom division), but this was harsh as several weaker teams dropped out before the end of the season. In the summer of 2009 they moved from their Utley base to Bradford & Bingley RUFC – renaming themselves Bradford & Bingley Pumas in the process & joined the Pennine League, where they played only a handful of games in division 7 before folding.

KEIGHLEY RANGERS - (1) Informal side operating during the 1885-86 season.
(2) Played between 1908-10 in the Keighley Intermediate League. Possibly champions in 1910, but did not reappear the following season.
(3) A Keighley Rangers side started the 1931-32 season in the Bradford League's Intermediate Section. However they appear to have folded half way through the season
(4) 1937-39 Keighley & District League, playing home fixtures at Marley playing fields, Worth Village. (See also **Keighley League Combinations**)
(5) A team of this name was to be formed for the 1948-49 season, but did'nt appear.

KEIGHLEY ROVERS - (1) Informal side operating between 1885-88. Played on a field at Woodhouse Road from at least 1887. A Keighley Rovers played some fixtures during the period 1889-91. Whether this is the same club or not is unclear.
(2) Northern union club playing 'friendly' fixtures during the 1902-03 season.

KEIGHLEY SHAMROCKS - (1) Formed in 1885 at the town's Shamrock club at the bottom of Turkey Street. Played at Highfield Lane 1885-1886, and at Oakworth Road (Holycroft) from 1886-1888. Were possibly based at Dalton Lane 1888-89, but were at West Lane (probably former ground of the first Keighley AFC who had recently become defunct) by 1889-90. Moved to another new ground prior to 1891-92 season - this one at Highfield, adjacent to the local reservoir. Another new ground at Calversyke Hill was used from the 1894-95 season.
1894-95 West Yorkshire League *(winners - their most successful season ever, achieving the 'treble')*
1895-98 Yorkshire No3 Competition.
Were to have played in Yorkshire No.2 Competition (Bradford section) 1898-99 but disbanded during the summer of 1898. Shamrocks 'A' team entered the Keighley Charity Cup League 1897-98 but withdrew early in the season.
Reformed briefly to play as **'Shamrocks Old Boys'** against St.Annes Juniors during 1900-01 season (northern union rules) and played some 'friendly' fixtures during 1901-02 season, again under northern union rules.
Honours: Keighley Charity Cup, Wharfedale Cup, West Yorkshire League, all in 1894-95
(2) 1909-10 Keighley Intermediate League. Nothing else is known about this side, which lasted only one season.
(3) Shamrocks were the first local side to be revived after the Great War, playing in the Bradford & District League between 1920-22. Ground was at Calversyke Hill. Reverted to the Keighley & District League for the 1922-23 season. Ran only youth sides in the Keighley League the following season, after which they appear to have become defunct again.
(4) 1937-39 Keighley & District League (Junior Division). Began life as **Highfield Shamrocks**, changing their title prior to the 1938-39 season to **Guardhouse**

116

Shamrocks. However, they were actually known as Keighley Shamrocks from that point on. (See also Keighley League Combinations)
Honours: Keighley League: Junior Division 1938-39,
(5) An other, albeit brief, revival occurred in the summer of 1953.
1953-54 Keighley & District League
1955-56 Keighley / Dewsbury League
1956-57 Halifax League (withdrew during the season & disbanded)
(6) Yet another attempt by the Shamrocks club came in the 1968-69 season when the newly reformed side played in the Bradford League, they continued in this competition for a further season before discontinuing around the summer of 1970.

Below, a rare Keighley Shamrocks Baines shield from the early 1900s

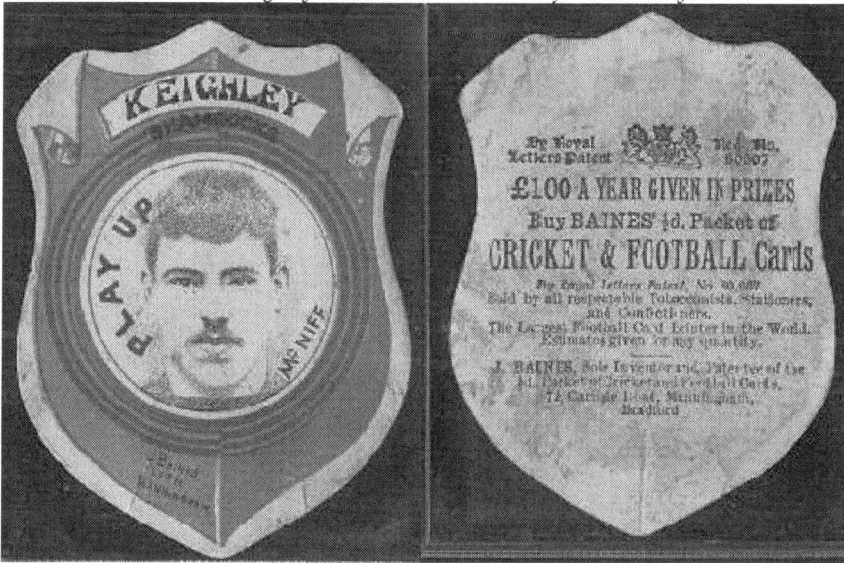

KEIGHLEY ST.ANDREWS - A church-based rugby union side of this name was around during at least the 1939-40 season. Since the mass defection to northern union / rugby league, only Keighlians (now Keighley RUFC) and St.Andrews have been formed specifically to play rugby union. The outbreak of war put paid to any hopes of progression for this club.

KEIGHLEY
SHAMROCKS
1894-95

KEIGHLEY ST.ANNES - (1) First referred to as a result of a 'scratch' game played against Shamrocks at Oakworth Road around Christmas 1886 to raise funds for St.Annes Church -no severe tackling was permitted due to the pitch being a quagmire ! It is of no co-incidence that at the time both sides represented the town's Irish / catholic population.

(2) A St.Annes Northern Union side was formed around 1900.

1900-01 Keighley & District Junior League

1901-04Bradford & District Junior League

Honours: Keighley & District Junior League 1900-01, Keighley Charity Cup 1902-03,

(3) A new club hoped to compete in the 1922-23 Keighley & District League but this never materialised.

(4) A revived club played briefly between 1937-39 in the Keighley & District League (Junior Division)

ST.ANNES GUILD - Between 1901-03, this side played in Keighley & District League, winning the league title in their second campaign. Run separately to the Keighley St.Annes side which played in the top division of the Bradford League at the time.

By the 1903-04 season the club was in the Bradford & District League (division two), but it seems that they had disbanded before season's end.

Honours: Keighley & District Junior League 1902-03

KEIGHLEY ST.PAULS - (1) Informal side operating in the 1885-86 season.

(2) A northern union side of this name also played friendly fixtures from 1900-03.

KEIGHLEY STAR – Between 1981-88 they competed in the Pennine League, initially based at Keighley RLFC's training ground at Lawkholme before a move to Marley. Began the 1988-89 season as **Great Northern**, to reflect their new base, but withdrew from the league in the first half of the season.

KEIGHLEY SUPPORTERS CLUB - Also referred to as **Keighley RLFC Boys**. Formed at the beginning of the 1925-26 season, playing in the West Yorkshire Supporters League from 1925-27.

Played in the Intermediate Section of the Bradford & District League from 1927-29.

Also fielded two teams, successfully, in the Keighley Intermediate League from 1926-1929.

Honours: Bradford & District League (Intermediate Division) 1928-29, Keighley Intermediate league 1926-27, 1928-29, Keighley Hospitals Charity Cup 1927-28,

A Keighley Junior Supporters Club was formed in time for the 1966-67 season, playing in the Bradford Junior League, where they were beaten in the final of the league's under 19's Harry Hornby Cup. Also ran under 18 & 20's sides during the late 60's & 70's. They officially became the professional club's under 19 side in 1972.

Honours: Bradford Sunday Junior League, under 18's league cup 1968-69, under 19's league cup 1971-72,

KEIGHLEY TEMPERANCE CLUB - (1) 1922-23 Keighley & District League. Merged with Lawkholme Clarence March 1923but not around the following season. (2) Revived prior to the 1932-33 season, playing friendly fixtures only this, and the following season.

KEIGHLEY TOWN - Formed following the merger of Worth Village & Keighley Celtic prior to the 1999-2000 season. Known as Worth Village Celtic for first few matches. Have played in the Pennine League since the merger, playing home games at Marley. The 'Town' suffix refers to the fact that following Keighley Albion's removal to Crossflatts, the team were by then the only amateur rugby league team still based in Keighley.

KEIGHLEY TOWN REPRESENTATIVE SIDE - The town team of the 1990's consisted of players from the Keighley Albion, Worth Village, Keighley Celtic, Silsden Rangers and Silsden clubs and represented the Keighley in the BARLA inter-town competition. The combination side's first game was against Keighley RLFC at Lawkholme Lane, (Keighley's last match before changing to the Cougars). The District side beat the professionals with a Chris Kelly try under the goal posts in the last minute and won 22-26. After representing the district four times, each player received a Keighley & District tie.

KEIGHLEY TRADESMEN - Played fixtures against Manningham Tradesmen in 1885-86 season, and in later seasons took part in the Yorkshire Tradesmen's Cup, playing at the Keighley Hornet's ground in Dalton Lane. Still playing around 1887.

KEIGHLEY (HOLY) TRINITY -(1) **Keighley Trinity** was an informal side operating in the 1886-87 season. 1887-88 saw **Keighley Holy Trinity** playing fixtures, with the vicar evidently intending to play for them! Holy Trinity Choir played Parish Church Choir in March 1889. The Holy Trinity side then played home fixtures at Lawkholme Lane from 1889-90 season.
(2) Keighley Trinity became more established from 1893. Joined the Bradford & District League for the 1895-96 season. Played friendlies during the 1896-97 season, then joined the Keighley Charity Cup League for the 1897-98 season *(finishing the season as champions)* when they returned to Lawkholme Lane. Joined the Yorkshire No.2 Competition (Bradford Section) for the 1898-99 season but withdrew in January 1899 due to financial & playing problems.
Honours: Keighley Charity Cup League 1897-98
(3) Keighley Holy Trinity reformed as a northern union side prior to 1900-01 season, playing at Bradford Road. Did not compete in any league competition and seem to have become defunct again around the summer of 1902.

KEIGHLEY VOLUNTEERS - Informal side operating in the 1885-86 season.

KEIGHLEY WANDERERS – (1) A side formed specially to play in the 1902-03 Keighley Charity Cup competition - unfortunately without much success ! Unheard of again after this time.

KEIGHLEY YMCA - Played at least one 'friendly' fixture during the 1912-13 season.

KEIGHLEY ZINGARI - (1) The Zingari name first appeared when a 'scratch' played two 14-a-side fixtures against Red Star during the 1882-83 season. Several of the Zingari players also played for Keighley Parish Church, whom they did not meet themselves. Keighley Zingari C&FC re-appeared during 1884-85 season. By 1886 they were playing at Bradford Road, Stockbridge, establishing themselves as one of the top sides in town. The side joined the Yorkshire No.3 competition (group A) in 1895-96 but finished bottom of the league. Disbanding during the summer of 1896, there was an unsuccessful attempt to reform to play a Yorkshire Challenge Cup-tie the following season. Zingari briefly reformed for a benefit match for a former player, playing Worth Village early in 1900.
Honours: Keighley Charity Cup 1892-93, 1893-94,
(2) Reformed in September 1908, playing at Lawkholme Lane when the senior Keighley club were playing away. By the 1914-15 season, Zingari were effectively Keighley's 'A' team (players were not debarred from assisting junior clubs until they had played 10 times for a senior club), although the town's professional club chose not to revive the name following the Great War.
1908-09 Bradford & District League
1909-10 Yorkshire Combination / Bradford & District League
1910-11 Friendly Fixtures only
1911-12 Leeds & District League
1912-13 Leeds & District / Halifax & District League (played fixtures in both)
1913-15 Halifax & District League
Did not reform after the Great War.
Honours: Halifax Charity Cup 1911-12, 1913-14,

KILDWICK - Something of an unknown quantity. Played the newly formed Keighley club on 7th October 1877, could only raise 14 players and were beaten by 1 goal to 5 touchdowns. Never heard of again and were therefore more than likely a scratch side raised specially for that match. For the record, the Kildwick team that day was: *W.Wilson (back), W.Vint (three-quarter back), F.Wilson (captain), A.Hargreaves (half backs), E.Hargreaves, R.Whitaker, J.Laycock, A.Smith, J.Davy, S.Thompson, C.Petty, W.Wilcock, J.Wilson, G.Jackson (forwards)* It is more then likely that there was at least one set of brothers in the Kildwick line-up !

KILDWICK PARISH CHURCH - Played at least one fixture during the 1887-88 season.

KNOWLE PARK - 1922-24 Keighley & District League. Appear not to have played during the 1924-25 season, but by 1925-26 were again in the local league for one season.

LAWKHOLME - see Keighley League Combinations

LAWKHOLME CLARENCE - (1) The first side to use this title played friendly fixtures during the 1899-1900 season under the old rugby union rules, despite most other clubs in Keighley playing northern union from this season.
(2) A new Lawkholme Clarence played in the 1921-22 Bradford & District league (Intermediate Division). By 1922-23 they were in the Keighley & District League. Merged with Keighley Temperance Club in March 1923, but were not around the following season.

LONG LEE ALBION - Northern union club playing 'friendly' fixtures during the 1902-03 season.

LONG LEE C&FC - see **Thwaites Brow**

LORD RODNEY - Played at least one 'friendly' fixture during the 1962-63 season but did not play any competitive fixtures.

LOW MILL - Northern union club playing 'friendly' fixtures during the 1902-03 season.

MALTONIANS - 1923-24 Keighley & District League
1924-25 Bradford & District League. Nothing else is known about this side.

MILL HEY WANDERERS – Informal, Haworth-based side operating in the 1885-86 season. At the time there were a number of clubs operating in the village on an informal basis.

MORTON - (1) Formed prior to 1884-85 season. Changed grounds in the summer of 1886. Became defunct December 1887.
(2) A new village club is known to have played fixtures during the 1894-95 season.
 (3) Reformed as a northern union club around November 1901, originally playing friendly fixtures only. Played in the 1902-03 Keighley & District Junior League, but withdrew early in 1903.

NEW ROAD SIDE - (1) Informal side operating in the 1886-87 season.
(2) Northern union club playing 'friendly' fixtures during the 1902-03 season.
(3) The third team of this name managed to complete more than one season! They appeared between 1937-39 in the Keighley & District League (Junior Division), based at Hermit Hole (In 1938-39 they also ran a team in the Intermediate Division).

(see also Keighley League Combinations). Considering their Charity Cup success in 1939 they were surprisingly short-lived.
Honours: Keighley League: Junior Charity Cup 1938-39,

NEWTOWN CLARENCE - Northern union club playing 'friendly' fixtures during the 1902-03 season. Possibly played home fixtures on a ground on Shann Lane.

NEWTOWN LIONS - Northern union club playing 'friendly' fixtures during the 1901-02 season.

NEWTOWN WANDERERS - Informal side operating in the 1886-87 season.

N.S.F. RANGERS - The National Switch Factory works team first appeared late in the 1962-63 season when they took part in the Keighley Cup competition. Between 1963-66 they played in the Bradford League, playing home fixtures at Marley. Played pre-season fixtures as NSF in the 1966-67 season but prior to opening their league fixtures changed their name to **Worth Village.**

OAKWORTH - (1) An informal village-based side that played at least one match in the 1885-86 season.
(2) Reappeared early in 1889, playing on a more firm footing than previous side but did not compete in any league competition. Became defunct in the summer of 1894.
(3) An Oakworth team played friendly fixtures during the 1896-97 season.
(4) A revived club played in the Keighley Intermediate League, albeit unsuccessfully, during the 1908-09 season. Went over to 'Soccer' in the summer of 1909.
(5) Following a failed attempt to revive a club in the village around the summer of 1924, the next club in Oakworth appeared late in the 1937-38 season, playing in the Intermediate Division of the Keighley & District League. Played in the same competition the following year but withdrew before the end of the season.

OAKWORTH RANGERS - Early northern union club that played at least one friendly fixture the 1902-03 season.

OAKWORTH ROAD HORNETS - Between 1925-27 they played in the Keighley Intermediate League, apparently disbanding during the summer of 1927.

OAKWORTH WANDERERS – Formed originally as **The Wanderers** by Allan Bancroft & David Ingham, they played in the Pennine League from 1980-82, adopting the Oakworth title in November 1980. Ground: Adjacent to Oakworth Cricket Club on Wide Lane, with changing and training facilities at Oakbank School. Headquarters were at the Golden Fleece in Oakworth.

OXENHOPE - (1) Formed late 1889/ early 1890, becoming defunct around the summer of 1893
(2) A new village club, playing northern union rules, was formed in November 1903 - playing friendly fixtures, as well as competing in the Keighley Charity Cup competition during the 1903-04 season. Appear not to have been around the following season as the local rugby scene went into decline.

PARK LANE – A side of this names played at least one 'friendly' fixture during the 1908-09 season, but little else is known about it.

PARK LANE ALBION – Around for two tears in the early 1900's. 1901-02 Keighley & District (northern union) Junior League, 1902-03 - playing friendly / ordinary games only.

PARK LANE ROEBUSH - Informal side, played at least one fixture during the 1884-85 season.

PARKWOOD – Apparently around for only one season, 1937-38, playing in the Keighley & District League (Intermediate League)

PARKWOOD HORNETS - 1923-26 Keighley & District League. Also ran a youth team during at least the 1923-24 season. *Honours: Keighley Intermediate League 1923-24,*

PARKWOOD WANDERERS - Played one, informal, fixture at Dalton Lane against Red Star on November 4th 1882. Lost by 3 goals, 2 tries & 3 touchdowns to nil. Never heard of again!

PRINCE SMITH & STELLS - During World War 2 this works team played in the 1943-44 Keighley Workshops Junior League and the 1944-45 Huddersfield & District League.
Honours: Keighley Wartime League 1943-44
(2) Reformed in time for the 1948-49 campaign, playing at Strong Close Park.
1948-53 Bradford/Keighley League
1953-55 Keighley & District League
(3) Revived during the summer of 1961, acquiring many of the players from the struggling Silsden club. At this time, Prince Smith's sports club ran also soccer and cricket teams, which played in local leagues.
1961-65 Bradford League
Honours: Keighley Cup 1962-63

RED STAR - Possibly an informal side who played several 14-a-side fixtures against other local sides during the 1882-83 season. Won 3, the other two 'drawn in their favour'.

RIDDLESDEN - (1) Formed prior to 1895-96 season. Joined the Horton & District League for 1896-97 season, playing in the Keighley Charity Cup League the following season. Played in Bradford & District League between 1898-1900, the second season in which they, along with the rest of the league, moved to northern league rules. Disbanded in the summer of 1900.

(2) A revived club joined the Keighley Workshops Junior set-up in Keighley for the 1943-44 season, playing friendly fixtures against other local sides. Also played friendlies the following season.

(3) A new reformed club appeared for the 1948-49 season, playing on the fields which are now part of the new St.Marys / old Grange school site.

1948-53 Bradford / Keighley League

1953-55 Keighley & District League

Honours: Keighley Cup 1950-51,

SHOWFIELD - (1) Northern union club playing 'friendly' fixtures during the 1901-02 season.

(2) A club of this name hoped to play in a reformed Keighley & District League during the 1937-38 season, but did not take a place in the new league.

SILSDEN (1) The original Silsden rugby team was said to have been formed in 1883, although the first fixtures located in the local press were in the 1884-85 season. They first played at Daisy Hill, playing in blue & white jerseys, before moving to a field called the 'Wyveries' on Skipton Road. A later move was made to Keighley Road, which they vacated until their demise and which has since been used by the village soccer team.

1893-94 Yorkshire No.3 competition

1894-95 Yorkshire No.4 competition (a renamed No.3 competition),

1895-96 Yorkshire No.3 competition,

1896-98 YorkshireNo.2 Competition, the second season of which they finished bottom of the table.

1898-99 Were to have played in Yorkshire No.2 Competition (Bradford section), but played friendly fixtures only.

1899-1900 Bradford & District Junior League

1900-01 Bradford & District Junior League - now NORTHERN UNION

Possibly dormant 1901-02, playing some friendly fixtures 1902-03.

Honours: Keighley Charity Cup 1889-90, 1890-91,

(2) Reformed in 1921, and known also as **Silsden Northern**. Ground on Hainsworth Road. Disbanded May 1963.

1921-22 Bradford & District League (Junior Division). 'A' team played in the Intermediate Division of this league

1922-24 Bradford & District League

1924-25 Yorkshire Senior Competition

1925-30 Bradford & District League (open age/junior & intermediate sections)

(1922-30 'A' team in Keighley & District League)

1930-32 Leeds League (also ran teams in Bradford & District Lge)

1932-34 Bradford & District League
1934-35 Leeds League (also ran teams in the Bradford & District League)
1935-37 Bradford & District League
1937-38 Initially played friendlies, then joined a new Keighley & District League (Junior Division) which was formed early in 1938
1938-39 Keighley & District League (Junior Division)
1939-46 Closed down for the duration of the war
1946-47 Halifax & District League *(took over the fixtures of Hunslet Engineering Company)*
1947-48 Bradford & District League
1948-53 Bradford / Keighley League
1953-55 Keighley & District League
1955-56 Keighley / Dewsbury League
1956-57 Dewsbury League (withdrew in November 1956)
1957-62 Bradford League (actually resigned from league early in the 1961-62 season. Officially wound up May 1963)
Honours: Bradford & District League: Champions 1929-30, Intermediate Division 1929-30, League Cup 1926-27,
Keighley Cup 1949-50, 1951-52, Keighley League 1929-30, 1937-38, 1952-53, 1955-56, Keighley League Medal Competition 1953-54,
'A' team honours: Bradford League: Supplementary League Cup 1921-22, Keighley League 1925-26,
(3) Reformed in October 1978. Ground at 'The Arena', Silsden Park, although early games were played on a number of fields in the village. Played in the Pennine League from the 1979-80 season until their merger with **Silsden Rangers** in the summer of 1992.
Honours: Silsden Shield 1985-86, 1986-87,
(4) Silsden Park Rangers were renamed 'Silsden' in the summer of 2010, continuing in the Pennine League

SILSDEN RANGERS - (1) Informal side operating during the 1887-88 season.
(2) Formed as a breakaway from **Silsden** in 1984, playing alongside their rivals in the Pennine League. A number of grounds were used, notably the Drabble House Field, one on Keighley Road, and from the 1991-1992 season at South Craven School, Crosshills. Re-merged with Silsden for the 1992-93 season.
Honours: Tommy Holmes Cup: 1986-87, Silsden Shield 1987-88, 1988-89,

SILSDEN PARK RANGERS - Formed when Silsden & Silsden Rangers amalgamated in the summer of 1992. Played in the Pennine League until they renamed themselves Silsden in 2010.
Honours: Tommy Holmes Cup: 1997-98, Pennine League Division 4 2000-2001,

SILSDEN YOUTH CLUB - Appeared in the 1959-60 season, when they played fixtures against other local under 19 sides. Disbanded around 1962.

SOUTH CRAVEN CRUSHERS – Formed by Robert Ferguson and Paul 'Ned' Kelly, Crushers joined the Pennine League for the 2000-2001 season, but failed to complete their fixtures. Home matches were played at South Craven School, Crosshills. Their first ever match was a 20-40 friendly defeat to Silsden Park Rangers.

SPRINGFIELD HORNETS / WANDERERS - Played in the Keighley & District League during the 1927-28 season. Local references were made to either 'Wanderers' or 'Hornets', and it is more than likely that this was one team rather than two.

SPRINGFIELD MILL - Northern union club playing 'friendly' fixtures during the 1901-02 season.

STEETON - (1) First club initially said to have disbanded around 1886, although details of this club are sketchy. Their date of formation is unknown.
(2) Reformed under northern union rules. Played friendly fixtures only during the 1900-01 season. In 1901-02 they joined the Bradford & District League. Disbanded due to lack of a field just months after their cup success, several of their former players going on to play for Keighley.
Honours: Keighley Charity Cup 1901-02
(3) Reformed in time for the 1908-09 season when they played in the Keighley Intermediate League. HQ at the Goats Head. Appear to have gone over to soccer at the end of the season. A Mr.J.Williams of Whitley Head was said to have placed a field at the club's disposal.
(4) A new club hoped to compete in the 1922-23 Keighley & District League but this never materialised. Possibly based around a workshops team that had been successful the previous season.

STOCKBRIDGE - 1902-03 Keighley & District Junior League (northern union). Appear to have been around for this single season only.

SUMMERSCALES EMPLOYEES – An informal works side operating in the 1886-87 season.

SUN STREET MISSION - Northern union club playing 'friendly' fixtures during the 1901-02 season.

SUTTON - Known to have played Keighley Juniors in 1880 & 1881, although there are also references to possible alternative title of **Sutton Mills**. Both titles were again used during the 1882-83 season. Subsequent reports in the local press refer to Sutton, **Sutton Parish** (1885-86) & **Sutton Rovers** (1888-89), which may all be related. 'Sutton' re-appear from the 1891-92 season. Joined the Bradford & District League in 1895-96, finishing joint champions. Moved up to the Yorkshire No.3 Competition (group A) for the 1896-97 campaign but struggled. Played in the

Keighley Charity Cup League in 1897-98, finishing runners-up. An advert in the Keighley Labour Journal, 16th July 1898 refers to a 'Sutton Football Club, Annual Sports and Gala Day, at the Football Field, Crosshills'

Possibly played some friendly fixtures during the 1898-99 season. Joined the northern union Bradford & District league for the 1899-1900 season but withdrew early in the season. Played in the Keighley & District Junior (northern union) League in 1900-01 but suffered many heavy defeats. Initially a club called 'Glusburn' was going to play in the competition instead of Sutton – whether these are one and the same is unknown. What is known, however, is that Sutton club ceased in the summer of 1901.

Honours: Bradford & District League (joint champions) 1895-96

SUTTON BAPTISTS - Formed in 1903 as successors to the old village club. Poorly supported, so changed to 'association' football later that year as Sutton United FC, who would become one of the Keighley district's most successful sides prior to World War 2.

THE WANDERERS – see Oakworth Wanderers
THWAITES – An informal side operating in the 1887-88 season.

THWAITES BROW - (1) First appeared 1886-87, playing at Worth Village. Later moved to a sloping pitch at Parkwood Top, also playing some games at Worth Village. Also referred to as **Long Lee C&FC**. Seem to have become defunct in the summer of 1888.
(2) Northern union club playing 'friendly' fixtures during the 1901-02 season.

THWAITES ROVERS – A club that played for one season only, participating in the 1924-25 Keighley & District League

UPPER GREEN - Informal side operating in the 1886-87 season.

UTLEY - 1901-02 Keighley & District League
1902-03 same league, but withdrew in November 1902.

UTLEY ST.MARKS - 1921-22 Bradford & District League (Intermediate Division)
1922-23 Bradford & District Junior League. Reverted to playing soccer the following season. *Honours: Bradford & Dist. League (Intermediate Division) 1921-22,*
A **St.Marks** side played at least one 'friendly' fixture during the 1962-63 season, although this was not an open age team and may be unrelated to the Utley Church.

VICTORIA PARK - (1) A side of this name played at least one 'friendly' fixture during the 1922-23 season
(2) A new club bearing this name played between 1937-39 in the Keighley & District League (Intermediate Division), very successful in their second season.
Honours: Keighley League: Junior Cup 1937-38, 1938-39, Junior League 1938-39,

VICTORIA PARK RANGERS - Played at the town's Greyhound Stadium.
1953-55 Keighley & District League
1955-56 Keighley / Dewsbury League
1956-58 Halifax League
1958-59 Bradford League
Honours: Keighley League 1957-58,

VICTORIA ROAD - Played at least one 'friendly' fixture during the 1908-09 season.

WARD - Joined the Keighley & District League for the 1937-38 season but do not appear to have played any fixtures.

WOODHOUSE – An informal side operating in the 1887-88 season.

WOODHOUSE RANGERS – Formed prior to the 1937-38 season, initially playing friendly fixtures, before joining the Keighley & District League (Junior Division) later in the season.

WORTH VILLAGE - (1) **Worth Village Free Wanderers** played fixtures, probably informally, during the 1884-85 season.
(2) A new Worth Village club commenced playing friendlies during the 1894-95 season. The team joined the Horton & District League for the 1896-97 season, playing at Lawkholme Lane, moving to the Keighley Charity Cup League the following season, when they swapped grounds with Keighley Trinity. Played in the Bradford & District League from 1898-99. This league moved *en bloc* to Northern Union in the summer of 1899, Village continuing in this league until 1903-04, during which time they lifted the Bradford & District Cup. Withdrew from their league in January 1904, becoming defunct.
Village also ran a junior team in the first Keighley & District northern union league during the 1900-01 season. Ran a soccer section in the local league also - Harry Myers was on their players' register.
Honours: Bradford & District Cup 1899-1900,
(3) Probably based around a workshops team that had been successful over the previous two seasons, a revived Village flourished in local leagues between 1922-26. They became defunct when Ayrton Anderson, who ran the club, formed a new club in town – Keighley Highfield.
1922-23 Keighley & District League
1923-26 Bradford & District League (1923-25 also fielded a team in the Keighley & District League)
Honours: Keighley Intermediate League 1922-23, 1924-25,
(4) Another club bearing the Worth Village name played between 1937-39 in the Keighley & District League (Intermediate Division)
(see also Keighley League Combinations)
(5) Little is known about the Worth Village team of 1959-60, except that they played in the Dewsbury League, fielding several players who had previously turned out

for the recently defunct Victoria Park Rangers club. The side defeated Silsden in the Keighley League final that season but were not around the following season.

(6) Reformed originally as works team **NSF Rangers** in 1963. Changed the name of the club to Worth Village prior to the 1966-67 season. Played home fixtures at Marley.

1966-67 Bradford League (expelled during the season)

1967-71 Leeds League

1971-73 Bradford League

1973-74 Huddersfield / Halifax League

1974-99 Pennine League

Honours: Huddersfield / Halifax Combined League division three 1973-74, Pennine League division 1 1993-93, division 2 1974-75,1985-86, Halifax Cup 1976-77, 1979-80, Tommy Holmes Cup: 1973-74, 1978-79, 1979-80, 1980-81, 1983-84, 1987-88, 1989-90, 1990-91, 1992-93, 1993-94, 1994-95, 1996-97, Jessop Marine /Keighley 'A' teams Trophy: 1993-94, 1995-96, 1998-99,

Merged with Keighley Celtic prior to the 1999-2000 season, initially as **Worth Village Celtic** but as **Keighley Town** weeks later.

KEIGHLEY RUGBY UNION FOOTBALL CLUB: Formed as Keighley Old Boys in December 1920, by old boys of the Keighley Trade & Grammar School. The side played a number of fixtures towards the end of the 1920-21 season on a ground at Utley, the club's first ever match being against Bradford 'B' (which was won). There was 'substantial financial backing' for the new venture and its first president was T.P.Watson (headmaster of the Grammar School). Known as Keighlians from the 1921-22 season, a field was utilised at Stockbridge which had previously used by Keighley Town AFC.

The club won the Yorkshire Rugby Union Cup in the 1947-48 season, in their first campaign on a new ground at Thwaites, defeating Otley 14-9 in the final. They also won the Yorkshire Shield this season, becoming the first team ever to win this particular 'double'. Now located at Utley, following an extended tenure at Marley the history of this club is a different story, to be told elsewhere.....

(See also **Keighley St.Andrews**, the town's only other 'rugby union' club for a short time)

BIBLIOGRAPHY

Lawkholme Lane – 100 Years of Rugby,
        Trevor Delaney (ed), 1985
Seasons To Remember - Keighley Albion 1948-1998,
        Don & Dave Kirkley, 1998
The Story of Rugby League in Silsden,
        Steve Pyrah, 1997
Riddlesden Reflections,
        J.D.Lee & K.Davies, 1994
A Village Tapestry (Silsden),
        Roy Mason
Chasing Glory - The Story of Association Football in Keighley, volume 1,
        Rob Grillo, 1998
Glory Denied - The Story of Association Football in Keighley, volume 2,
        Rob Grillo, 1999
Sutton-In-Craven - The Old Community,
        Alec Wood (ed), 1993
The Grounds of Rugby League,
        Trevor Delaney, 1991
Rugby Disunion,
        Trevor Delaney, 1993
Glory Days - A History of English Rugby Union Cup Finals,
        Graham Williams, 1998
The Rugby League Myth,
        Michael Latham & Tom Mather, 1993
Rugby's Great Split - Class, Culture and the Origins of Rugby League,
        Tony Collins, 1998
Football's Secret History,
        John Goulstone, 2001
'The Keighlians',
        Francis Coakes, Yorkshire Illustrated, February 1951,
A History of Keighley,
        Ian Dewhirst, 1974
Halifax & District R.L 'Joseph Fee Memorial Trophy' Brochure, 2002
Newspapers: The Keighley News, Keighley Herald, Bradford Telegraph
        & Argus

12667041R00072

Printed in Great Britain
by Amazon

EXPLODING RATS
AND OTHER DEVIOUS DEVICES OF
SOE

EXPLODING RATS
AND OTHER DEVIOUS DEVICES OF
SOE

THE CAMOUFLAGE SECTION 1941–1945

Edited by

CRAIG MOORE

FONTHILL

First published in Great Britain in 2025 by
Fonthill
An imprint of
Pen & Sword Books Ltd
Yorkshire – Philadelphia
www.fonthill.media

Note from the Editor and Appendix F © Craig Moore, 2025

ISBN 978-1-78155-965-9

The right of Craig Moore to be identified as Editor of this work has been asserted by him in
accordance with the Copyright, Designs and Patents Act 1988.

A CIP catalogue record for this book
is available from the British Library.

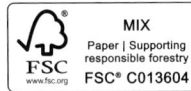

FSC
www.fsc.org
MIX
Paper | Supporting
responsible forestry
FSC® C013604

The Publisher's authorised representative in the EU for product
safety is Authorised Rep Compliance Ltd., Ground Floor,
71 Lower Baggot Street, Dublin D02 P593, Ireland.
www.arccompliance.com

For a complete list of Pen & Sword titles please contact
PEN & SWORD BOOKS LIMITED
George House, Units 12 & 13, Beevor Street, Off Pontefract Road,
Barnsley, South Yorkshire, S71 1HN, England
E-mail: enquiries@pen-and-sword.co.uk
Website: www.pen-and-sword.co.uk

or

PEN AND SWORD BOOKS
1950 Lawrence Rd, Havertown, PA 19083, USA
E-mail: uspen-and-sword@casematepublishers.com
Website: www.penandswordbooks.com

Contents

Note from the Editor

THE REPORT

James Bond had Q branch to supply him with equipment he would require on a mission, and during the Second World War, the Special Operations Executive (SOE) had the Camouflage Section. They supplied equipment and explosive devices to British field agents dropped behind enemy lines in Europe and, to a lesser extent, the Far East.

I am a military historian and specialise in the development and use of armoured vehicles from 1915 to 1952. I was at the National Archives at Kew in London, looking for information on camouflaged tanks used for Operation Bertram in North Africa during the Second World War, when I stumbled upon a file entitled 'History and Development of the Special Operations Executive Camouflage Section 1941–1945'. It was not what I had been looking for, but its content was fascinating. The ingenuity of some of the devices developed and deployed in wartime Europe was extraordinary. I decided that this was an archive report that deserved to be made available to the wider public.

At the end of the Second World War the Camouflage Section, alongside many other units, was disbanded. However, a requirement was made to write an official history recording the work of the section for the purpose of internal research and record keeping. This file, to which a number of individuals seem to have contributed, was restricted under the 1911 Official Secrets Act, but was later declassified. The front of the file states, 'Note: I understand this is the only copy of this volume in existence.—21 February 1946.' This book is essentially a copy of that file.

I have retained the punctuation, grammar and style of the original report. There is a degree of repetition in the text, which has been left in, and despite the variable quality of some of the original photographs, all have been included. I want you to be able to read this archived history as close to its original format as possible. The British abbreviation for inches has been used; 7″ and 11″ means 7 inches and 11 inches.

THE MISSION OF THE CAMOUFLAGE SECTION

Most people believe that, in the Second World War, German-run factories were put out of action almost exclusively by RAF and USAAF bombing. Some factories, however, were out of range of Allied bombers. These factories often used coal- or wood-fired boilers to produce power. If a boiler that provided power to a factory could be put out of action by a (carefully manipulated) dead rat, a replica piece of coal or a hollowed-out lump of timber packed with explosives, production would be stopped in just the same way as if the factory had been the target of a successful bombing raid. For other factories which lacked an explosive boiler—for example, those that produced food or clothing for the Wehrmacht—setting fire to the building and its contents with an incendiary device produced by the SOE Camouflage Section would achieve the same result: a stop in production.

Devious devices were also used in the war against Japan, shipped out to agents in the occupied territories. Tourist trinkets packed with explosives were sold on the dockside to Japanese infantry waiting to board troop ships. Explosives were also packed into tins of food, water and oil and added among other supplies for loading onto ships.

Some of the devices manufactured by the SOE Camouflage Section during the Second World War were not new ideas. For example, during the 1861–1865 American Civil War, Captain Thomas Courtney of the Confederate Army manufactured a device he called the 'coal torpedo'. It was a hollow iron casting, packed with explosives and covered in coal dust so that it resembled a lump of coal. It was intended to be secreted in the coal supply of a Union Navy steam ship and cause damage when shovelled into the ship's boiler.

To the modern reader the name 'Camouflage Section' may seem misleading. For the most part, the section's activities did not include painting camouflage patterns on objects. However, they camouflaged objects in other ways—as everyday items—to disguise their true nature, so the term 'Camouflage Section' is applicable in this context. One of the most important tasks of the section was in providing field agents with appropriate clothing, hats, shoes, boots, documents, toiletries, tools, work clothes, bags and briefcases, that would pass the scrutiny of German security services. Gestapo officers in occupied countries were instructed to look out for people wearing foreign-style clothing and using suspicious papers. A button sewn the wrong way, socks with labels showing a foreign manufacturer, the seams on sleeves or the buttons on a shirt opening in a style contrary to European fashion could raise suspicion, resulting in arrest, torture and execution. The work of the SOE Camouflage Section was absolutely critical to the safety and survival of Allied field agents, and therefore the war effort as a whole.

Not many people are as lucky as I am to live near the National Archives at Kew and be able to read original reports such as this one. I have carefully transcribed the report's pages and reproduced the images to give you that opportunity. My hope is that, in addition to being a fascinating resource for historians and the general reader, especially those interested in SOE operations, this book will serve to inspire and inform writers of wartime spy novels.

The Report

SPECIAL OPERATIONS EXECUTIVE, HISTORY 28

'HISTORY AND DEVELOPMENT OF THE
CAMOUFLAGE SECTION 1941–1945'

NATIONAL ARCHIVES HS 7/49

Preface

These records provide contemporary or near contemporary historical accounts of the activities of the various sections of the Special Operations Executive, and daily 'diary' accounts of the activities of the territorial sections. The section histories and war diaries, written in the closing months and in the immediate aftermath of the Second World War, provide a broad overview of SOE activities.

In the lead up to the Second World War, Department EH (after its headquarters, Electra House), a war propaganda unit, a section of The Secret Intelligence Service (MI6) called Section D, and a third unit renamed from GS(R) to MI R, were all engaged in related covert operations and research. Operations were co-ordinated and combined to form The Special Operations Executive in 1940. Its main purpose was to carry out espionage, sabotage and reconnaissance in the occupied areas of Europe and to help resistance movements in those and other countries, during the fight against Germany and its allies during the Second World War.

It was a Top Secret section of the war effort and the few that knew of its existence referred to it as 'The Baker Street Irregulars', 'Churchill's Secret Army', or the 'Ministry of Ungentlemanly Warfare'. Its activities often took place under more mundane descriptive operational titles such as 'The Joint Technical Board' and the 'Inter Service Research Bureau'. The organisation had 13,000 men and women under its command and helped supply or support resistance groups in occupied countries during the conflict.

Introduction

In 1941, the Special Operations Executive Camouflage Section was formed. The Director of Camouflage was Lt. Col. J. Elder Wills R.E. The Camouflage Section was based in four locations called 'Stations' around London. Station XV was located in the Thatched Barn, Barnet By-Pass, Elstree and went by the name Camouflage Research I.S.R.B. Station XVA was based in 56 Queen's Gate, London SW7 and went by the name Clothing Assistance Board (C.A.B.) or Military Operations 1 Special Projects (M.O.1 S.P.). Station XVB was housed in The Natural History Museum, Cromwell Road, London SW7 and had a name that sounded like a location, War Department Lecture Hall. Station XVC was moved into 2 & 3 Trevor Square, London SW7 and was called Military Operations 1 Special Projects (M.O.1 S.P.) Photographic Department. [See the plate section for photographs of locations used by SOE.] The Special Operations Executive also had Sections that specialised in the war in particular countries, for example there was the French Section, Belgium Section, Dutch Section.

It was through the foresight of the AD/Z Directorate that a camouflage expert was engaged by the SOE organisation in November 1941, to advise on the various needs of concealment which were becoming a demand for the various countries' sections. It was however, quickly realised that advice was not sufficient, and a small workshop was formed at Station 9 in January 1942 with a staff of one officer, one 'other' rank, and one civilian. Country Sections were quick to appreciate the importance of good camouflage and requests were immediately forthcoming.

While the work was naturally experimental at first, effective methods of production were soon developed. Close cooperation with Country Section Representatives was an asset in dealing with their requirements where advice was needed on the suitability of commodities, method of transport, the area in which the camouflage was to be used, and in the case of the agent's personal equipment, the type of man or woman, together with their cover story.

In February 1942, larger workshops were taken over at the Victoria and Albert Museum in Kensington. As distinct from the more usual forms of camouflage used by the armed forces, the main job of the Camouflage Section was to produce concealment devices for the transportation and the use of arms, explosives, operational money, codes, documents, radio transmitters and receivers, together with special stores for the equipment of agents in the field.

The staff was supplemented by an additional six 'other' ranks, most of them one time film studio technicians, and it proved that their experience in the reproduction of authentic articles with studio properties and set dressings was useful training for the type of work to be produced. Further assets which could be attributed to studio experience were the correct mental attitude in adapting themselves to the somewhat unusual work to be carried out, and the speed of production so essential to film work and even more important to this new venture.

To illustrate the versatility of the Camouflage Section's work, the first orders produced, were a lipstick holder to take a small message, a pair of sabots carved in wood and fitted with a false sole, filled with plastic explosive and the time delay to act as an explosive device. The glass floats of a fishing net were drilled and filled with a fluorescent substance to act as night markers for underwater containers. Pit props were produced in plaster to hide 3-inch mortar barrels, and latex rubber sheets, representing various barks of trees, were produced for the quick concealment of parachute containers dropped in enemy territory.

Many unusual articles had to be obtained which were not available through the normal Service channels, although contraband material was used whenever possible. Therefore, the services of a buyer whose experience enabled him to contact sources of unusual supplies was procured. Again, a man from the film industry was employed, a man whose job it was in peace time was to go out and procure anything from a sable coat to a Dickensian horse drawn coach within an exceedingly limited timeframe. His new job proved even more fantastically varied than his past studio occupation. 150 rat skins to be cured, filled, and armed as explosive devices, one hundred varieties of coal, stones, and logs to be produced from fibrous plaster as means of containers for the articles to be infiltrated into enemy country. A Belgium gas metre, a French mechanics tools, Polish patent medicines, a German toothbrush, this is a fairly representative list for one day.

Advice on the correct geological structure of stone to make tyre bursters had to be obtained, and therefore the services of a geologist was sought. Tins and containers of innumerable sizes filled with various commodities and fitted with the many methods of false bottoms, also liquid containers, each carrying the authentic label, had to be produced. This called for commercial artists, printers, and metalworkers. The plaster and papier-mâché work needed expert painters and plasterers to imitate the various types of geology and the many kinds of vegetation in order to complete the final perfect picture. Carpenters and cabinetmakers were needed for subtle joinery work, in contrast to the making of packing for the many devices.

The agent's clothes and equipment had to be made to look old and the money needed and carried by the agent could not appear new, therefore studio property men were employed. The fairly simple process of printing labels developed into the production of foreign matches and cigarettes. The reproductions of codes printed on silk created a further demand for professional printers and compositors. All these men, apart from one or two exceptions, were obtained from the Forces, and where possible, personal recommendations were accepted, which led to a high degree of cooperation and security, both so necessary to the successful fulfilment of the Camouflage Section's commitments.

These increases of staff, together with the large-scale demands which involved the handling of many tons of explosive material, demanded the acquisition of new premises. In June 1942, the Thatched Barn, a pre-war Roadhouse on the Barnett bypass, became known as Station XV and dealt with all large-scale production, leaving a small staff at Kensington to deal with prototypes and personal contact with Agents. Kensington was now known as Station XVA.

A special supplies section was already in existence to deal with the equipment of Agents proceeding to the Field. It was realised that better cooperation and results could be procured if this section was incorporated into the Camouflage Section. The authenticity of detail was of paramount importance. The type of clothing needed for the various European countries had to be exact as continental styles are entirely different from those of Britain. The methods of sewing and making are as different as chalk from cheese. A collar button hole on a continental collar is vertical, whilst that on an English made article is horizontal. A dangerous giveaway to the enemy. Suits, hats, shoes, socks, braces, handkerchiefs, brushes, all had to be specially made, and by June 1944 over 90,000 articles were being issued per year, an average of 16 Agents were being fully equipped down to the smallest detail per day.

A new demand arose, the need for disguising the Agent himself. Film makeup experts and eminent plastic surgeons were engaged to cope with this new difficulty. Men and women were sent out into the field either temporarily or permanently disguised beyond any possible recognition.

In order to further their security, a photographic section dealing with the production of fake passport photographs was also absorbed into the Camouflage Section. From March 1, 1943 to November 15, 1944, this section photographed 1,620 Agents.

In order that the Agent should receive every possible help and avail himself of 'food for thought', a demonstration room was formed in the Natural History Museum, this exhibition contained not only examples of the many facilities available from the Camouflage Section, but examples of all the devices produced by the AD/Z directorate.

The Camouflage Section now consisted of four Stations. Station XV being the headquarters and the main production station, Station XVA consisting of prototypes, ageing workshops, together with the clothing department, Station XVB being the demonstration room and lecture hall, and Station XVC which was occupied by the photograph and multimedia department. In all, eighteen officers and nearly 300 'other' ranks. Meanwhile camouflage activities had spread overseas, and sections were formed in Italy, Algiers, and Cairo. As the war moved eastwards, two further sections were formed in India and one in Australia. With the advance of our armies in Europe, a Camouflage Section dealing with German agents was sent overseas in January 1945 and established workshops outside Brussels.

Ideas were developed from suggestions made by the staff, the country sections, Agent's reports, foreign trade journals, customs officials, and MI5. The CID were brought in to vet and try out new gadgets. No new idea was rejected without a trial, and every effort was made to try and not repeat a device which had already been used. Originality was the chief aim, but as most operators were dropped by parachute, the question of weight and size meant very severe restrictions. Wherever possible any article which should work normally was made to do so, for example gramophones carrying radio transmitters could play records, batteries concealing ammunition could be tested, torches either carrying messages or in the form of a new anti-personnel device, could function in the normal fashion.

Many millions in foreign currency which was needed for operational purposes were hidden in a great variety of carriers: toilet articles, suitcases, briefcases, workmen's tool boxes, tea cans, thermos flasks, writing pads, toys, tins of food stuff, were in general demand. Foreign oil stoves, vibro massage outfits, sythe stones, shoe trees, alarm clocks, even toilet rolls, are typical of the many schemes devised for the particular characteristics to be supported. Identity cards, ration books, micro prints, codes, messages and letters required smaller articles, preferably to fit in the pocket, such as wallets, cigarette cases, pencils, fountain pens, match boxes, and notebook covers.

While the wireless sets presented an additional problem owing to their delicate nature and the careful packing required vacuum cleaners, adding machines, portable gramophones, scales, breezeblocks, petrol, and oil tins, proved successful forms of camouflage for the larger type of wireless sets, while bibles and other books, brandy flasks, ornaments, tea cans, mangelwurzels and turnips, were used to hide smaller transmitters and receivers.

At one time over 30 tons per month of arms and ammunition were camouflaged for one Country Section alone. These stores were camouflaged as current commodities, like barrels of fish offal, cement sacks, broken spas, and driftwood.

Incendiary suitcases and cigarettes, explosive ration tins, oil cans, the moulding of TNT in the form of Balinese carvings and other Far East ornaments were made. Dummy tuna fish packing crates carrying arms, aerials camouflaged as clothes lines, rope and tender drills, the production of tropical fruits and vegetables for carriers and sabotage devices, invisible printing on clothes and every description of cloth, formed many of the oddities that were produced. The making of sniper suits, portable observation posts, the camouflage of small craft, the production of decoy tanks and armoured vehicles, the reproduction of foreign uniforms complete to the identification discs, were other essentials that came under the ever-increasing cloak of the Camouflage Section.

CAMOUFLAGE SECTION STAFFING

The Camouflage Section as required for such an organisation as ours, is entirely different, and must not be confused with, camouflage as known by the Forces. As pointed out previously, the name itself is camouflage for the makeup and clothing of the Agent going into the field, the concealment of all necessary paraphernalia, together with the disguising of all sabotaged devices.

It was therefore, a perpetual difficulty throughout the existence of this section, to try and convince the War Office of our essential need for certain personnel who are not included in the category of Army Tradesmen.

The following are examples of such trades needed for this work and for which there are, at present, no army equivalents:

1. Makeup artists and hairdressers—required for dealing with facial hair, and general alterations of appearance of students. The man must be experienced in the making of wigs and the handling of crepe hair dyeing and tinting.

2. Property man—a trade used extensively by the theatrical profession and the film industry. The qualifications of such a man are exceedingly varied. He is a Jack of all trades and master of all.
3. Artist—this man is essentially a commercial artist, and is required for the reproduction of line and colour drawings, for the making of blocks and engraving of stones in order to produce a large variety of foreign printing matter, such as labels stamps, and identification cards.

This non-existence of these particular trades, resulted in many difficulties connected with the men themselves. One case was that of a man who was admirably suited as a key man in the plasterer's shop, but who had been placed by the army into the Catering Corps. Consequently, there was continued difficulty in holding this man because he counted against the authorised ceiling of numbers in that Corps. Likewise, when he was promoted, he again counted against the ceiling of ranks in the catering core. His pay was that of a cook instead of a plasterer, so that he had to be paid temporary tradesman's rates of pay under article 846 of the Royal Warrant 1940.

There were a number of infantry soldiers employed in the Camouflage Section as tradesmen, and as many as 25% of these men employed had to be paid a temporary tradesman's rate of pay because personnel were either in non-trade Corps, or of the wrong trade in Trade Corps. A man could not be transferred into appropriate Corps because the Corps in question were not prepared to accept the men against tradesman ceilings, giving the reason that the men would not have been available for postings within the Corps establishments. Considerable personal hardship was inflicted on many 'other' ranks because of loss of their temporary pay when posted within the Organisation and the loss of trade pay, and sometimes rank when posted outside the organisation.

It was not practical to show tradesmen in the War Establishment as belonging to a definite arm of the Service, because a great number of the staff employed were chosen personally by Colonel Wills who had employed them prior to the war, and also they had already served a certain period of service in their Units before it was intended to organise such a section.

A probable solution to the whole of these troubles would have been a non-military establishment, and the employment of civilians together with the release of men and women from the services on the W.T. Reserve.

BUYING DEPARTMENT

It was found essential that men employed in buying had to be civilians. As already mentioned, the variety called for was tremendous, and the buyers had to use their ingenuity to think of cover stories as an excuse for their peculiar purchases. For example, the purchase of rats was done under the guise of a laboratory student from the University College Hospital, requiring rats for experimental purposes. The cover story of a buyer from a film studio was very often successfully used because of the variety of requirements needed in film production.

The purchase of clothing presented many more difficulties, especially as all articles required had to be of a foreign nature. The men that were employed had vast experience of continental clothing. These men were able to obtain practically all examples from the many refugees residing in the country at the outbreak of the war, but a large number of firms had to be taken into our confidence in order that articles could be produced in bulk. In one case a manufacturer started a shirt factory purely for the use of the Organisation. He employed a staff of continental refugees, who made shirts as they had always made them, that is with usual continental stitching and cut, and therefore they were never aware that they were making anything unusual.

The camouflage section was not formed until 1941, and consequently the two previous years were wasted and much valuable data lost. The following are essential contacts and although we acquired a certain amount of useful material from them, the bulk of their prize stores had disappeared during the previous two years:

(i)   The Admiralty Marshal should have been immediately contacted and all such parts of enemy cargo as found necessary should have been commandeered. The same applied to the Kings Customs House.
(ii)   MI5 was especially useful in putting at our disposal all the personal effects of arrested 'suspects.'
(iii) Warehouses dealing in foreign merchandise should have been contacted and their stock purchased at the outbreak of the war.

PROPERTY MAKING DEPARTMENT

One of our biggest problems was the ageing of all new clothing and articles. It is impossible to lay down definite rules for ageing except that a strict system is essential. The cover story of the man who is to wear or carry the articles must be given in order that 'agers' know exactly what he is representing to be (businessman, farm worker, factory employee etc.).

It was found essential that specific teams were appointed to work on the effects of each man. For instance, in the mending and washing of his clothes, it had to be decided whether the man had a good wife or a bad one, or whether he had to mend his clothes himself. This ensured a continuity not only in the general aspect of his clothing, but the more detailed points such as the darning and mending.

It was essential that no article carried by the Agent should appear new as it was impossible to obtain ersatz (fake) material which was of a much poorer quality than anything that we could obtain in this country. This especially applied to all leather goods, braces, and suspenders.

The German was extraordinarily thorough in his search and considerable care had to be taken to see that manufacturers of shoes and suitcases did not use old British newspapers for linings. We provided them with Continental newspapers to be used according to the allocation of the articles. It was even necessary to provide exact replicas of all cottons and threads used in the making of these articles. We even reproduced canvases made from plaited string such as was being used on the Continent.

Close contact with the Country Sections is essential. They are the Agent's guardians, and as such can inform both sides as to what is needed. They can assure the Camouflage Section that the Agent is instructed to give them information, and at the same time they can advise the Agent on the many facilities available from the Camouflage Department.

The following is a copy of a questionnaire that was issued to all Agents returning or proceeding to the Field:

1. Did you find a need for Camouflage?
2. If so, what forms were most useful?
3. Did you find that the Camouflage supplied was satisfactory? If not, please give reasons.
4. Did you receive any form of disguise before going into the field? (i.e. facial alterations, hair dyed, etc).
5. Was it satisfactory?
6. Did you have any need for temporary disguise?
7. Can you suggest any improvements or additions?
8. Were your clothes satisfactory? Did they conform with those worn in the country you visited?
9. Should they have been aged?
10. Is it true that British cloth and cigarettes could be bought in the black market?
11. What differences in the equipment supplied to you could have been more beneficial?
12. Give any information you can on the following:
    a) Hats
    b) Overcoats
    c) Suits
    d) Shoes and Boots
    e) Shirts
    f) Underclothing
    g) Toilet requisites
    h) Cigarettes
    i) Matches
    j) Suitcases
    k) Tinned Foods
    l) What were the most common objects seen being carried?

1

The Camouflage Section

As man acquired defensive methods, and became more and more civilised, his instinctive desire to hide as a means of preservation gradually dwindled, and finally disappeared. It was modern warfare that reawakened these last instincts and brought him again the imperative need of concealment.

Therefore the art of camouflage has been developed to give protection to the soldier and his equipment. In the same way, camouflage has been introduced into this Organisation for the purpose of safeguarding the Agent proceeding into the 'field.' It supplies his correct clothing to the smallest of detail. It provides means of disguise, so that he can pass amongst hostile acquaintances. It aids him in the concealment of the necessary equipment, which has to accompany him, and it facilitates the infiltration of arms and explosives into the country in which he has to work, so that he can organise and carry out operations against the enemy. It provides him with every aid in order that he can fit himself into the existing background.

The Camouflage Section is divided into the following categories:

a) The introduction of a 'shell' over stores in order to transport in bulk. For example, in an operation during 1943 some 20-tons of equipment per month was camouflaged in this manner, success depending on the variety of the represented commodities in order to confuse the Gestapo.

b) The more complicated method of hiding each article in a tin or package as an extra precaution to the outer 'shell' and with each tin or package fitted with a liquid container or false bottom carrying a quantity of the purported commodity. If needs be this 'shell' can be used to get articles already camouflaged to a destination, e.g., a broken spa carried ashore, containing cans of putty, concealing plastic explosives.

c) The camouflage of devices, where standard or special charges are designed as instant vehicles such as oil cans, coal, or stones.

d) The introduction of camouflage into booby traps such as tins which explode when opened, or the innocent military manual left lying on the desk.

e) The camouflage of wireless sets can be divided into two categories; firstly, that of a carrier as described in category 'a' or secondly as a permanent camouflage where the wireless set is in constant use, such as a calculator or an ordinary domestic radio receiving set.

f) The concealment of small articles which are needed to be carried by the Agent upon his person, e.g., codes, microscopic photographs, and messages hidden in pens, pencils, or wallets, etc.

g) In this Section the Agent's clothing is dealt with, particular importance being placed on the necessity for ensuring that everything he wears or carries fits in with his cover story.

h) This Section shows how the Agent's physical appearance can be altered, either temporarily or permanently by makeup, disguise, plastic surgery, or other means, and how he can change his personality so that he can move about freely without fear of recognition.

i) It is often necessary to use methods of camouflage as laid down by the Armed Forces, as in many cases operations are carried out by small military or naval parties. The principles involved in disruptive painting are explained in this section, which shows how objects are so painted to break up their shape and to help them become immersed into their background. This method applies mostly to small craft and the personal equipment of the men taking part.

j) The camouflage of tyrebursters. This is done by three different methods, illustrations of which are applied to the text.

k) All the labels and printing matter necessary to complete the fake commodities as described in the previous sections, are produced by the Printing and Art departments. This also includes production of armlets for invading forces, insignias for foreign uniforms, and the printing of codes.

l) The Photographic Section exists chiefly for the purpose of producing the necessary photographs for faked documents. It is also responsible for the illustrations required for the various catalogues and technical journals.

m) Miscellaneous. Included in this section are all the smaller and more unusual items of camouflage which cannot be properly classified under any of the above headings.

While it is not possible to include in a catalogue of this nature all the many and varied camouflage items that have been produced, it will be found that the above sections cover all the main branches of camouflage work, and any items not included vary only in details from the chief principles set out in the succeeding pages.

'SHELL' OVER STORES

The introduction of a 'shell' over stores is usually for camouflaging single units of bulk stores such as arms, ammunition, food, etc. Where possible this principle is aided by the additional tricks of subterfuge such as the introduction of a liquid container in tin flagons, or drums, but in the majority of cases, the camouflage consists of only the outer covering. A list of articles that have been used is applied below:

Bricks, barrels, plaster bandages, plastic bottles, bottles of mineral water, drums of pitch, drums of size, driftwood, drums of paint and oil, fish boxes, fish barrels, food tins, plaster logs, plaster vegetables, papier-mâché oil bottles, soap powder cartons, food cartons, skittles, ships' spars, stones, tunny fish and water carriers.

DRUMS OF OIL PAINT, ETC.

Different types and sizes of metal drums are designed to represent normal commodities in the countries concerned. They are used for concealment of arms, ammunition, explosives, and are painted and stencilled to appear as paint, TA, tallow, creosote, herring oil, etc. As illustrated these drums can be fitted with a bung-hole, and the section inside the drum is filled with the liquid which it is supposed to be carrying, so that it will stand scrutiny when a dipstick is inserted into the drum.

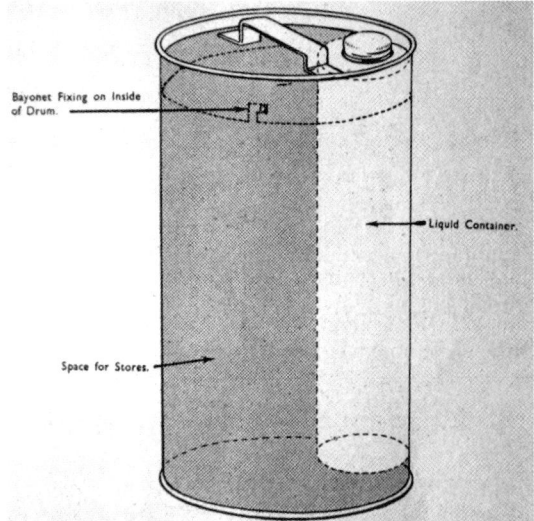

FISH BARRELS

If a fish barrel of a type fairly common to most countries is used for shipping of arms and ammunition. A metal drum is filled with the stores, sealed down with pitch to protect from damp, and then placed in the barrel. It is packed round on all sides with rock salt, or cod roe (fertiliser) and the barrel top is then nailed on and banded.

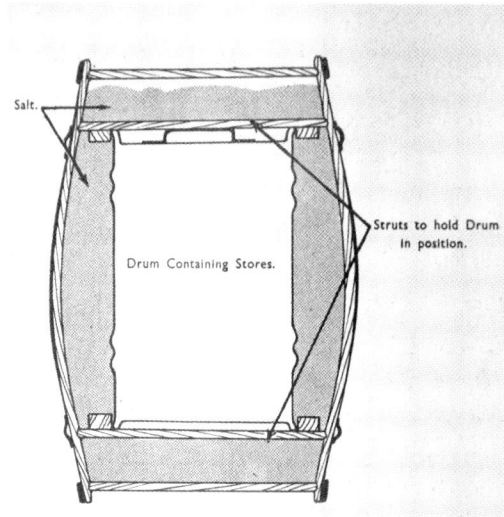

METAL FLAGONS

Metal containers of various types and shapes are used for concealment of ammunition, small stores, grenades, crystals, money, etc. A great range of tins and labels of all countries is kept in stock. Below is an illustration of some of the tins used, but as almost any type of label can be copied and produced by the team, it is not necessary to give an illustration of them all. Liquid containers etc., are fitted to each tin so that when shaken it appears to be full of the purported contents.

PLASTER LOGS

A range of plaster logs designed for shipping arms and ammunition. The arms are packed in cardboard containers and sealed to protect from damp. They are then built into dummy logs made of plaster, which are modelled on actual types of trees common to the countries to which the shipments are being made. The plaster is then painted and garnished with moss, green lichen, or other tree fungi. Wooden logs with a hollow cavity in the centre are also used for concealment of stores and ammunition.

PLASTER VEGETABLES AND FRUIT

Vegetables such as potatoes, swedes, parsnips, etc. and tropical fruits are made of plaster or clay and used for concealment of ammunition, plastic explosive, incendiary material, etc. The result is an excellent imitation of the actual vegetable or fruit. This type of device when filled is useful for depositing in ammunition dumps and mixed with real vegetables or fruit until distributed.

PACKING CASES

A series of packing cases in wood and cardboard designed to represent commodities in everyday use in the countries concerned. Arms and ammunition are sent out in these boxes representing such articles as china and glassware, jam, tinned foods, electric goods, mineral waters, etc. These cases are designed to fit the standard dump unit and variations are made to the outside appearance by means of cross members, handles, wire banding, stencils, and destination labels. In some instances, the box is given a coat of paint or stained according to the type required.

DRIFTWOOD AND SPARS

Driftwood, such as old railway sleepers, and struts used in bridge building, are made with a cavity, and used for the concealment of Sten guns and ammunition. To guard against the effects of dampness, the stores are packed in tin containers, and then placed in the pieces of wood. The same principle is used in the construction of ships' spars, accept that the entry to the concealment chamber is from the bottom instead of from the side.

CEMENT BAGS

Bags of cement are used for carrying arms and ammunition. The arms are packed into tin containers around which a plaster shell resembling cement hardened by damp or water, is modelled. The whole is then put into a cement bag, which is printed and aged to look like the genuine article.

FISH BOXES

A fish box of normal type is used for packing arms and ammunition. The arms are first packed in a sealed tin box, placed in a fish box with a salt or fish covering, and a wooden lid nailed or banded down. The boxes are made from new wood if actual fish boxes are unobtainable. They are aged with paint, dyes, and various solutions of fish and oil.

'DOUBLE SHELL' CAMOUFLAGE

The term 'double shell' camouflage describes the method of introducing arms, ammunition, and other stores into a foreign country disguised as normal merchandise. These stores are first packed in a manner that ensure they do not rattle, or otherwise expose the camouflage, and then these packages are placed into cartons, tins, etc., appropriate to the commodity under which they are being disguised.

An example of this 'double shell' packing is as follows:

It is required to send grenades to Norway. Each grenade is greased and packed into a tin which is an accurate copy of a current brand of Norwegian fish cakes. Each tin is specially constructed with a liquid container which is filled with an appropriate amount of water. Special attention is paid to weight. The tin is correct as to size and label and sounds genuine when shaken. The tins are sealed by the same method that the fish cake manufacturer would use, and packed in reproductions of its crates.

Obviously careful selection of commodity containers is necessary to ensure that (a) the weight of packages is similar to real goods, (b) that weight for space is closely related, i.e., it would be wasteful of space to send rifle ammunition in tins of tobacco on the account of the small number of rounds which could be packed in, say, 1/2 pound tin, and still keep the weight down to that of the original quantity of tobacco.

A complete variation of 'double shell' camouflage can be employed in the following way:

A reproduction of a broken ship's spar is constructed of wood. It is hollow and provision is made for it to be opened to contain a considerable volume of stores. Inside the spar may be packed grenades, etc, which have been concealed in plaster reproductions of vegetables or other camouflage.

The hollow spar is waterproof and may be left on the beach, or collected by a 'beachcomber' who, of course, will be a person connected with the particular operation. He can distribute the camouflaged articles as necessary or keep them concealed in the spar.

For the purpose of double shell camouflage a comprehensive range of foreign boxes, tinned goods, and labels are kept in stock, covering the following countries: Norway, Hungary, Italy, Germany, Belgium, Denmark, Holland and, France, Portugal, and Japan.

CAMOUFLAGE OF WIRELESS SETS

The size and shape of wireless receiving and transmitting sets used in the field, and the fact that they are mostly required to be assembled ready for use, presents a difficult concealment problem, but, as the following list shows, a large number of articles have been successfully used to conceal wireless sets:

Artist paints box.	Electrical testing metre.
Blocks of granite.	Portable gramophone
Bundles of fagots.	Munro adding machine.
Bathroom scales.	Paint and oil drums.
Car batteries.	Rocks, rubber, tin, papier-mâché.
Concrete posts used in fencing.	Rubber arm chairs.
Cement sacks.	Vacuum cleaners.
Driftwood.	Vibro massage sets.
Domestic wireless sets, continental type.	Workman's tool boxes.

Each item is 'manufactured,' e.g., made with papier-mâché, plaster, etc., or, in the case of bathroom scales and other mechanical objects, the machinery is replaced by the wireless set, and the outside appearance remains as the original innocent domestic appliance. The following examples and illustrations are typical of wireless concealment devices:

BUNDLES OF FAGGOTS

This type of concealment is used for country districts. Care must be taken to ensure that the fagots correspond to the kind of trees found in the neighbourhood. A rope aerial can be used to bind round the bundle of fagots. The construction of the bundle is shown in the illustrations overleaf. The first operation is to gather a real bundle of sticks, and then to select those which are to be used for the centre and cut out the middle of each stick. Holes are bored in the end of the box and the short end of the sticks firmly secured into them. The outer casing of sticks is nailed onto the box. In the field the agent can alter the bundle by placing more locally gathered sticks on the outside and binding them on with his rope aerial.

MUNRO ADDING MACHINE

This machine is manufactured in America, but it is in common use on the Continent. The machine is used to conceal the A. Mk.II wireless set. If the vibrator pack is required, it must be sent under separate camouflage. When the set is fitted into the machine it is still possible to operate the keys, but the machine does not work. This latter fact would help to substantiate a cover story that the machine was being taken for repairs if an Agent was stopped in the street.

DOMESTIC WIRELESS SETS

Domestic wireless set cabinets constructed to appear identical to those in use on the Continent can be very satisfactorily used as a concealment for an Agent's wireless set. The outside controls are dummy, and the Agent's set is hidden in the false case.

PORTABLE GRAMOPHONES

The A. Mk. II wireless set fits conveniently into a Continental style gramophone. By removing the gramophone motor, substituting a dummy spindle to carry the turn table,

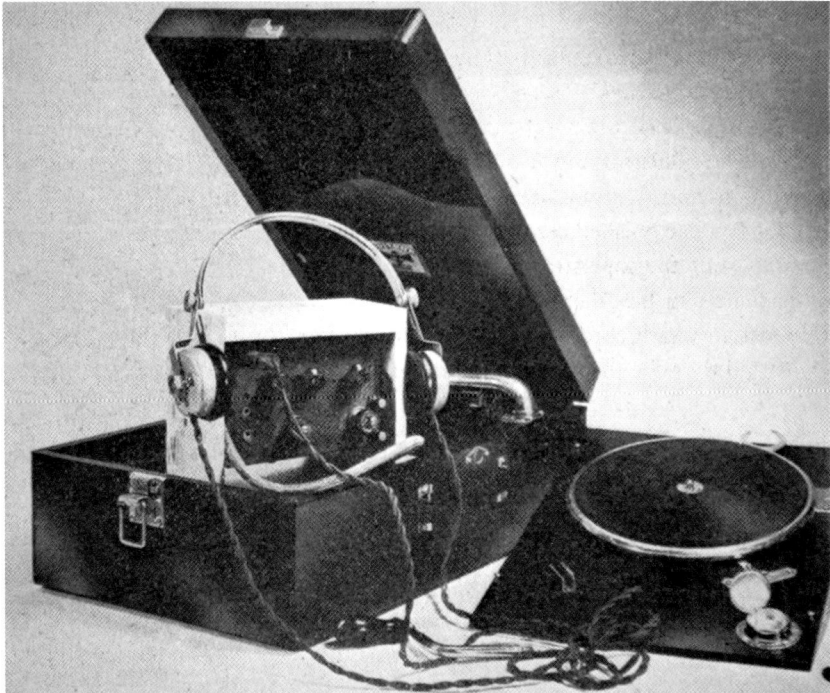

and cutting away the sound horn inside the gramophone, enough room is provided to take the four packs of the A. Mk. II wireless set. This concealment is only for carrying purposes and the wireless set must be taken out of the gramophone and assembled for working. Whenever possible the gramophone is made to play and appropriate records are supplied.

VACUUM CLEANER

The images below show the method of concealing the four packs of the A. Mk. II wireless set, crystals and spares in a Continental type Electrolux cleaner and its carrying case. The cleaner can be plugged in, and although not actually operating as a cleaner, the noise produced will give an appearance of it doing so. If an agent was stopped carrying the cleaner in the street it would be normal to tell the story that it was being taken for repair, or to be sold.

AERIALS

A good aerial always improves the performance of a wireless set, and an Agent can make use of one with little fear of detection if it is concealed in a rope clothesline or window sash cord. The first illustration shows an aerial disguised as a tendril in its natural surroundings on a tree. The second illustration shows the finished clothes line aerial. This aerial is made by twisting the rope strands over the aerial: a rope making machine can be adapted to do this work. In the case of the window sash cord, the centre core of the cord is withdrawn, and the wire threaded back in its place.

ROCKS

These rocks are devices for depositing a wireless set on beaches or in open country. A papier-mâché shell is constructed and is lined inside with a tin case which conforms to the outline of the rock at the top and is flat at the base. The shell is realistically painted and finished to blend with the geological types of the district in the country in which operations are being carried out, providing they are used with discretion to fit into their correct surroundings. These rocks are weatherproof when finished and quite safe to leave in an appropriate

place without fear of detection or damage to the wireless set. Hollowed out spars or blocks of driftwood are also successfully used for concealing wireless sets out-of-doors.

RUBBER ARMCHAIR

This device is constructed like a balloon. When it is inflated with a pump it has the outline of an ordinary armchair. The wireless set can be placed under the seat. The effect is perfected by covering the chair with a loose cover, placing a cushion on the seat and the chair can be used in the normal way. Care must be taken to keep it normally inflated. When deflated the chair folds up to a package about 15-inches by 9-inches. And boulders can also be produced in the same way. This type of camouflage takes up very little space and is easily manipulated.

CONCEALMENT OF MINIATURE COMMUNICATION RECEIVERS (M.C.R.)

The following pages of illustrations show various devices used for the concealment of miniature communication receivers M.C.R. Antique German clocks copied from originals, and suitably aged and painted are illustrated on this page. The concealment chamber at the back of the clock is sufficiently large enough to accommodate an M.C.R.

ARTICLES CARRIED BY A STUDENT

This section could very well be a catalogue in itself; the many articles mentioned in the following pages do not in any way cover the whole field of material which comes under this heading. Almost anything which a person carries or makes use of professionally, by way of trade, for personal convenience, or toilet purposes, can be adapted for concealment.

PERSONAL ARTICLES

The following is a short list of some of the articles which have been adapted:

Collar stud.
Collar stiffener.
Coat button.
Cigarette holder.
Door key.
Fountain pen.
Finger ring.
Pocket petrol lighter.

Pocket torches.
Penknife.
Pipe and pipe cases.
Pencils.
Shoe trees.
Shoulder paddings
Shoe heels and soles.
Spectacles.

The following examples show what can be done with these articles:

Collar stud. A metal collar stud with a celluloid back can be used for concealing micro prints. The celluloid back is removed, and the micro print placed in the cavity. The celluloid is replaced and secured with a small application of Seccotine.

Necktie. A necktie can conceal a small code printed on silk. The code is secured to the back of the tie with two small press studs. This method is used in order that the code may be very speedily used and replaced. A tie adapted in this manner is worn quite normally and without any bulkiness showing.

Door key. A door key has been successfully adapted for the concealment of small micro prints. The shaft of the key is drilled to about three quarters of its length, and a small stud is made which fits into the hollowed shaft by means of a left-hand thread.

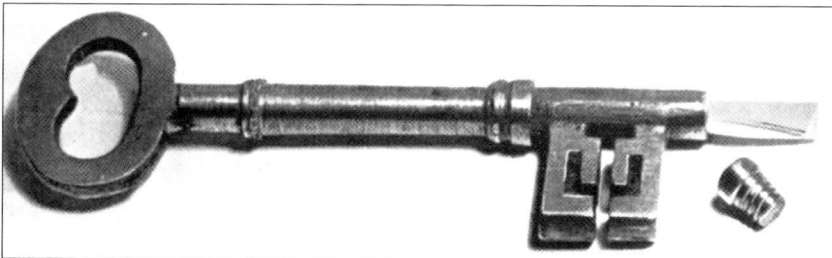

TOILET ARTICLES

In the following list are some of the toilet articles which have been used for concealment purposes, and which form some of the personal equipment of a student.

Bath salts.
Razor box and razor.
Shaving stick and shaving
    soap.
Lipsticks.
Folding mirror.

Sponge.
Talcum powder.
Toilet roll.
Manicure accessories.
Toilet soap.
Toothpaste.

Sponge. A suitable place in the sponge is chosen, and a hole is cut to conform to the natural texture of the sponge. A small amount of the sponge fibre is cut away from the inside to leave sufficient room to insert a message or code printed on silk. The object inserted in a sponge must necessarily be of a soft nature in order not to make a hard lump and to avoid a rustling sound which would be made by paper. The cavity in the sponge is closed by replacing a small sponge plug and securing with Seccotine or by stitching.

Toilet soap. It is necessary to procure a copy of a cake of soap common to the district where the student is proceeding. The piece of soap is carefully split open, and the centre is hollowed out. Pins are used to help keep the two halves together. When the object for concealment is in place, the soap is pressed together. To render the joint unnoticeable a little moisture is rubbed around the joint, or the soap is used in the normal way.

Toothpaste in tubes. These tubes have a number of uses. The student naturally requires toothpaste appropriate to the country to which he is proceeding. Some of the brands which are made-up by the camouflage section are shown in the image below. Glass frosting ointment is also dispatched under this disguise. For concealment purposes the tubes are completed with the supposed makers trademarks, etc., and the top of the tube is filled with toothpaste. If the object to be concealed requires to be proofed against damp (e.g. a code printed on silk), it is inserted into a rubber balloon. The object is placed in the tube, packed with a little cotton wool and the end of the tube is folded over in the normal way. This device is safe enough because the toothpaste can be used and should arouse no suspicion.

Shaving cream in tubes. This method is exactly similar to the toothpaste tube, except that there is a larger concealment space.

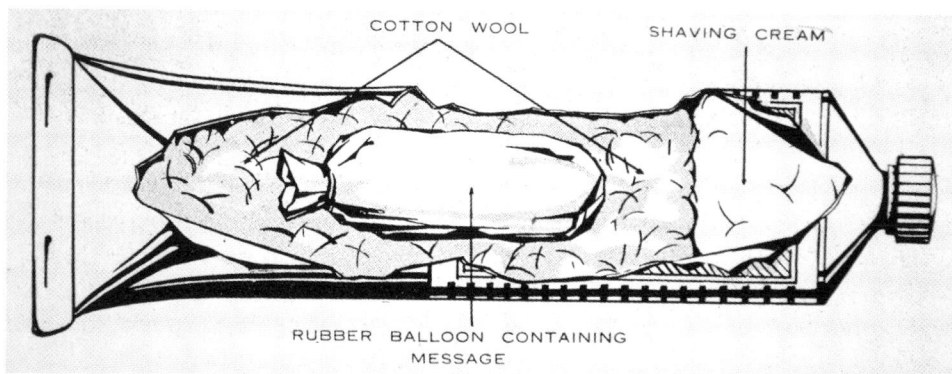

COTTON WOOL   SHAVING CREAM

RUBBER BALLOON CONTAINING MESSAGE

BRUSHES

The following is a list of some of the brushes used for concealment:

Hair brushes, celluloid backs, wooden backs, and swivel side.
Shaving brushes.
Clothes brushes.
Tooth brushes.

Nail brushes.
Shoe brushes.
Paint and distemper brushes.
Wire brushes.

These are used for concealment of codes, money, documents, etc. There are two principal methods used for brushes. When the brush is used to carry money, etc, to the field and is not reused, the back of a celluloid brush, for example, is removed, money is packed inside the cavity, and the brush is sealed up. The brush must be split open to extract its contents. If the brush is for use on a number of occasions the swivel sided type of brush is supplied. The following are some descriptions of typical brush concealments.

Celluloid hair brush and shaving brush. The illustration below shows a complete toilet set in a leather case. The case itself has a concealment pocket and the hair brush

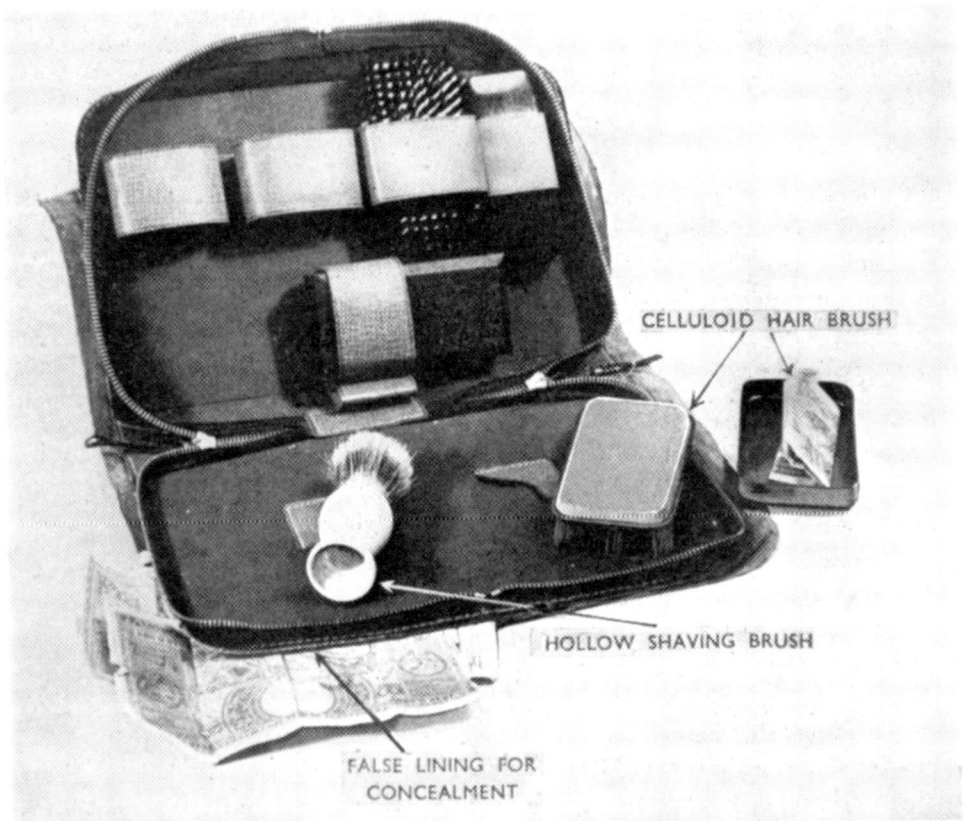

CELLULOID HAIR BRUSH

HOLLOW SHAVING BRUSH

FALSE LINING FOR CONCEALMENT

is of the celluloid back type. The shaving brush is hollow as shown, these three devices are single use only, as each article must be forcibly opened to extract the hidden contents.

Shaving brush. This brush is also for quick and frequent use. The bristles are held in place by a tight metal ring which clamps them to the handle. This brush must not be confused with the type, shown on page 38, which can only be used once.

Swivel-type celluloid hair brush. The photograph shows the working of the swivel sided hair brush. The cavity is approximately 3-inch × 2-inch × 3/8-inch.

Tooth brush. A celluloid handled toothbrush can be used for concealment of small micro prints. The handle of the brush is drilled, the print inserted, and the hole sealed by softening the celluloid with acetone and smoothing off on a buffering wheel. To extract the message the handle of the brush must be broken.

LEATHER GOODS

Various types of leather goods can be used for the concealment of codes, money, documents, etc. A list of these is given below:

Brief case.	Suitcase, various types.
Cycle saddle bag.	Tobacco pouches.
Cigarette cases.	Pocket notebooks, various types.
Card cases.	Toilet cases, various types.
Handbags, ladies'.	Wallets, photo and money.
Needle cases and housewives (mending kits).	Writing cases, various types.
Pocket chess set.	Leather belts and braces.
Razor Strop.	Hair brush cases.
	Tool bags.

Two methods are used in the camouflaging of codes, documents etc.

1. Where the article is used only once for transporting money and documents to the Field, it can be sealed and ripped open when needed.
2. In the case of codes when the article would have to be used many times, a concealed flap device is incorporated into the design so that the code can be readily accessible.

Brief cases. These are of Continental design in various sizes and colours, having double sided partitions with fake sewing along the top. Partitions are glued together after the documents have been inserted.

Suitcases. Varying types of continental suitcases are used for the concealment of codes, documents, money, etc. In some cases, the handle is also used as a concealment device for small articles. A handle made of metal and constructed in two parts, is held together by threaded rivets: a nut is soldered on to the inner side of the bottom half thus facilitating the removal of the two parts, and easy access to the article concealed therein.

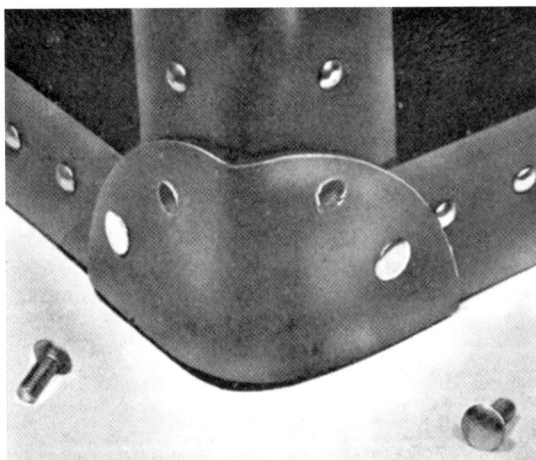

The double button suitcase, as shown below, is constructed so that a sliding panel is held in position by threaded rivets, which when unscrewed allow the panel to be withdrawn. The cavity exposed is about ½-inch deep and covers the area of the bottom of the suitcase. From these measurements it can be seen that this type is extremely useful for large amounts of money. In the double-sided type of suitcase an inner casing is made to lift out exposing a shallow cavity on all four sides.

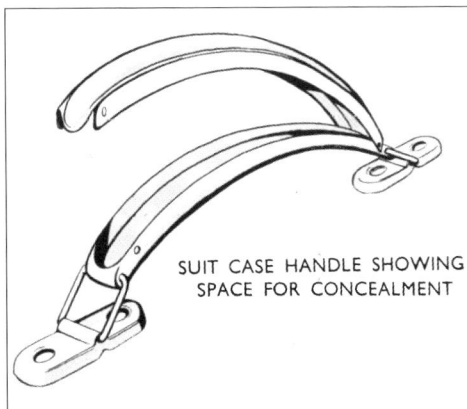

SUIT CASE HANDLE SHOWING SPACE FOR CONCEALMENT

Ladies handbags. These handbags are stocked in various designs and colours. An opening concealed in the fold at the bottom of the bag gives access to the hidden compartment, which is between the lining and the outer covering. This allows easy insertion and withdrawal of the code etc., which is concealed therein.

Razor strop. In this case the Razor Strop handle is used for concealment of small messages and micro prints. The handle is opened up, and the message inserted into the padding. The handle is then re-sewn.

Needle cases and 'Housewives' (mending kits). Needle cases and 'Housewives' being quite normal things to carry, are used for the concealment of silk codes and messages. The concealment is in a false lining. Cotton reels, woolcards, needles, scissors, etc., used for the contents of the housewife are authentic. Labels are printed copies of the originals. Spools and reels of cotton or silk can also be used as further carrying devices for drugs, micro prints, etc.

Leather belts. Double sided belts of various colours and designs, with grip on buckles are used for the concealment of micro prints. When the buckle is removed, the open end is revealed, giving quick and easy access to the hollow centre of the belt where the micro prints are inserted.

Braces. The leather connecting pieces between two braces can be unstitched and used for the concealment of micro prints. Continental designs are used as far as possible.

Wrist straps. Wrist straps can be used on the same principle as braces.

STATIONERY

A selection of stationery articles which form part of the normal equipment of a writing desk have been adapted for the concealment of codes, money, documents,

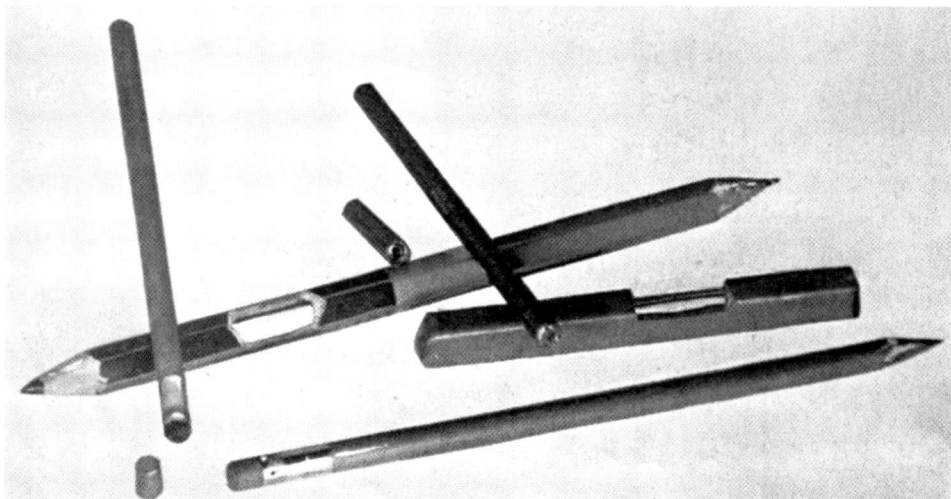

and tablets. Included in this list are book ends, uncut books, desk blotters of both the flat and curved varieties, fountain pens, inkstands, message carrying pencils, pencil boxes, pen knife handles, rubber stamp pads, sealing wax and rubbers.

Uncut books. Uncut books are a quick and easy method of concealing silk and paper micro prints. These books are authentic copies of current volumes on sale in the countries of origin. The codes are inserted between the uncut leaves at the back of the book. A few pages at the beginning of the book are cut purposely to give the impression the book is being read.

Rubbers and sealing wax. Rubbers and sealing wax are used for the concealment of B, K and L tablets. A cavity is bored in the centre of each of these articles, the tablet inserted, and the article buffed up to remove any signs of the join.

Matches. A large stock of various types of foreign matches is carried for the personal use of students in the field. These can be adapted with false bottoms for concealment purposes when required, but normally they are issued as part of the Agent's cover

Japan.

Holland.

Thailand.

Germany.

France.

Denmark.

Norway.

story. Below is appended a list with illustrations of the various types of matchboxes and the countries of origin.

French	Portugal	Sweden
Allumettes soufrées	Nau	Sakerhets tandstickor 222
Allumettes amorphés	Patria No. 2	Sakerhets tandstickor Swallow
Allumettes de sûreté	Patria No. 3	Kampion
Allumettes gitanes		
Casque D'or	**Norway**	**Spain**
Drapeaux	Nitedals	Compania Arrendataria
Timax	Hjelpestikker	Phosforos de papel
La Cocarde		
	Japan	**Denmark**
Dutch	Eagle matches	H.E. Gosch safety
Gaai	Two Lion matches	H.E. Gosch paraffin
Molen Lucifers		
Oehoe	**Poland**	**Germany**
	Polski Monopol	Schubert
Italian		Haushaltungsware
Allumettes 120	**U.S.S.R.**	Welt-Holzer
S.A.F.F.A.	Lenin matches	

BATTERIES, ELECTRIC

Various types and makes of foreign batteries have been used from time to time for camouflage of codes, etc. Types such as the three-cell battery, three segregated round type, the single unit 3-volt battery, and the large bell battery are used. These carry labels authentic to the country where they are to be used. The three-cell flat battery of the usual type is the one most frequently used. The centre cell is removed and replaced with a thin tube of the same size. It is then connected up in series by means of a wire so that current still flows through the circuit. Therefore, the light is generated by the two outside cells. The empty cell is used for concealment of micro film, codes, money, etc.

In the three-cell, round battery, shown in the illustration, the centre unit is hollowed out for carrying purposes. The large bell battery consists of a hollow shell, with a small battery to generate the light, fixed in the top of the casing and the remainder of

the space used for concealment. As the concealment space is larger, this type of battery is particularly useful for carrying wireless crystals, etc. These are of course, used in conjunction with the torch itself.

RAZOR BLADES

Various types of razor blade covers are printed and issued with blades for the general-purpose equipment of the Agent.

France.

Germany.

France.

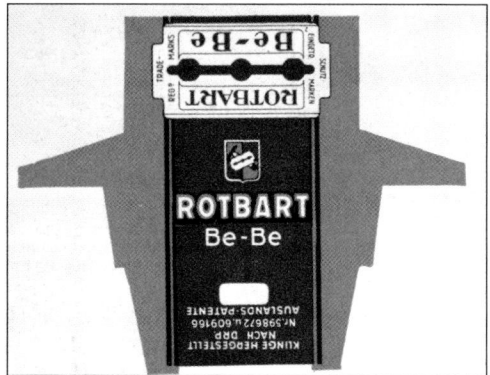

Germany.

France.

CIGARETTE CASES AND WALLETS

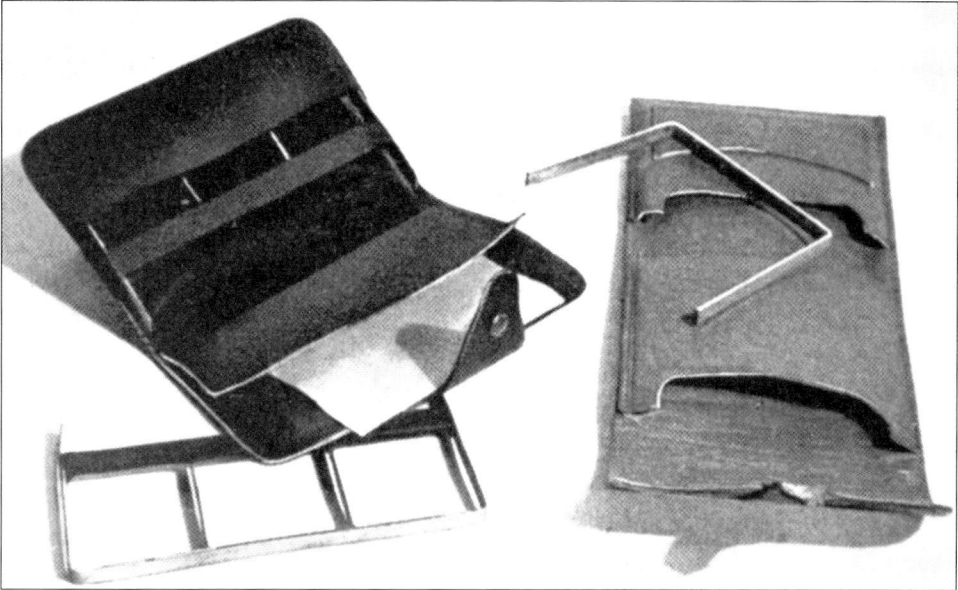

Two types of cigarette cases, showing concealment devices.

Wallet as used for the concealment of codes, etc.

WORKMAN'S TOOLS AND EQUIPMENT

Articles of this kind give us great scope for concealment of documents and money. These are necessarily controlled by the cover story of the Agent, for instance, a carpenter would have chisels, planes, and hammers, whilst an engineer would carry an oil-can, files, pliers, etc. Naturally, all the tools possible for concealment are not listed below as they cover such a wide field and almost anything of any size can be used for concealment of codes and money.

A carpenter's work bag containing innocent looking tools, but most have concealment cavities.

This photograph shows a carpenter's mallet and planes fitted with their concealment compartments covered.

This photograph shows the concealment cavities in a carpenter's mallet and planes.

Among tools that have been used are the following: blow lamp, builder's level, car dynamo, car Jack, dentists drill, dentist's chair headrest, drawing instruments case, cycle oil-tin, engineer's oil-can, grinding wheel, oil-stone, scythe stone, hammers, screwdrivers, chisels, mallets, planes and drill stands.

CIGARETTE PACKETS

A variety of foreign cigarettes and packages are kept in stock for the personal use of Agents in the field, or as a concealment device for small articles or micros, or incendiaries.

French	German	Greece
Gauloises Blue	Overstolz	Papastratos
Gauloises Buff	Privat	Arista
Gauloises Green	Merkur	
Gitanes	Juno	**Italy**
Golden Gate	Cairo	Stella
Deka	Milde Sorte	
	Reemtsma Sorte	**Thailand**
Norwegian	Club	Pratu Chai
Gold Flake	Roth Handle	
South State	Hoco	**Japan**
Marmara		Aeroplane Cigarettes
Golden West	Belgian	
	Vega	

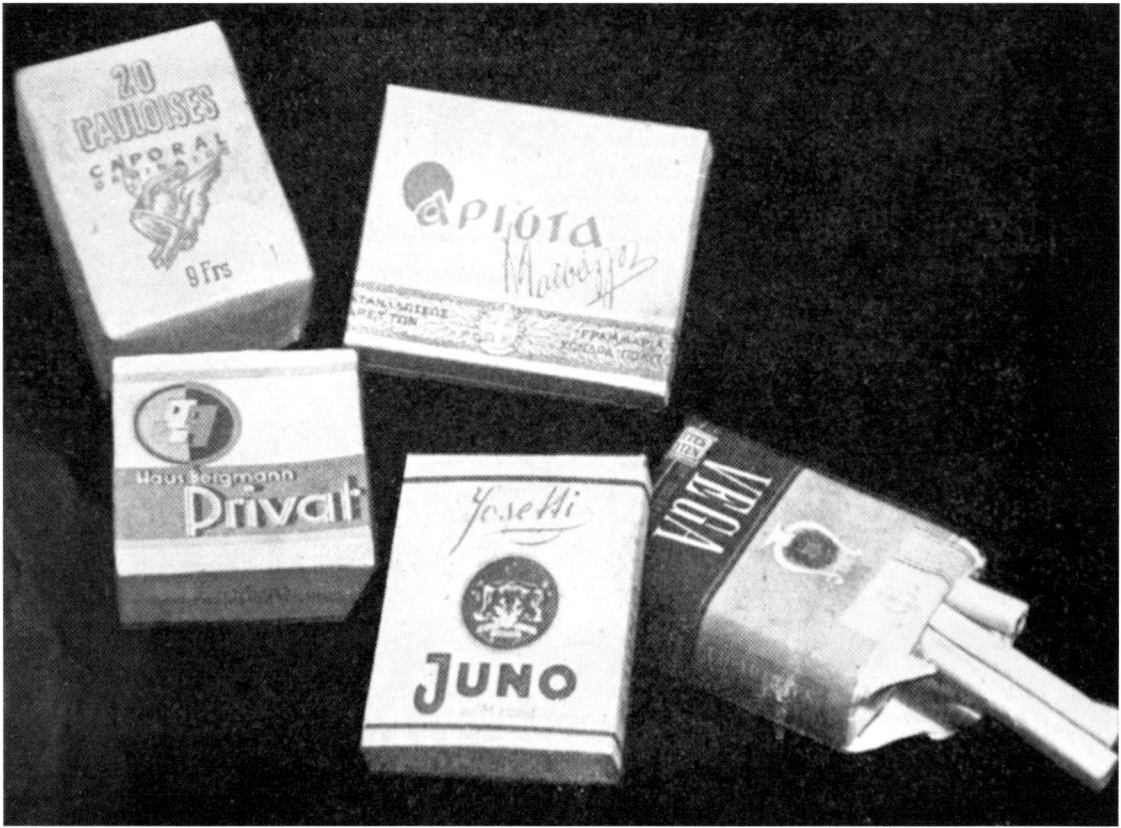

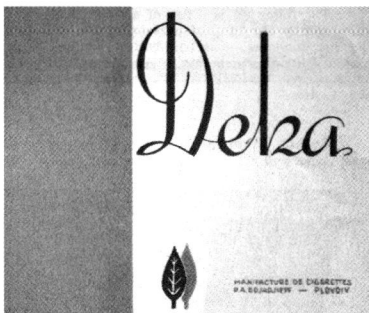

Above left: German reproduction cigarette packet label.

Above right: French reproduction cigarette packet label.

Left: Balkans reproduction cigarette packet label.

Top: A selection of German, Belgian, Greek and French reproduction cigarette packets.

PIPES

Pipes were used for carrying small messages and codes.

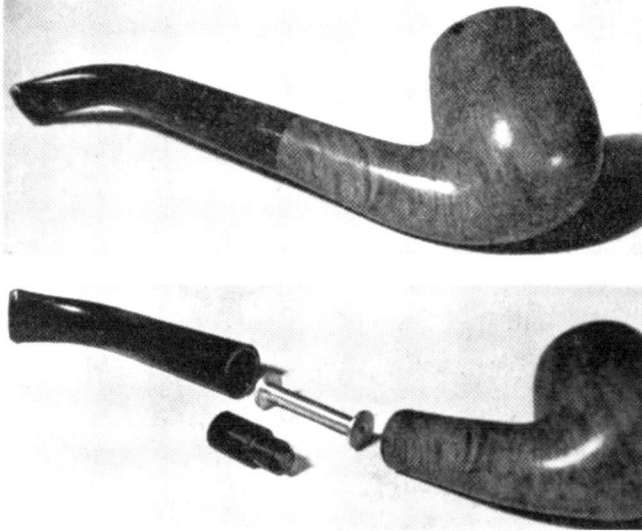

MISCELLANEOUS

The following is a list of articles that can be adapted for camouflage and can be carried by the student personally but cannot be classified under a general heading. The list includes: electric bulbs, candles, crucifixes, corks, cotton reels, electric irons, fishing floats, hollow faggots, gas masks, life jackets, musical instrument cases, mouth organs, medical kits, piano-accordions, toys, thermos flasks, walking sticks, and wine bottles.

Corks. A normal cork as used in a wine bottle is used for the concealment of small codes and micro prints. The cork has a hollow centre with a sliding panel.

Cotton reels. The cotton reel is composed of two parts, firstly, the outer casing which comprises one end and the body of the cotton reel around which the thread is wound, and secondly the removable centre shaft which is attached to the other end. When the reel is taken apart the silk code is wound round the centre shaft and the reel is then reassembled.

Explosive Devices

INTRODUCTION

Explosive and incendiary devices produced by the Camouflage Section are arranged in five groups.

1. Explosive devices—These consist of standard or extemporised charges, operated by ordinary safety or delayed action fuses, which are concealed in, or camouflaged by, some commonplace object.
2. Booby traps—These consist of charges activated by mechanisms which are called into operation by some unsuspecting person either moving, opening, or operating the article which camouflages the mechanism and charge.
3. Protective incendiary devices—These consist of cases for the concealment of documents; any unauthorised person proceeding to open the case in an incorrect manner would initiate the mechanisms firing the device. Two types are produced, electrical and mechanical.
4. Incendiary devices for destruction of documents by design of operator.
5. Delayed action incendiaries—Incendiaries camouflaged to represent commonplace objects.

EXPLOSIVE DEVICES

EXPLOSIVE OIL CAN

1. Description. An engineer's oil can is prepared to take an explosive charge. Under the opening in the lid of the can a small container is built, this is filled with oil so that on inspection, the can may pass muster. The charge is initiated by a pencil fuse, No. 27 detonator and CE primer.

2. Method of use. To prepare for operation, the spout is unscrewed, the prepared PTF and detonator pushed home, and the spout replaced. The can is then placed on, or alongside the target to be attacked.

3. History. At Station IX, Peter Henry produced the explosive oil can in the latter part of 1941. Early in 1942 the can was illustrated and described by Peter Henry in the shipping section of the sabotage handbook, Fig 34. Later Staff Sergeant Jones at Station XV produced cans for this device.

4. Prepared at Station XV. 106 cans were produced up to December 1944. A development of the oil can was the application of the same idea to the ordinary 1-gallon bulk oil tin.

EXPLOSIVE COAL

1. Description. Dyed plaster cast to represent lumps of coal, in which a filling of plastic explosive or other high explosive is initiated by a match headed Bickford fuse, detonator and CE primer.

2. Method of use. Lumps of explosive coal are placed in both railway engine coal supplies and those for industrial boilers, so that they may be fed to the fire in a natural manner.

3. History of Development. In "Brown Book of Devices", published at the end of 1939, explosive coal, coke, briquettes, logs, scrap iron etc, are dealt with. The actual materials were bored out to take explosive charges. These were the forerunners of camouflage coal, etc, which now take the place of the genuine article. Coal is also mentioned in the blue book published early in 1941. Halex Ltd produced celluloid shells at the end of 1941, which were not satisfactory.

Regimental Sergeant Major Bull, under the direction of Lieutenant Colonel J. Elder Wills, experimented with different kinds of plaster and dye in order to obtain a result which would stand up to handling, and if chipped still appear like coal. Staff Sergeant Nunney developed the production of camouflage coal until the following formula became standard:

a) Herculite plaster, mixed to a creamy gauge.
b) Dextrine 25%.
c) Black Ebony Water Dye No. 46164, made by John Nyland, Stockwell Road, Stockwell.

The plaster coal is cast in the form of half shells in moulds, each half shell being reinforced with fine scrim. When thoroughly dry, the interior of each shell is painted with shellac, the explosive charge inserted, and the two halves joined together with plaster and secured by metal cleats. Finally shellac varnish is used to coat the completed lump prior to a dressing of coal dust to give an authentic appearance.

A later development was the use of the GP charge as the explosive medium, instead of plastic explosive. This enabled the coal to be cast without a join. The GP charge, being in a metal container, permitted the pouring of liquid plaster around the charge in the mould, scrim being used as before; thus, production was simplified, the only drawback being that the shape of the GP charge limited the variation of size and shape of the finished coal.

4. Prepared by Station XV. Approximately 3.5 tons between 1941 and 1945.

EXPLOSIVE WOOD

I. Description. Natural wood, in the form of logs or sawn blocks, is hollowed out to take an explosive charge. Built up blocks made to represent tarred road blocks are similarly filled. In each case the charge is plastic explosive initiated by a CE primer, No. 27 for a matched headed Bickford fuse.

2. Method of use. Explosive wood is placed among similar wood used as fuel for wood fired boilers.

3. History. In January 1944, Colour Sergeant Major Waldron experimented with hollowing out pieces of wood, logs, road blocks, sawn timber etc. with a view to use them as concealment devices. In February 1944, Lieutenant Colonel J Elder Wills asked for explosive woods as an alternative to explosive coal where wood fired boilers were in use. The types already prepared were adapted to take approximately 1 1/2 lbs of plastic explosive each.

Logs: logs of slightly greater length than the requisite finished length were split with an axe, the two halves hollowed out, and, after filling with plastic explosive and primer, joined together with Beetle Cement, a hole having been first bored to give access to the primer. The logs were held fast in clamps until the cement had set, then the ends were sawn off at an angle to disguise the ends of the split. A small piece of bark was prepared, as a plug to fit the hole bored, to take the fuse and detonator. Until the detonator was inserted a length of dowelling remained in position so that the primer could be located. In some cases, adhesive tape, painted to represent bark was used to conceal the hole.

Sawn Timber: preparation was the same as for logs.

Road Blocks: hollow cases, the same dimensions as roadblocks, were prepared from 3/8-inches thick pine boards. One end was made a sliding fit to enable the explosive charge to be filled in. Prior to filling, the blocks were creosoted, tarred, and aged. After filling, the removable end was cemented in. A hole for the insertion of the initiating unit was made as before, but in this case, it could be camouflaged with a small quantity of tar. All types of explosive wood have the cavity treated with Copal Varnish.

4. Prepared at Station XV. 700 assorted pieces prepared up to December 1944.

EXPLOSIVE CLOGS

I. Description. Wooden sabots have a cavity made in the thickness of the sole. The explosive filling is plastic explosive. Initiation is by means of a PTF, No. 27 detonator and No. 6 CE pellet.

2. Method of use. Single or pairs of wooden sabots are placed in rooms occupied by enemy personnel or placed on selected targets.

3. History. First prepared early in 1941 at the request of the French and Belgium Section.

4. Prepared at Station XV. 36 pairs prepared at Station XV.

EXPLOSIVE RATS

I. Description. A rat is skinned, the cured skin being sewn up and stuffed to the correct shape with plastic explosive to assume the shape of a dead rat. A Standard No. 6 Primer is set in the plastic explosive. Initiation is by means of a short length of safety fuse with a No. 27 Detonator crimped on one end and a copper tube igniter on the other end., or, as in the case of the illustration a P.T.F. with a No. 27 Detonator attached. The rat is then left amongst the coal beside a boiler and the flames initiate the safety fuse when the rat is thrown on to the fire, or as in the case of the P.T.F. a Time Delay is used.

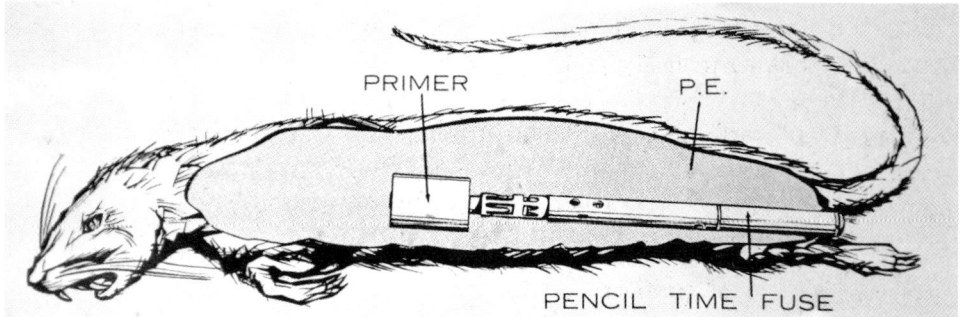

PRIMER   P.E.

PENCIL TIME FUSE

2. Intended method of use. The rat is left near the fuel beside a boiler. To dispose of the rat the boiler man might throw the body into the fire which initiates the safety fuse.

3. History. First prepared early in 1944 at the request of the French Section.

4. Prepared at Station XV. 100 rats were prepared.

This device caused considerable trouble to the enemy, but not in quite the way that it was intended. A container containing explosive rats was found by the enemy before any of the rats could be used for operational purposes, but their discovery had an extraordinary morale effect and the device was exhibited at all German military schools, a wide search being organised to find the 'hundreds of rats' which the enemy believed were distributed on the continent. The trouble caused to them was a much greater success to us, than if the rats had actually been used. It is obvious that in the latter case no evidence would have remained, and the enemy would not have discovered their existence. It was a device with a limited operational use, and the happy discovery of it by the enemy was considerably more advantageous to us.

EXPLOSIVE TORCH

I. Description. A German Torch (Daimon type) has a cylindrical deeply grooved bomb filled with Baratol in place of two of the three batteries normally used in the torch. Initiation is by means of an igniter safety fuse, electric, Bickford safety fuse and a No. 27 detonator. The delay is between 4 to 5 seconds. The switch on the outside of the torch has been adapted so that current can flow to the torch bulb, or, after the removal of a safety pin, to the 'igniter safety fuse, electric.' This safety pin prevents accidental initiation prior to operational use.

2. Method of use. The safety pin is removed, the switch pulled back to the rear thus causing ignition of the safety fuse. The torch is then thrown as a grenade.

3. History. In 1943, Lieutenant Cameron carried out the first experiments which consisted of converting a standard German torch into an anti-personnel weapon. Improvements were later made by Captain Starlee and Captain Porter in the design of the grenade in order to ensure good fragmentation.

4. Prepared at Station XV. 50 torches were made-up to December 1944.

EXPLOSIVE BOLTS, CHIANTI BOTTLES ETC.

I. Description. An explosive charge may be concealed in, or camouflaged by, any suitable article, or an artificial representation of such an article can be produced to contain a charge. Big rusty bolts, made of wood and painted to complete the camouflage, are made to hold a standard clam or a made-up charge of plastic explosives. They were provided with magnets to enable the completed article to be fixed to the iron or steel target selected for an attack.

Also a Chianti wine bottle, made of celluloid, is used to contain a plastic explosive charge, initiation being by means of a suitable delay action fuse. The introduction of the fuse, anti-removal (air-armed), enables a charge to be prepared as a booby trap with a large variety of types of camouflage. Examples of this are the explosive book, and explosive cotton waste. A delay-action fuse and fuse anti-removal, may be used in the same charge, an example of this being the explosive fish plate.

BOOBY TRAPS

EXPLOSIVE BICYCLE PUMP

I. Description. A bicycle pump camouflages as a small bomb, filled with plastic explosive which is initiated by means of a pull switch and detonator. Any person operating the pump would cause the pull switch to function.

2. Method of use. The safety pin is removed prior to the prepared pump being placed on a bicycle in hostile services. To encourage the enemy to use the pump one of the tyres may be deflated.

3. History. In 1943, Lieutenant Cameron carried out the first experiments. The basic idea of the device is that a metal cylinder, filled with plastic explosives, is fixed inside a bicycle pump. Initiation is by means of a detonator functioned by a pull switch.

The cylinder is fastened to the inside of the pump by means of a screw at the pump connection end. The pull switch is fastened to the other end of the cylinder and is also connected to the piston of the pump, which has to be short to permit these additions. The safety pin in the pull switch is withdrawn through a hole camouflaged by the makers name plate. This is a straightforward mechanical job. Trials were carried out in 1943 at Station IX.

4. Prepared at Station XV. 138 pumps were made up to December 1944.

EXPLOSIVE FOOD TIN

1. Description. A food tin of press on or lever lid type is partially filled with plastic explosive. A release switch set vertically in the tin is engaged by a lug attached to the lid so that it cannot function. Initiation is by means of a No. 27 detonator in the spring snout of the release switch: The detonator fitting into a CE primer in the plastic explosive charge. Prior to use the safety pin in the switch is pulled out through a small hole in the side of the tin.

2. Method of use. The tin prepared for use, maybe left in billets, kitchens, etc., where hostile troops can find it. Easing of the lid permits the release switch to operate.

3. History. Initial work on this device was carried out by Lieutenant Cameron who developed the lever lid type only. There were no technical difficulties with this device. Later Captain Porter and Staff Sergeant Jones adapted the design to the press on type of lid.

4. Prepared at Station XV. 24 tins were made-up to December 1944.

PROTECTIVE INCENDIARY DEVICES (ELECTRICAL)

    A. Incendiary Suitcase
    B. Incendiary Briefcase
    C. Incendiary Document Case

1. Description. The appearance is that of a normal case. The Suitcases carry two Thermit charges suitably camouflaged. The Attaché and Briefcases carry one charge each. Initiation is electrical.

2. Method of use. The right-hand lock brakes the electrical circuit, thus enabling the case to be opened safely. Any unauthorised person operating the left-hand lock, closes the circuit and fires the case.

3. History.
Incendiary Suitcase and Attaché Case—A requirement was received in May 1942 for a charge which could be fitted into a suitcase so as to destroy the contents at the will of the owner. This was primarily designed to achieve the destruction of the Eureka radio

set, but was found to be impractical and was abandoned for that reason. However, the requirement remained insofar as the destruction of documents was concerned and development began, but bearing the following points in mind.

First, the charge was to be fitted to a suitcase in such a way that it was not obvious to casual inspection. Secondly, the charge should be capable of being initiated at the will of the owner. Thirdly, the charge was to be initiated by a booby trap switch should the case be opened by an unauthorised person. The work was carried out by Major Critchfield at station IX.

Early experiments showed that the explosive charges were undesirable from a technical point of view, quite apart from the risk they presented to the operator. This was because papers attacked by explosives were found to be blown into many pieces, but not completely destroyed. They could therefore, with patience, have been pieced together by the enemy. Slow burning incendiary materials were unsatisfactory because of the difficulty of oxygen supply to the contents of the case. After many experiments therefore, it was decided to use a Thermit as the incendiary material.

The Thermit was concealed in the bottom of the case by means of a false bottom and the fabric pocket, respectively. The charge in the fabric pocket was usually camouflaged as a book. Some considerable trouble was experienced in initiating the charge safely, the first method being to push the switch which the operator could reach by inserting his finger through a hole in the case. This hole was covered by a paper label pasted over it. The system which was eventually used was one developed for the incendiary briefcase and consisted of fitting modified locks in the following manner.

Each lock was suitably modified so as to form a small electrical switch; one switch being normally closed and the other normally opened. For operational purposes it was standardised that the right-hand lock would normally be open. Since the two switches were in series with each other and with the batteries, the operation of the left-hand lock alone would activate the circuit and fire the case.

In order to open the case safely, it was necessary to hold the right lock in the open position, while the left-hand one was operated. This, after practise, can be done quite unobtrusively. For use as a booby trap, all that was necessary was to leave the case with the right-hand lock, i.e. the closed switch, locked into place with the key. Any person then attempting to open the case would invariably complete the firing circuit through the left-hand switch.

After the initial electrical troubles had been overcome, trials on the case were held. They proved that large quantities of paper could not be satisfactorily dealt with unless a quantity of oxygen bearing materials, such as potassium nitrate were provided. This was done in the form of quilts of potassium nitrate placed among the documents in the case.

At the end of 1943, an improved incendiary unit was designed and made by Captain Porter and Staff Sergeant Jones.

Incendiary Briefcase—While experiments were proceeding on the development of an incendiary suitcase, a further requirement was received for a briefcase fitted with an incendiary demolition charge. This was chiefly for use in this country and was required to function as a booby trap should the case be opened by an unauthorised person.

Since most of the experimental work had by this time been carried out on the suitcase, this presented little difficulty except in the matter of camouflage. It was finally decided to incorporate the Thermit charge, battery, and safety switch on one unit which could be camouflaged as a parcel or a book lying at the bottom of the case. The development of this device proceeded side by side with that of the suitcase, and, to a large extent, the results of experiments which were carried out were applied to either or both.

4. Prepared at Station XV. 30 suitcases were made and dispatched up to December 1944. 39 attaché cases were made and dispatched up to December 1944. 81 briefcases were made and dispatched up to December 1944.

PROTECTIVE INCENDIARY DEVICES (MECHANICAL)

D. Tobacco Tin.
E. Cigarette Box.
F. Lady's Workbox.

1. Description. The workbox looks normal from the outside but is fitted internally with an incendiary charge and salts adequate for the destruction of all documents. The quantity of paper must be restricted to 35 sheets of foolscap paper or its equivalent for the workbox and 10 sheets for the cigarette box. The firing mechanism is mechanical. A pull-switch has been altered so that it is armed but does not fire on closing the lid of the box. On opening the box in the normal way, the charge fires. By opening the box upside down, a shutter falls across the path of the striker and ensures safe opening.

2. Method of use. To open the box safely, turn the box upside down, give it a little shake to ensure the shutter has fallen into position, and open the lid. The striker is prepared for loading by compressing the spring. This is best done by seizing the projecting arm with the tool provided in the box, pulling it back till it is clear of the switch body, and then raising it to an angle of approximately 45° from the horizontal, but still pointing towards the front of the box. It is recommended that this operation be done with the box upside down, so that the safety shutter is in position.

The slide door is raised, and the documents are placed in the lower compartment. A 'quilt' containing potassium nitrate salts will be found in the lower compartment. This is placed among the paper to assist combustion. The slide door is replaced. On closing the lid, the switch is armed. If the box is now opened in the normal manner, the charge of Thermit is ignited. By opening the box in the upside-down position, the shutter, as described in paragraph one, falls and prevents initiation.

3. History. Lieutenant Cameron carried out the initial work on these devices. The object was to conceal documents in boxes fitted with a simple operated device for igniting a Thermit charge. Should the box be opened by any person unfamiliar with the correct method of opening, the concealed papers are thus destroyed. Later Captain Porter and Staff Sergeant Jones improved the shutter.

4. Prepared at Station XV. Up to the end of 1944 the following number were produced and dispatched.

Tobacco tins	19
Cigarette Boxes	6
Ladies Work Boxes	6

INCENDIARY DEVICES FOR DESTRUCTION OF DOCUMENTS AT WILL

DEED BOX

1. Description. A standard security box is fitted with thermit charges. Initiation is by means of dual pull switches housed in waterproof caps and accessible from outside the box. The addition of these caps is the only external difference from a normal box.

2. Method of use. Remove waterproof caps and actuate pull switches in the normal manner.

3. History. The first Canadian Army Headquarters forwarded a request on the 28 May 1943 for a security box—Deed box or Box Sealed, Stationery Large—to be fitted with Thermit Charge so that documents contained therein could be destroyed at will. Lieutenant Cameron prepared two Deed Boxes for trial on the 22 June 1943. The first box had one 15 lb charge of 'Cendite'. The second box had an additional charge riveted to the lid. The results in both cases was incomplete combustion of the contents.

As a result of these tests the type with two charges was adopted, and in order to supply additional oxygen to ensure combustion of contents, quilts containing potassium nitrate were provided in the proportion, one quilt for every 60 sheets of foolscap paper likely to be kept in the box with a top limit of 600 sheets. Each quilt holds half a pound of potassium nitrate.

4. Prepared at Station XV. 11 Deed boxes were prepared and dispatched up to the end of 1944.

DELAYED ACTION INCENDIARIES

INCENDIARY CIGARETTES

1. Description. To outward appearances the device is an ordinary cigarette. Actually, the cigarette paper contains a pellet of match composition, PN196, which is nearer at one end than the other in the case of full length round cigarettes, and in oval section cigarettes, which are shorter, the pellet is at one end. The cigarette is filled with cotton wool previously dyed brown and treated with potassium nitrate, the ends being finished off with the type of tobacco appropriate to the cigarette.

When the pellet is ignited by the glowing cotton wool, it gives a flame of about 5 seconds duration in the case of round cigarettes, the delay is about two minutes if a cigarette is lit at the end near the pellet; if lit the other end the delay will be three or four minutes. The cigarettes can be lit at either end according to the delay required, by means of a match, petrol lighter, or from the glowing end of a normal cigarette. Oval cigarettes have one delay only of from 2 to 3 minutes. The pellet can be located by touch.

The incendiary cigarette is really a delayed action igniter and not an incendiary proper. It is intended to ignite ordinary kindling material such as a pile of paper, shavings, oily rags, dry hay etc after the selected delay. The cigarette is described as Item No: NS302 in the 1944 catalogue of supplies.

2. Method of use. The cigarette is lit at one end, according to the selected delay for round cigarettes, and either placed or thrown onto the kindling material.

3. History. A device of this sort was first asked for by the Italian Section, in a note to DSR in April 1942. It was proposed to use it as a small delay incendiary for starting fires in offices, stores, etc, where loose inflammable material is available. The experimental work was carried out by Major Walker and Mr. King at Station IX. Prototypes of an incendiary cigarette were prepared which contained an incendiary pellet consisting of a rod of celluloid capped at either end with SFG. The balance of the cigarette was filled with dry tobacco previously impregnated with a solution of potassium nitrate. The final layer of tobacco at each end being cemented in with a solution of celluloid in acetone. These were acceptable to the Italian Section, and instructions for making 200 cigarettes were passed to Station XIII. In August 1942, 130 cigarettes were supplied to the Italian Section. As an improvement, short cylinders of NCT were substituted for the rods of celluloid.

In June 1943, Station XV received orders for incendiary cigarettes and took over from stations IX and XIII at this stage of development. Captain Starley, in charge of production at station XV, found that failures resulted from faults in the design. The two principle faults were due to the SFG not providing a sufficient hot or prolonged flame to ignite the NCT, and due to the tobacco, being loose, falling out after being cemented and having been consumed, thus breaking the train of combustion. To provide a hotter flame match composition, PN 196 was used to cap the ends of the NCT cylinders, and to prevent the tobacco falling out it was cemented in for the entire length. The result was satisfactory, but the cigarette was heavy and of poor appearance.

In one operation, sticks of cordite were substituted for NCT and cotton wool, dyed brown and impregnated with potassium nitrate, were used for the filling, with the ends being closed with cemented tobacco as before. The chief drawback of this design was the difference in diameter between the cigarette to be reproduced and that of available cordite. The celluloid cement used to close the ends of the cigarette resulted in a strong smell of camphor when ignited in a closed space; in consequence a solution of cellulose acetate in acetone was used instead and was found to be satisfactory.

Towards the end of 1943, oval section cigarettes to represent Turkish and Egyptian cigarettes, were called for. To produce oval section pellets, PN196 was worked into a paste with a solution of shellac in methylated spirits; the resultant paste was extruded through a metal tube of the requisite cross-sectional dimensions. On drying, the pellets could be cut to the size required. As this method proved satisfactory for oval cigarettes it was also adopted for round cigarettes, thus the number of materials required in the makeup of a cigarette could be reduced.

It was found to be essential, in order to eliminate failures, that the ends of the pellets should be pointed or roughly domed so that their slow ignition from the smouldering cotton wool would be accepted.

4. Prepared at Station XV. 43,700 Incendiary cigarettes were made and dispatched up to the end of 1944.

TYRE BURSTERS

The tyre burster is a tool which lends itself to a variety of camouflage. As this device is primarily intended for use on roads and tracks it is necessary for the camouflage to resemble objects met with on roads. The following forms of camouflage have been used successfully:

1. Stones and rock fragments of 48 types and 240 variations.
2. Mud and brick.
3. Coal (for use in coal yards).
4. Cork.
5. Horse droppings.
6. Mule droppings.
7. Dog droppings.
8. Adhesive tape, painted to represent stones and mud. 48 types.
9. Waterproof material, made-up into bags to hold one tyre burster each, and painted to represent stones and mud, in all 230 variations.

Items 1 to 4 are in plaster, and items 5 to 7 were made out of Papier-mâché.

The geological formations of Europe, the Mediterranean and Eastern theatres of war were covered by the types of stones reproduced. For operational use the camouflage tyre burster is placed near similar natural objects, care being taken that the outline, in the case of No. 8 and 9, is broken by a stone, a rut in the road or a light covering of dust or sand.

Originally plaster half shells were made, the tyre burster inserted and the two half shells joined together. This method did not give a sufficiently robust product, consequently a later development was casting the camouflage, reinforced with scrim, round the tyre burster. The plaster used was dyed with the basic colour of the particular stone so that there would be no great contrast if a piece became chipped.

To meet requirements where the weight of plaster camouflage, or the bulkiness of Papier-mâché would be a drawback, adhesive tape of a natural colour or waterproof material made-up into bags, were used. In each case painting was carried out to conform to the geological formation of the district where the tyre burster was to be employed.

Numbers of tyre bursters produced up to the end of 1944:

Plaster	80,650
Papier-mâché	11,450
Taped	70,688
Bags	23,025
Total	185,813

CAMOUFLAGE OF EXPLOSIVE DEVICES
(including booby traps and anti-personnel incendiary devices)

This section explains the camouflage of devices where standard or special charges were disguised as innocent vehicles. The following list gives examples of some of the methods used: bridge limpets filled with plastic explosive and made to represent rusty nuts and bolt heads, incendiary cigarettes, explosive coal, dummy fish plates for railway lines, explosive oil cans, explosive rats, wooden roadblocks filled with plastic explosives, explosive wood fuel, Chianti wine bottles, clogs, lifebelts, driftwood, ship's fenders. Explosive tins and containers and various devices for the Far East, including oriental carvings cast in TNT and coloured to represent wood or porcelain. Also included in this section are incendiary briefcases, suitcases, attaché cases and various types of boxes, all of which are fitted with protection against anyone other than the owner opening the vehicle.

RUSTY BOLTS OR NUTS

A hollow wooden imitation of an iron bolt or nut is made and is painted to give it the appearance of rusted iron. Two horseshoe magnets are fixed inside the bolt. When the device is to be used a general-purpose charge is clipped into position in the bolt.

Initiation is by means of a pencil time fuse and No. 27 detonator. The assembled device is then fixed by means of a magnet onto the target to be attacked.

EXPLOSIVE COAL

A hollow cast of a piece of coal is made in two sections. The interior is filled with plastic explosive, in which a 1oz Primer, Field, is set. The two sections are then clamped together, and the join sealed. The coal is finished off with a coating of black shellac which is garnished with coal dust. A length of dowelling keeps the passage to the primer clear until the insertion of the initiation unit. Initiation is by means of a match head safety fuse to which a No. 27 Detonator is crimped, or by means of a length of safety fuse with a No. 27 Detonator crimped on one end and a copper tube igniter crimped on the other end. The match end is dusted over with coal dust prior to operational use.

WOODEN LOGS, EXPLOSIVE

This device can be made in two ways. Firstly, the log can be hollowed out from one end. Secondly, the log can be split in two and hollowed out. In both methods the log is filled with plastic explosive and a 1oz Standard Field Primer set in it. Initiation is by means of a short length of safety fuse with a No. 27 Detonator crimped on one end and the copper tube igniter on the other end. A length of dowelling keeps the passage to the primer clear until the insertion of the initiation unit. The log can be used in many ways, particularly as fuel for boilers, furnaces, etc.

CHIANTI BOTTLE

This Chianti bottle is made of thick celluloid and is in two sections. The lower section is bowl shaped, the top section represents the neck and shoulders of the bottle and has the base of the neck closed by means of a diaphragm of celluloid so that the neck may be filled with wine to complete the camouflage when the bottle is assembled. Each section is filled with plastic explosive. A C.E. pellet is set in the top section but must be at an angle in order to permit the maximum length of space for the insertion of a detonator and 'L' delay fuse. The 'L' delay fuse is inserted through a hole in the base when required operationally. An A.C. delay fuse may also be used to initiate the charge, but a P.T.F. is too long.

When filling is completed, the two sections are fixed together and the joint sealed with acetone and buffed up, the inside of the celluloid having first been treated with transparent green paint, so that when the two portions are fixed together the whole takes on the appearance of green glass as used in the wine bottles. Next the raffia cover is attached to the bottle together with authentic labels. The finished effect is that of a genuine bottle of Chianti wine.

EXPLOSIVE BICYCLE PUMP

A hollow brass cylinder filled with explosive and fitted with a pull switch, is pushed inside the barrel of a bicycle pump. The piston rod is shortened, but air can still be pumped into the tyres; two grooves on the side of the cylinder acting as air passages. A nut is soldered onto the top of the pull switch, and the screw is fixed on the end of the piston. When required to operate as an explosive device, the piston is screwed onto the pull switch, and the safety pin withdrawn. This latter operation is done by removing a small brass name-plate from the side of the pump, pulling out the pin, and replacing the name-plate. The enemy's pump is replaced by the explosive one and his tyres deflated. When he uses the pump the device operates.

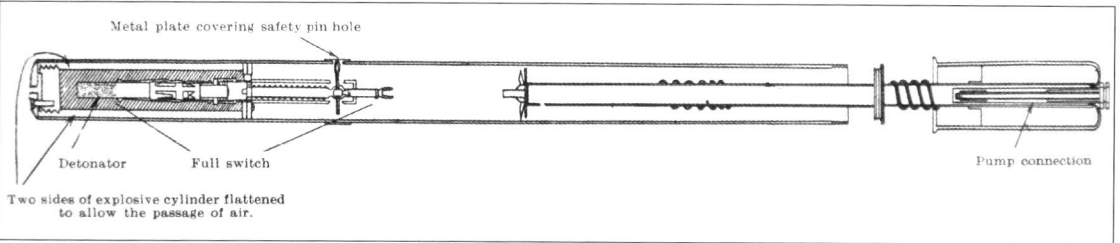

Metal plate covering safety pin hole

Detonator   Full switch   Pump connection

Two sides of explosive cylinder flattened
to allow the passage of air.

EXPLOSIVE FOOD TIN

This tin is of the lever lid type and is partially filled with plastic explosive. A pressure release switch is set vertically in the tin. A lug attached to the lid engages the shoulder of the release switch. Initiation is by means of a spring snout attachment with a No. 27 Detonator set in a 1oz field primer. The safety pin in the release switch is pulled out through a small hole in the side of the tin. When the lever lid is prised open the lug releases the shoulder of the pressure release switch which operates and fires the plastic explosive. The tins are made in varying designs and sizes with authentic labels attached. The devices can be left in damaged houses, food dumps, billets, etc.

INCENDIARY SOAP

A hollow cast is made of a cake of soap. The cavity is filled with pure metallic sodium and the joint is carefully sealed up with soap, so that the join cannot be seen. When the soap covering of the sodium wears thin through use, moisture seeps through causing it to ignite and burn fiercely. This device can cause a great deal of injury to the hands or face.

INCENDIARY SHAVING BRUSH

A normal shaving brush handle is hollowed out and filled with pure metallic sodium. A small hole is bored in the stub of the hairs of the brush to allow water to seep through, and when the brush is used the sodium is ignited by contact with the water. This device can cause a great deal of injury to the hands or face.

CIGARETTES, INCENDIARY PACKING OF

The illustration shows how a normal cigarette may be used as a message carrier, the message being rolled up into a small tube and inserted into the partially emptied cigarette. The tobacco is then replaced, sealing up the end of the cigarette.

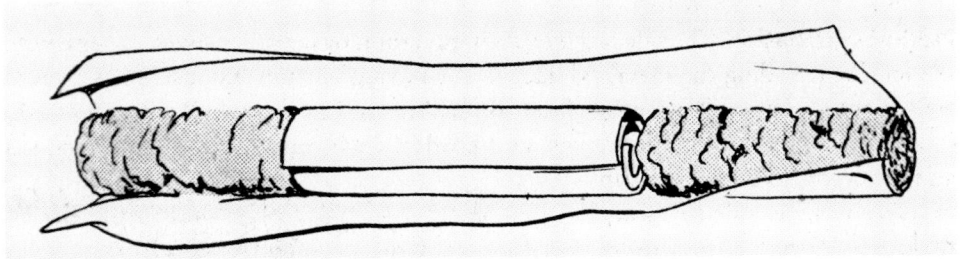

These are the labels from Greek cigarette packets. The incendiary cigarettes are packed ask if they were normal cigarettes and the usual government seal pasted around the packet.

EXPLOSIVE BOOK

This explosive book is a booby trap which may be placed on any flat surface preferably among other books on a tabletop. The inside of the book is cut away in order to leave sufficient space for a pound or more of plastic explosives. Initiation is by means of a Fuse, Anti-removal (Air Armed) to which is fitted a Type 6 Burster. The back cover is cutaway and reinforced with sheet metal if necessary, so that the fuse may be held rigidly flush with the outer face of the cover. The covers are fixed so that any attempt to open the book will cause lifting of the volume and immediate ignite the fuse. The book is camouflaged with any suitable book jacket, which is removed prior to placing the booby trap.

SHIP'S FENDER

This device containing a charge of 10 lbs of plastic explosive will detonate if upwards of 150 lbs crushing pressure is applied. It comprises of a thin metal cylinder containing the charge, which is initiated by Tyre Bursters, the whole being camouflaged as a ship's fender.

Method of initiation. The side stitching forming a running loop, may be eased open with the fingers, revealing the metal cylinder. On removing outside and inside lids at both ends, eight pockets will be visible. Insert Brass Priming Caps to Tyre Bursters provided in accessory box. Smear the threads and head of each cap with Luting Compound and cover with protective strip of adhesive tape. It is necessary to ensure that no Luting Compound enters the interior of the Tyre Burster. Place a prepared Tyre Burster in each pocket and replace inner and outer lids carefully to both ends, securing by passing the thin metal strips through the

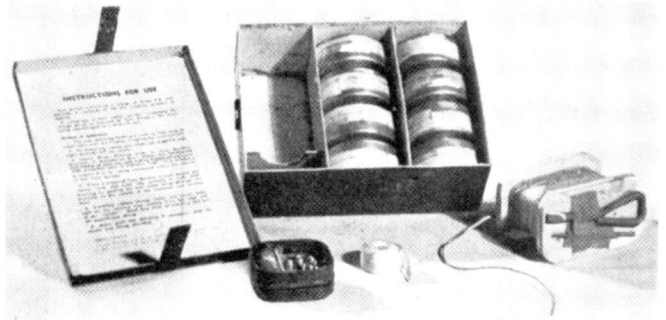

brackets on the outside of the container and turning back. Carefully replace charge inside jute cover, draw taut by the running loop—pulling from the rope end of the Ship's Fender. Knot loop close to the stitching and cut off superfluous string. Make good the stitching, if necessary, with the needle and string provided.

Important. These devices are to be identified by the knot tide at the junction of the rope of the Ship's Fender.

TORCH

A German pattern torch of the Daimon variety is used as an explosive device. Two of the three batteries normally present in the torch are removed, their place being taken by a cylindrical, deeply grooved bomb filled with Baratol. Initiation is by means of an

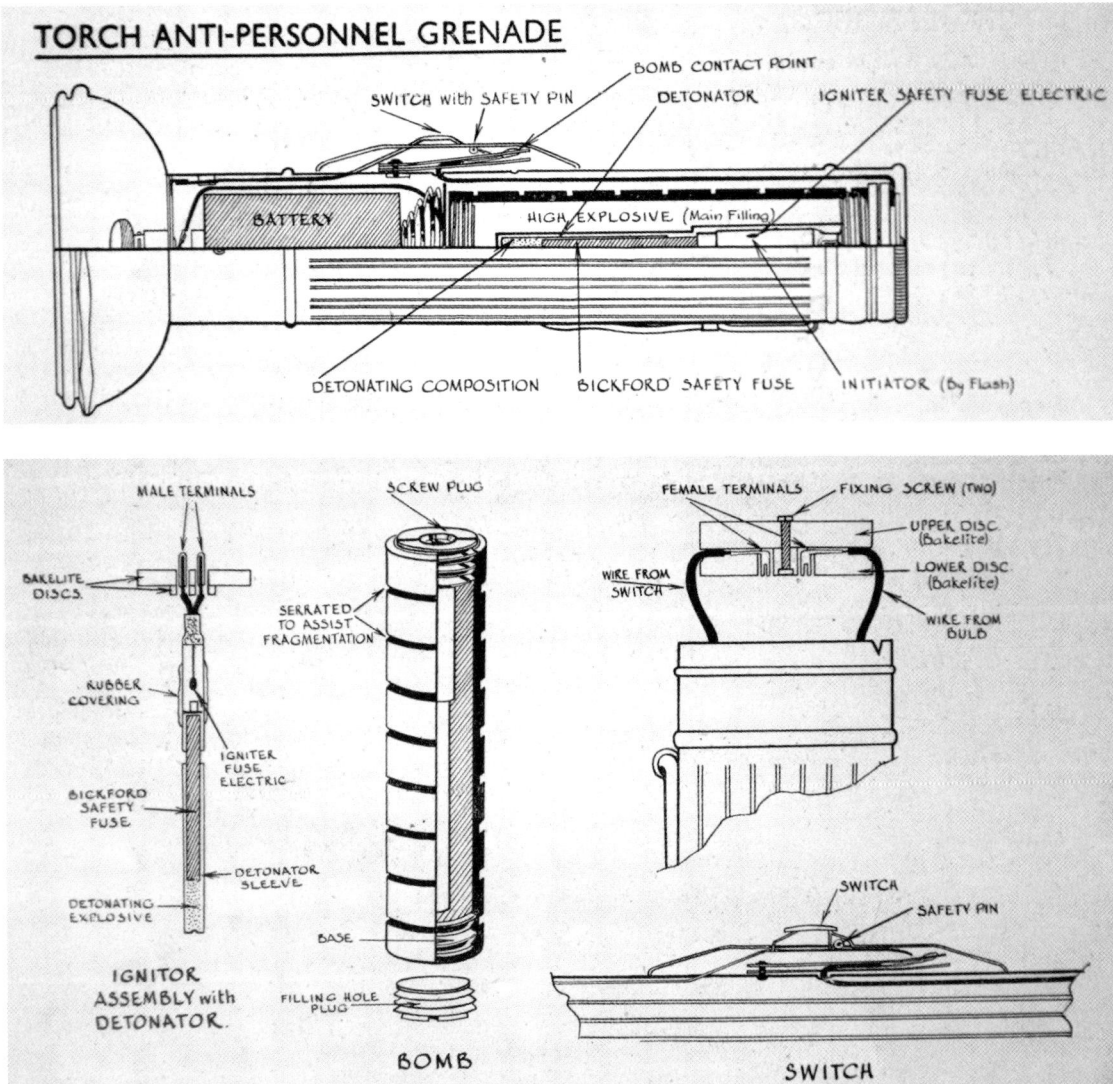

TORCH ANTI-PERSONNEL GRENADE

BOMB CONTACT POINT

SWITCH with SAFETY PIN   DETONATOR   IGNITER SAFETY FUSE ELECTRIC

BATTERY   HIGH EXPLOSIVE (Main Filling)

DETONATING COMPOSITION   BICKFORD SAFETY FUSE   INITIATOR (by Flash)

MALE TERMINALS   SCREW PLUG   FEMALE TERMINALS   FIXING SCREW (TWO)

BAKELITE DISCS   SERRATED TO ASSIST FRAGMENTATION   WIRE FROM SWITCH   UPPER DISC (Bakelite)
LOWER DISC (Bakelite)
WIRE FROM BULB

RUBBER COVERING

BICKFORD SAFETY FUSE   IGNITER FUSE ELECTRIC

DETONATOR SLEEVE

DETONATING EXPLOSIVE

SWITCH
SAFETY PIN

IGNITOR ASSEMBLY with DETONATOR.   FILLING HOLE PLUG

BASE

BOMB   **SWITCH**

igniter safety fuse, electric, crimped onto a length of safety fuse which has a No. 27 detonator crimped on the other end. The delay is from 4-5 seconds. The normal switch on the outside of the torch has been adapted so that current can flow to the torch bulb, or, after removal of a small safety pin, to the igniter safety fuse, electric. This safety pin prevents accidental initiation prior to operational use.

ENGINEER'S OIL CAN

A Continental type of oil can as shown in the illustration is used, with a small liquid container built around the oil filling well, so that when the cover is pulled back it gives the impression that the can is full of oil. The remainder of the oil can is filled with plastic explosive in which is set a 1oz Primer, Field, or No. 6 C.E. Pellet enclosed in a close-fitting metal container into which is embodied a guide tube leading to the spout of the can. Initiation is by means of a Pencil Time Fuse fitted with a No. 27 Detonator. For operational use, the spout of the can is removed, the P.T.F. slipped down the guide tube until the detonator fits into the Primer or C.E. Pellet. The spout is then replaced. As the device is quite innocent looking it can be left by the student beside machinery without causing undue attention. The delay should not be too long as an oil can is liable to be used frequently.

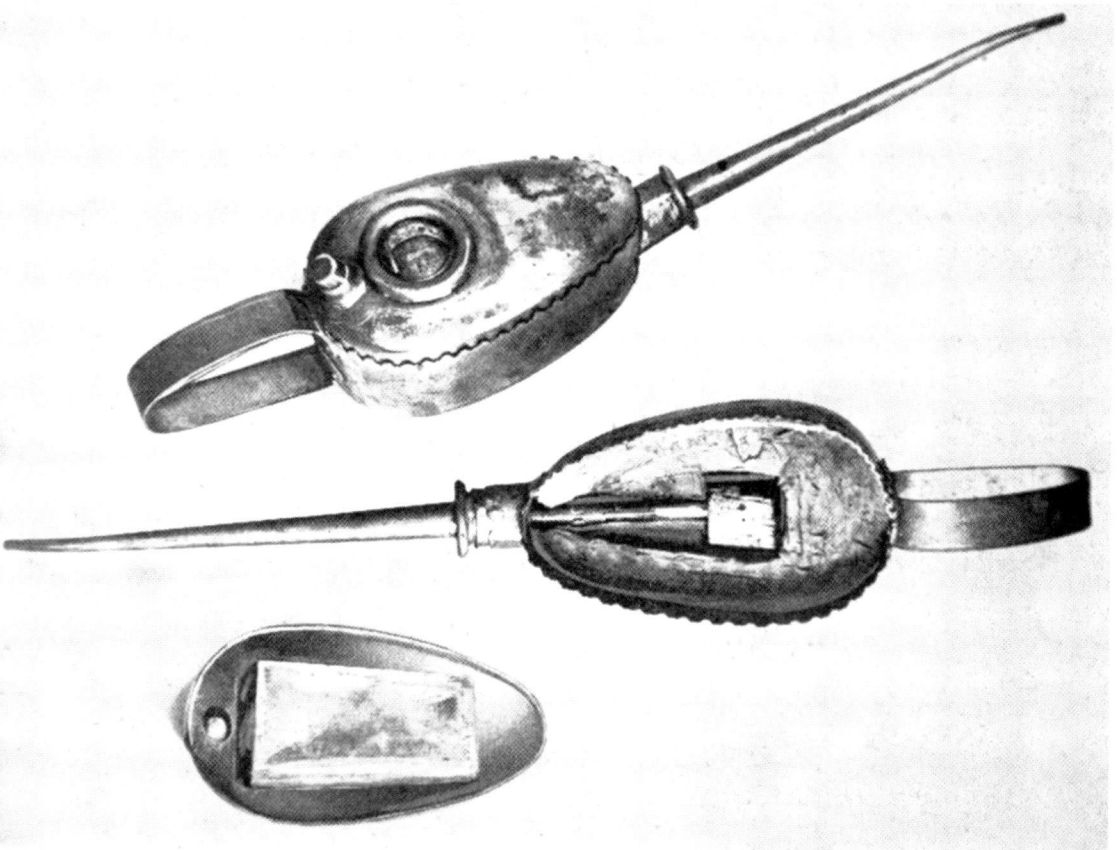

WOODEN ROAD BLOCKS

A tarred wooden road block of normal size is made with a hollow interior which is filled with plastic explosive, into which is set a 1oz Field Primer. Initiation is by means of a short length of safety fuse with a No. 27 Detonator crimped on one end and a Copper Tube Igniter crimped on the other end. A length of dowelling keeps the passage to the Primer clear until the insertion of the initiation unit. The whole is tarred and aged to resemble a worn road block which may be found in any pile or dump of wood.

CHINESE STONE LANTERNS

In the ordinary way the originals are made of solid stone, weighing anything up to half a ton. Camouflage section have reproduced these Chinese lanterns in light wood with a veneer of plaster and they resemble in every way the original. The device is divided into five separate compartments each of which can be filled with high explosive and fitted with a delayed action fuse or anti-removal switch, and can be assembled as in the illustration, or assembled as if the lantern had been knocked over. This is the reason why the lantern is made with arming devices in all five sections.

BALINESE CARVINGS

These are faithful reproductions of the famous Balinese wood carvings, but in this case, they have been cast in solid high explosive and coloured to represent wood, sandstone, or porcelain. Each head is mounted on a

wooden base and equipped for initiation by a time delay. It is intended to use these through native agents posing as hawkers frequenting the quaysides and selling them to Japanese troops about to embark on a ship.

JAPANESE SAUCE TIN

The illustration shows a reproduction of a Japanese tin which contains Shoyu Sauce. This type together with the many brands of kerosene tin which are in common use for carrying water and food in all parts of the Far East, have been adapted either as explosive devices or for the concealment of wireless sets and stores. Japanese ammunition boxes have also been put to similar use but with the addition of carrying an anti-removal switch.

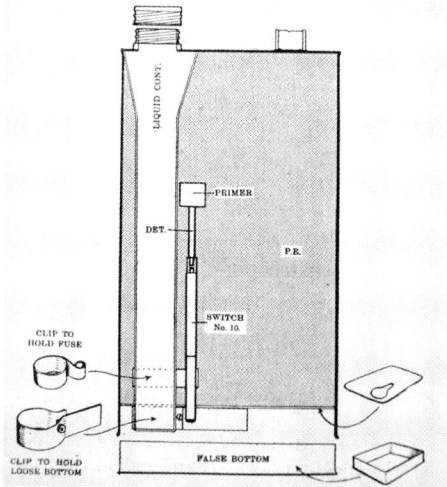

Explosive Japanese oil tin.

INCENDIARY BRIEFCASE (SINGLE LOCK)

The external appearance is that of an ordinary briefcase. A camouflage parcel inside the case contains a thermite charge, battery, and arming switch. The electric wiring is concealed in the lining of the case. One quilt of potassium nitrate is provided to assist

in combustion of the documents. The lock is converted to act as a switch. Another switch, under a patch of rexine inside the case, takes the place of the right-hand lock on double lock types. The arming switch is set to the 'on' position. To close and open the case safely, the switch under the patch of rexine must be depressed to its full extent and held thus while the outer lock is manipulated.

INCENDIARY ATTACHE CASE

The external appearance is that of an ordinary case. One camouflage parcel inside the case contains a thermite charge, battery, and an arming switch. The electric wiring is concealed under the lining of the case. Two quilts of potassium nitrate are provided to assist in combustion of the documents. The locks are converted to act as switches and control the firing of the charge. The arming switch is set to the 'on' position. To close and open the case safely, the knob of the right-hand lock must be pressed and held to the right. If this is not done the charge will fire when the left hand lock is moved.

INCENDIARY SUITCASE

The external appearance is that of an ordinary suitcase. Internally there are two camouflage thermite charges, one in the lid, the other in the bottom of the case. The electric battery and wiring are concealed under the camouflage and lining of the case. Five quilts of potassium nitrate are provided to assist in the combustion of the documents. The locks are converted to act as switches and control the firing of the charges. The arming switch incorporated in the lower thermite unit is set to the 'on' position. To close and open the case safely the knob of the right-hand lock must be pressed and held to the right. If this is not done the charges will fire when the left hand lock is moved.

SOE Camouflage Section Station
XVB War Department Lecture
Hall was housed in the Natural
History Museum, Cromwell Road,
London SW7.

SOE Camouflage Section Station
XVA was housed in 56 Queen's Gate,
London SW7, and went by the name
Clothing Assistance Board (C.A.B.) or
Military Operations 1 Special Projects
(M.O.1 S.P.).

Left: SOE Camouflage Section Station XVC was housed in 2 and 3 Trevor Square, London SW7, and was called Military Operations 1 Special Projects (M.O.1 S.P.) Photographic Department.

Below: The original SOE Camouflage Section stations XV and XVD were no longer suitable.

Above left: SOE
Camouflage Section
clothing store, XVA.

Above right: SOE
Camouflage Section
main gallery, XVA.

Right: SOE
Camouflage Section
lecture room, XVB.

SOE Camouflage
Section
photographic
section, XVC.

SOE Camouflage Section textile shop.

SOE Camouflage Section props shop.

SOE Camouflage Section carpenter's shop.

Right: SOE Camouflage Section outside storage.

Below: SOE Camouflage Section printing room.

SOE Camouflage Section Station XV at the Thatched Barn, Barnet By-Pass, Elstree. It was built in 1927 in the style of an American 'Roadhouse-motel' with an English twist. It was demolished in 1989 and replaced by a Double Tree, Hilton Hotel. It went by the name Camouflage Research I.S.R.B.

SOE Camouflage Section Station XV art department and testing station at the Thatched Barn, Barnet By-Pass, Elstree. There was a large swimming pool at the site.

SOE Camouflage Section printing compositor's shop.

SOE Camouflage Section plasterer's shop.

SOE Camouflage Section paint spraying shop, Station XV.

SOE Camouflage Section metal worker's shop.

3

Clothing Section

[Editor's Note: Although this report refers mostly to male SOE field agents, hundreds of female agents were kitted out by the SOE Camouflage Section and sent to enemy occupied countries. The clothing and equipment they were issued depended on their role and destination.]

PERSONAL CLOTHING AND EQUIPMENT

The old adage 'Clothes maketh the man' could well be a suitable title for the following notes. In fact, it could apply to the whole of the Camouflage Section, which does in fact make or remake the Agent in order to fit the cover story which is to be the background for his new life. Not only does this apply to his clothing down to the most minute detail, but to his makeup, his papers of identification, and his personal everyday requirements, such as cigarettes or the tobacco he smokes, his matches, his toilet requisites, and even the pen he writes with.

It is not sufficient to say "That is a German suit," or "These are genuine French braces." It is quite possible that the quality and style, although genuine, are quite unfitted for the job on which the man might be engaged. Thought must be given to the location in which the Agent is operating. His headquarters may be in the mountains, with only an occasional visit to town. In such a case it is most essential that he should be fitted with a good waterproof garment, and capes have proved the most satisfactory articles, as they can be spread out at night to act as ground sheets.

He must be given an overall coat for warmth, such as a sheepskin lined 'Canadienne', thick boots, heavy stockings, and under clothing. These clothes are of course quite unsuited for his visits to town, and are issued purely for personal comfort, in addition to the outfit which is essential for his cover story.

A shop was opened at station XVA, staffed with men who were experts on Continental clothing. This shop carried a great variety of everything that was needed. A competent tailor was always available on the premises in order to measure for suits and to make minor alterations. Various Continental tailors, shirt makers, and boot manufacturers, who had been passed by security, were employed in the making of the 'thousand-and-one' articles of clothing needed.

The following gives some idea of the variety of stock held in this unusual emporium:

Ready-made suits, shirts, overcoats and raincoats.
Leather jackets, Canadiennes, sheepskin waist coats and cavalry twill.
Shirting—Poplin, Woollen and Oxford.
Boots—ski, mountain and walking.
Shoes and Slippers—various.
Bends of Leather for soling footwear.
Crepe rubber.
Headwear—hats, caps, berets, balaclavas, and ski caps.
Gloves—lined or unlined, gauntlets, ski, woollen, ski mits.
Underwear—various.
Knitwear—pullovers, slipovers and cardigans.
Pyjamas—poplin and woollen.
Socks—wool, lisle, silk, ski, and golf.
Braces and suspenders—various.
Towels—Turkish and huckaback.
Dressing gowns—various.
Mackintosh capes and anoraks.
Boiler suits—various.
Ties, handkerchiefs and scarves.
Sundries—face squares and bags, laces, sponge bags, combs, elastic, colour studs, cufflinks, rock axes, snow goggles, and zip fasteners.

All these articles were available in various types suitable to the country in which the Agent was operating. The demand was raised by the responsible section, who in conjunction with the department, decided what was suitable for the Agent's cover story and needs.

IMPORTANCE TO DETAIL

It is very difficult to itemise and to explain the exact differences appertaining to the clothing required for each country, but the following short summary should give an indication as to the methods employed.

CONTINENTAL SUITS—TO BE READ IN CONJUNCTION WITH THE DIAGRAMS—JACKETS

1. Low setting top collar which gave a more square appearance and in consequence showed more shirt collar.
2. High shoulder seam which again gave a more square appearance.
3. Full pouch and draped back.
4. Close fitting around hips.
5. The top collar was extended and turned underneath but on top of the undercollar, i.e., on top of the collar Melton. This allows for easy alteration.

6. Inside welt pockets set in body lining always had a button and loop.
7. Body lining cutaway and facing extended to take inside jacket pocket.

The inside jacket pockets were standard. The lapels had a lower roll and a full drape given in the front. Very often the jacket carries a small ticket pocket which was cut from the inside facing on the left-hand side.

TROUSERS

A. The extension band as shown could be used in 1, 2, or 3, button style. An extension which was fastened in position by hook and eye was never used as this was typically English.
B. Inside extension. By far the most popular and could be altered in many ways.
C. Extension loops for braces. Always fitted to hip trousers in case the wearer should wish to wear his suit without a belt.
D. Two hip pockets were quite useful if required.

Black and white linings were very popular. If side straps were used on trousers the slide type without prongs were employed. Care was taken that fastenings did not bear markings and if any markings did appear on the cloth selvedge it was cut off.

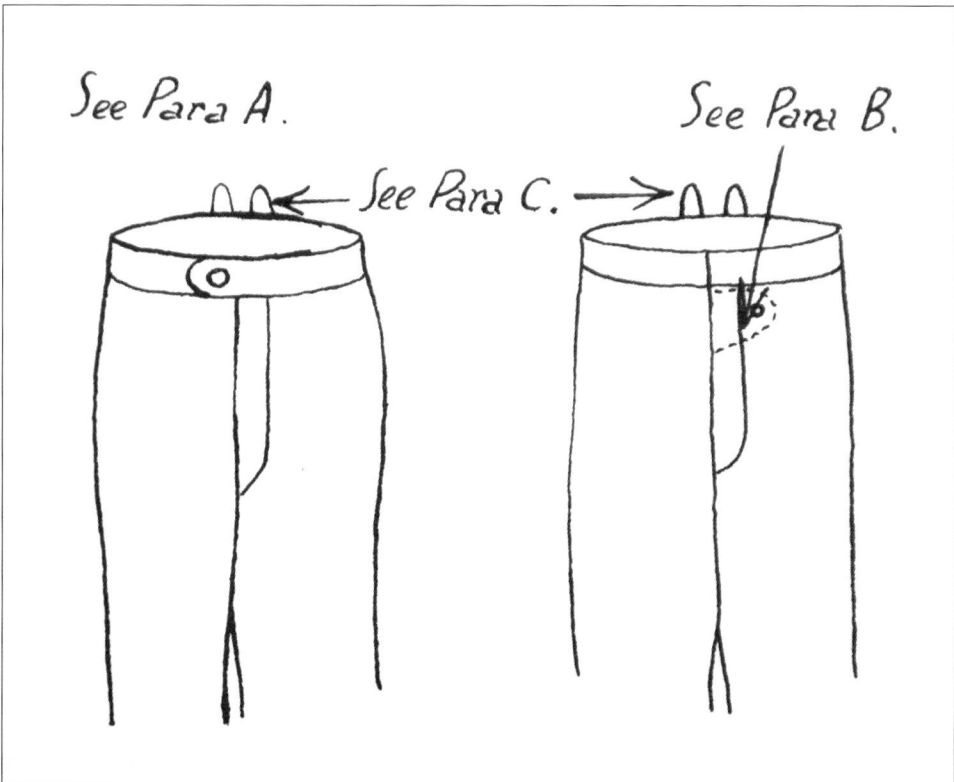

Continental style on the left and English style to the right.

MATERIAL FOR SUITS AND OVERCOATS

All cloth was specially manufactured. Quiet, unobtrusive patterns in worsted were mainly used but cheviots proved quite popular when hardware was essential. Fresco, which is well known Continental cloth, was always available.

BUTTONS FOR CLOTHING

Particular care had to be taken over the choice of buttons. The most popular was a fine rimmed type with two countersunk slots which ran parallel to receive the cotton. This method of sewing parallel applied to all continental clothing. It was not unusual to see a fancy button on a Continental suit.

RAINCOATS AND OVERCOATS

Considerably longer than an English garment. The Raglan sleeve type had to have one split sleeve (see diagram showing split sleeve on a shirt). This gave a square appearance on the shoulders. Normal variations of cloth were quite suitable.

CANADIENNES

These were made from rubberized cloth and lined with sheepskin. Only issued when warmth and waterproofness were essential. Otherwise, it could easily develop into a type of uniform.

SKI TROUSERS

Wind and showerproof material made-up into ski trousers of the Norwegian design.

ANORAKS

A smock which is worn over battle dress or ski outfit. Two split pockets in the front, pouched to take hand grenades. Could be worn fastened between the legs or unfastened for extra freedom of movement. Colours: white, khaki or Navy. Proofed material.

MACKINTOSH CAPES

Made to a special design from rubberised India cloth. Add a tight fitting hood with a pouched back to allow for a pack and it could be laid out flat to act as a groundsheet.

LEATHER JACKETS

Made in various colours and grains of full chrome leather in a variety of styles.

SHOES

Examples of Continental and English footwear are shown in illustrations. Careful note should be made of the main differences which are itemised below:

Continental shoes

1. The heel was considerably lower.
2. In consideration of the heel being lower the arch was automatically reduced.
3. Lower forepart which gave a more gradual rise from the toe and across the break.
4. A good type of German or French shoe could be recognised by placing the same against any flat surface when the heel and sole should lie almost perfectly in line.

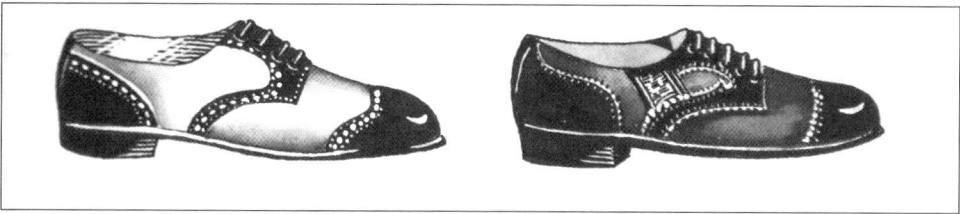

Continental style.

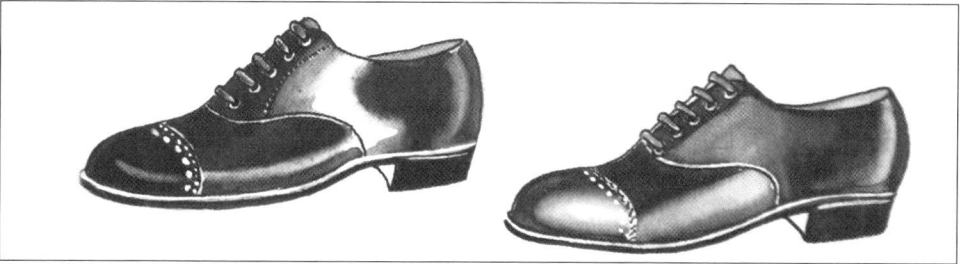

English style.

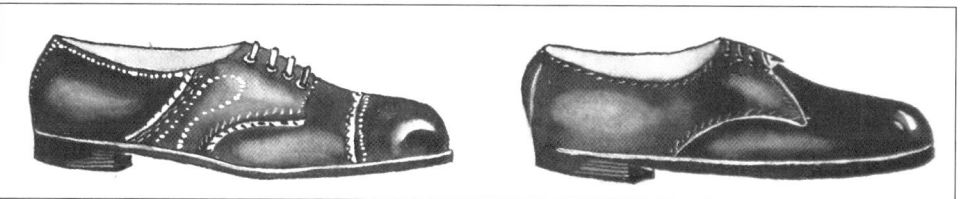

Continental style.

English style.

Generalities. It was impossible to alter an English shoe by taking off one layer of leather from the heel. It altered the pitch and in consequence made the wearer most uncomfortable. Reddish colours had to be avoided. Grained leather was never used. Normal variations in style such as brogues, semi-brogues, suede, etc., were quite usual.

BOOTS, SKI, AND MOUNTAIN

The boots had to be of superior quality leather as they had to stand up to the roughest wear. The English boot could never be as satisfactory as the genuine article. If possible, Norwegian made footwear was always purchased. Uppers were never varied in colour and design. Clingers and hobnails of wrought iron were supplied for mountain boots.

SLIPPERS

Several specimens were obtained from different countries, but these appeared to be quite an ordinary type. Therefore, special stocks were not essential, and it was quite sufficient if wide variations of colour and quality were made available. Soft soles were advisable for ease of packing.

ROPE SANDALS

These were issued to Agents who were to be engaged on a considerable amount of night work and inconsequence lack of noise was essential. Rubber soles were found equally suitable but owing to the shortage of this commodity rope soles made an admirable substitute.

SHIRTING AND SHIRTS

Cloth could be produced in many qualities, such as Poplin, Sea Isle, Oxford, Winceyette, Flannel etc. It all depended on the country and the cover story. The most universal designs were white grounds with a meat stripe running through. These were always popular with the middle classes and better dressed men right throughout the Continent. It was only when a man had no facilities for washing his clothes, yet may possibly have had to visit a town, that cloth with coloured ground shade was issued.

The making up of a continental shirt
The outstanding points over which care had to be taken are as follows: (see diagrams)

1. A very low setting collar.
2. On an English shirt front where the button holes appear there was an outside seam which gave a pleated effect. This could not appear on a Continental shirt which was quite plain on the outside.
3. If four-hole buttons were used, they had to be stitched parallel and not crosswise.

4. Two-piece, split sleeve as against the English single seam.
5. If detachable collars were being made the back stud hole had to be a horizontal and not vertical.

Apart from all these outstanding differences between Continental and English shirts, many alterations could be affected in the manufacture. The back yolk could be gathered or have either inverted or box pleats. The pleats could be placed in the centre or at each side. Cuffs could be round or square. The single variety had to have either one or two buttons.

Stitching could be single or double, and had to be varied according to the quality of the material being made-up, i.e., a long stitch for a cheap quality, and in the reverse ratio, if a good quality shirt was being made a small stitch had to be employed.

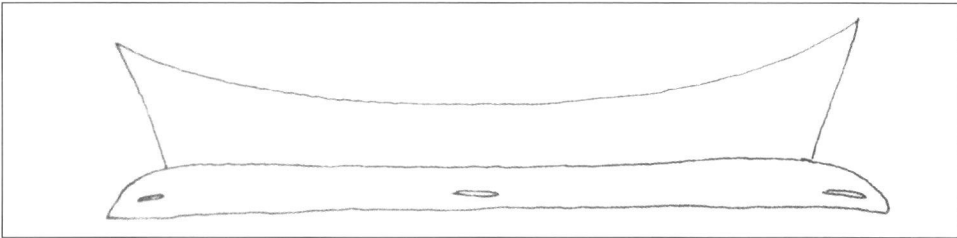

Continental collar.

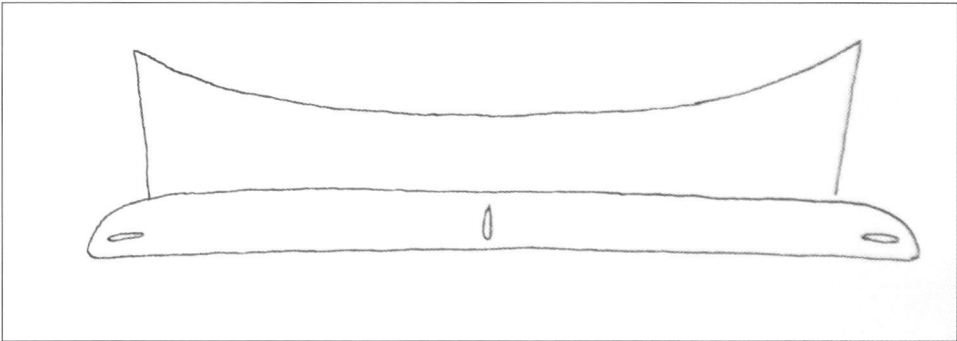

English collar.

Continental button style on the left and English button style on the right.

INVERTED PLEAT

SINGLE CUFF ROUND

BOX PLEATS

SINGLE CUFF SQUARE CORNERS

SINGLE CUFF TWO BUTTONS

MIDDLE GAUGING

GAUGING on SIDES

DOUBLE CUFF SQUARE CORNER

DOUBLE CUFFS ROUNDED ENDS

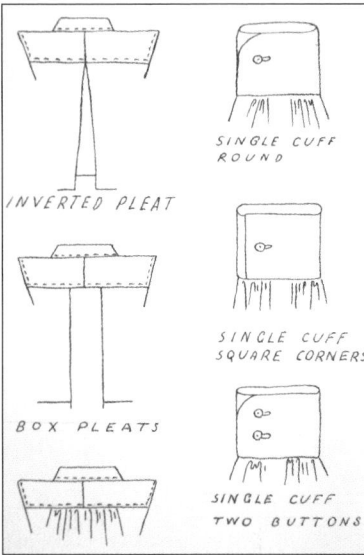

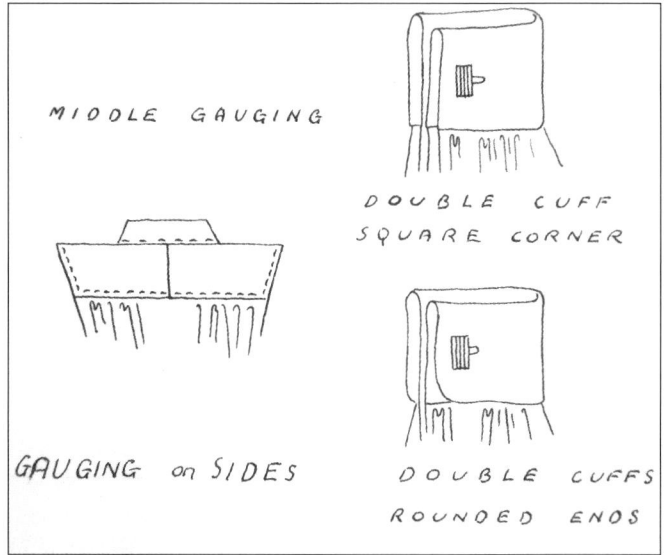

Above left and above right: Continental cuff styles.

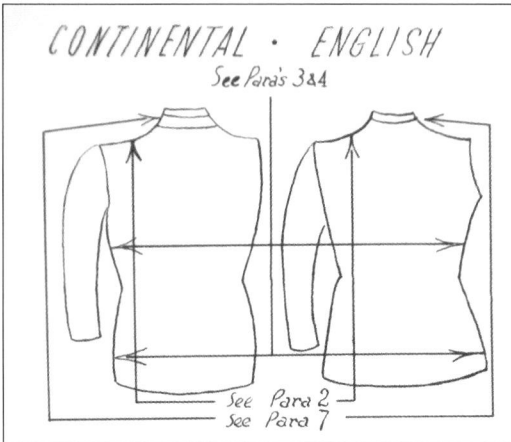

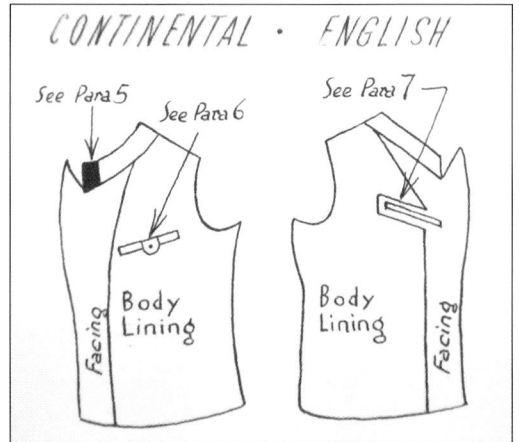

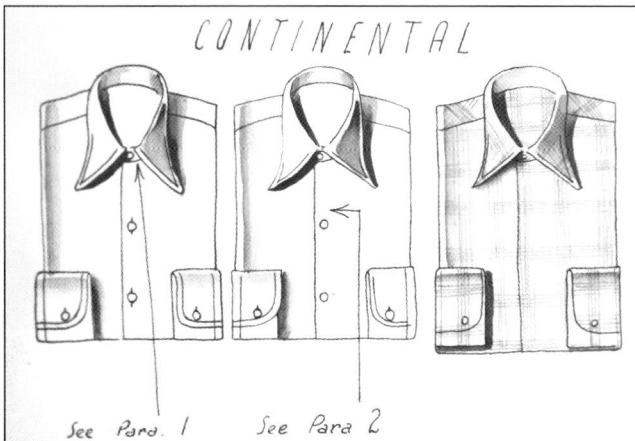

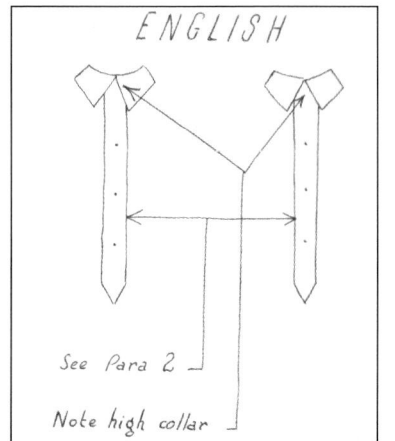

CONTINENTAL · ENGLISH

See Para's 3 & 4

See Para 2
See Para 7

CONTINENTAL · ENGLISH

See Para 5
See Para 6
See Para 7

Body Lining

Facing

Body Lining

Facing

CONTINENTAL

See Para. 1   See Para 2

ENGLISH

See Para 2
Note high collar

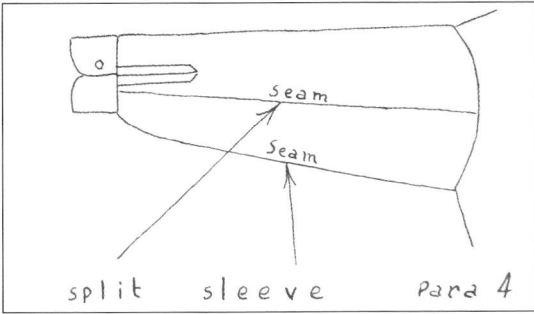

split sleeve   Para 4

Continental style sleeve.

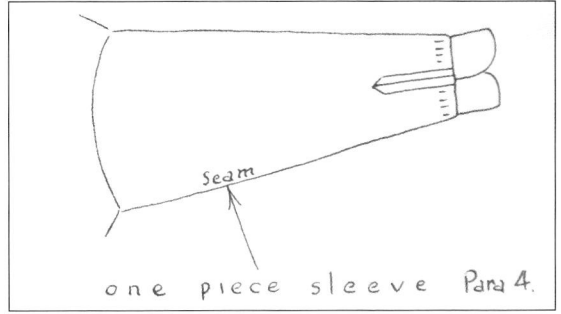

one piece sleeve   Para 4.

English style sleeve.

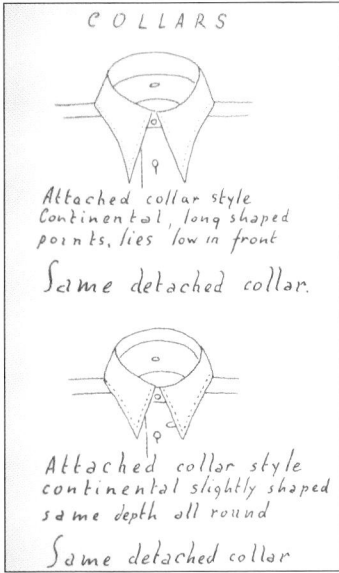

COLLARS

Attached collar style
Continental, long shaped
points, lies low in front

Same detached collar.

Attached collar style
continental slightly shaped
same depth all round

Same detached collar

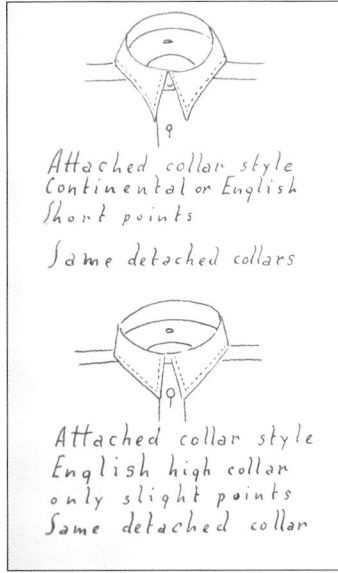

Attached collar style
Continental or English
Short points

Same detached collars

Attached collar style
English high collar
only slight points
Same detached collar

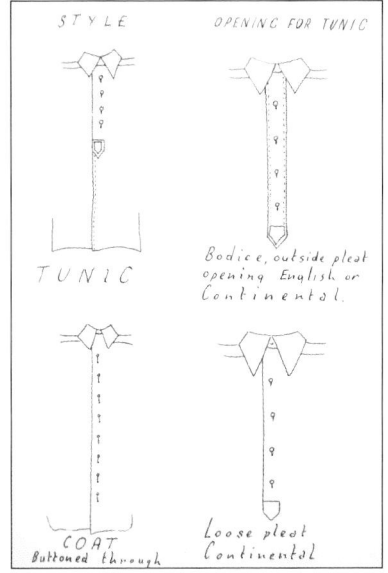

STYLE   OPENING FOR TUNIC

TUNIC

Bodice, outside pleat
opening English or
Continental.

COAT
Buttoned through

Loose pleat
Continental

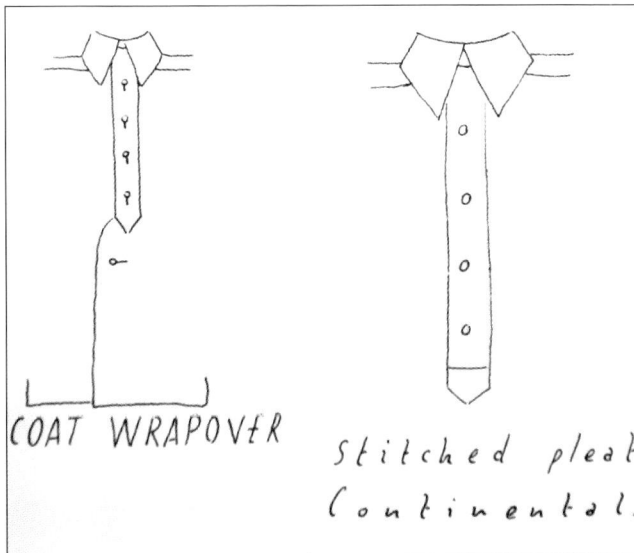

COAT WRAPOVER

Stitched pleat
Continental.

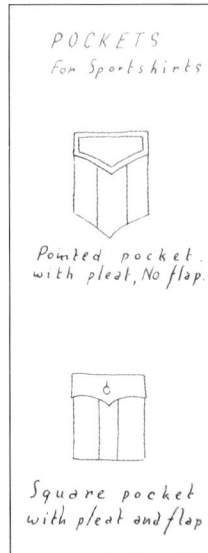

POCKETS
For Sportshirts

Pointed pocket.
with pleat, No flap.

Square pocket
with pleat and flap

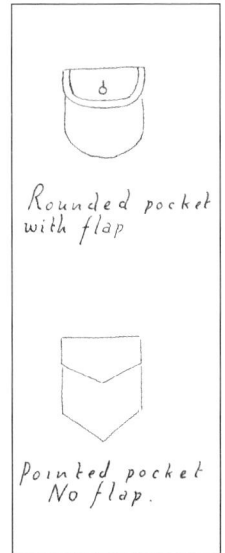

Rounded pocket
with flap

Pointed pocket
No flap.

HATS

The department successfully contacted a manufacturer who had a large stock of frozen goods which he had made for different Continental retail customers. Fortunately, the dyes, which were used for stamping the inside bands and lining with the manufacturer's name and address were still in existence (others were produced at Station XV). This ensured a constant supply of Continental hats together with the authentic quality felt, lining, trimmings, etc.

CAPS

These were unmarked throughout, and were specially made to order. A large shape was the most popular and this could be altered in appearance by having a wide range of materials. Care had to be taken that the peak press stud did not bear any markings and that the peak stiffener did not bear a watermark, or some makers name stamped there on.

BERETS

A Czechoslovakian was employed in making berets. These consisted of two types, the first having a small tight-fitting head and the other a rather more loosely fitting crown. All types were always left with a small strand of wool protruding from the top centre of the crown. Colours-Navy only.

SKI CAPS

These are made in various styles from proofed material which are mainly in demand by the Norwegians. The illustration shows a cap made from a knitted fabric, but wool was not as popular as waterproof material, as it did not keep out the rain or wind. In addition, ski caps were made from fully chromed leather which were lined with lamb's wool. The latter were only issued to Agents proceeding to cold climates.

GLOVES

These were supplied in various grains of leather with button cuff or pull-on type. Available unlined or lined with wool or fur. They could be altered in various small ways such as edge to edge stitching, hand stitching or pique stitch. The back part of the glove could be trimmed in various ways. In some cases, suede was available, but did not prove satisfactory owing to the lack of durability. A large assortment of woollen gloves was always available.

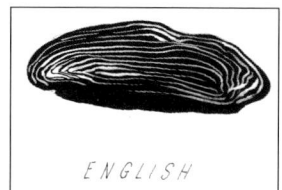

CONTINENTAL

ENGLISH

Leather ski gloves were in constant demand. The palms were made from fully chromed leather, extension arm made from proofed material with tunnelled elastic grip. Experience proved that these were the most satisfactory for skiing and were quite waterproof. Woollen ski mits, i.e., palm and thumb only, were supplied to go underneath.

UNDERWEAR—JOCKEY TRUNKS AND JOCKEY SINGLETS

Suitable for the French market only, and during summer months very popular. They were made from fine ribbed cotton or lisle thread. In some cases, a fancy weave was incorporated in the fabric. If flat elastic was used on the trunk, it could not be of the frilled type. Flat elastic could not be flatlocked or overlocked. There was insufficient stretch in both these stitches and a special machine was available for fixing elastic to this type of underwear.

The singlet had to be made with thin shoulder straps with a deep cut away arm hole. The bottom edge was rounded with a slit at each side to give freedom of movement. The singlet was not as long as ordinary athletic type, because it had to be tucked into the jockey trunk and could not leave a bulge. It was quite authentic for the trunk to have a fly front, but this was not very popular.

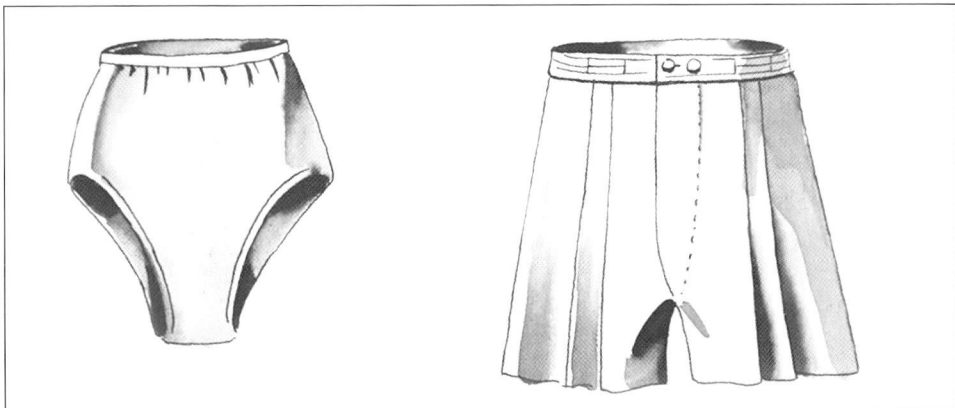

CALECON

These were quite suitable for France or Germany, in fact it was the most popular garment for both these countries, full wear in hot weather. They could be made from poplin, linen, cotton, etc., and very often were made from the same fabric as a man's shirt and sold in sets to match. Various styles could be made with 1, 2, and 3 button fronts (see diagram 3 we've dotted pencil line). In addition, it was possible to have an elastic insert at the sides or back (tunnelled or insert) and various kinds of crossover, adjustable French bands.

SINGLETS AND TRUNKS (UNIVERSAL)

Made from cotton mesh fabric. Care had to be taken to avoid any well known, branded cloth, such as Aertex. Interlock could be used as an additional variation. To effect alteration in the appearance differences in cuts and alternate art silk and cotton for the sewing gave variety.

LONG WOOLLEN PANTS AND LONG OR HALF SLEEVED VESTS

Made from either good quality all wool yarn, or a good wool and cotton mixture. There was no standard type for any one country, but imagination had to be used to vary the make and style. Welts could be laid, linked, flatlocked or overlocked. Seems could be flatlocked or overlocked. Trimmings could be of different qualities in either white or cream to match the fabric, and were put on either the inside or outside.

A two or four hole puff back could be used on pants, or alternatively on a cheaper garment a small V shape insert of the same cloth as used for trimming the other parts of the garments could be employed. Darted brace loops on a good class article were quite in order. Vests could be made with a round neck or button front, covered shoulder seams.

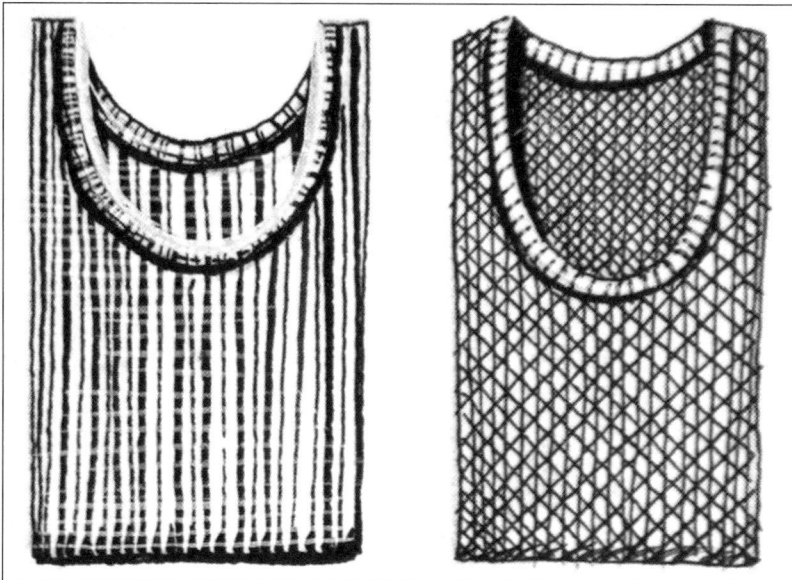

PULLOVERS, SLIPOVERS, CARDIGANS

These were supplied in various weights, weaves, colours, yarns, etc. The weight varied from a heavy pullover of approximately 3 lbs per garment with a high roll collar, to the lightweight slip over. All garments were supplied in V, round, or roll colour style.

PYJAMAS

Supplied in plain poplin, with or without contrast colour piping. Striped poplins were rarely used and if at all had to be in subdued colourings. Woollen materials were used extensively for cold climates, but care had to be taken that the patterns were not too striking. Normal English style was used, but all manner of small variations had to be thought of. The collar on the jacket was the most striking feature and had to have long, medium, or short points. Dummy cuffs to match the contrast piping were used extensively. A small proportion of pyjama trousers carried an elastic top instead of a girdle. A large assortment of buttons was necessary.

DRESSING GOWNS

A dressing gown specialist went to great lengths in order to obtain a variety of cloth and then made each gown slightly different. Some types had gauntlet cuffs, others dummy cuffs, wrap-over and button up fronts, self-material belt or cord. Pockets varied in all manner of ways.

BOILER SUITS

Ordinary workmen's type in either one or two piece. Colours: navy predominated but demands were received for brown and white.

SOCKS

A wide choice in seamless and fashioned half hose had to be made available. The most popular were plain ingrain shades made into 3x1 and 6x1 ribs. If fancy designs were demanded, socks with vertical stripes were issued. Fancy rings could not be used.

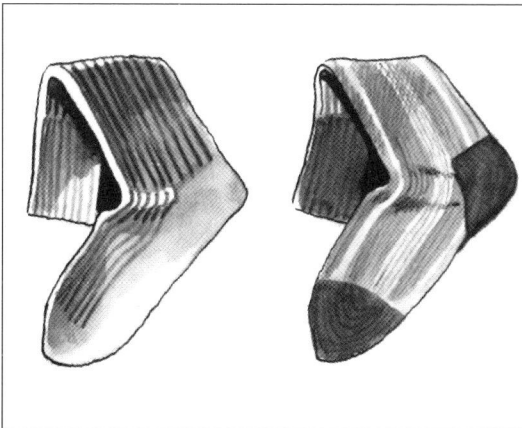

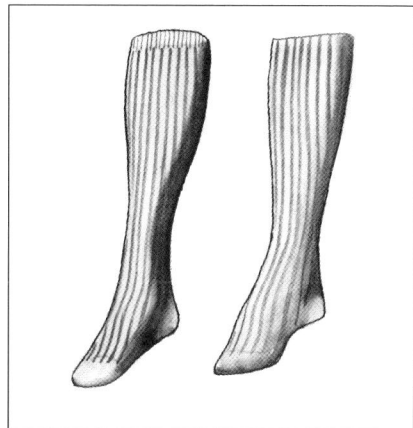

SKI SOCKS

Made from goats' hair and containing the original oil.

GOLF STOCKINGS

Dark plain colours were essential. In special circumstances subdued checks were made available. Elastic tops were authentic issue for all countries. Typical example in illustrations with tunnelled elastic support.

BRACES

The most famous of all French braces was the Chas Guyot. The Section were fortunate enough to find a manufacturer who had a good amount of webs and fittings available. This brace was only issued to well-dressed Agents. The bindings on these braces were put on by hand and the work was usually carried out in French Convents. For normal issue an elastic brace with a braided or leather end was quite suitable, but during the end of 1944 information that rubber, and leather were in very short supply on the continent was received. Therefore, a considerable quantity of braces with rigid webs and only a small elastic insert at the back were produced.

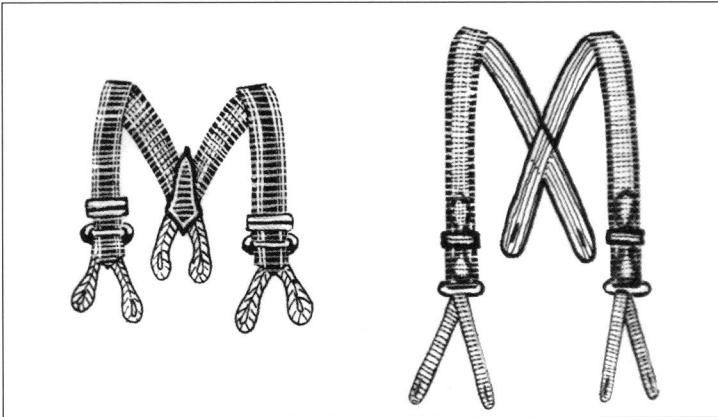

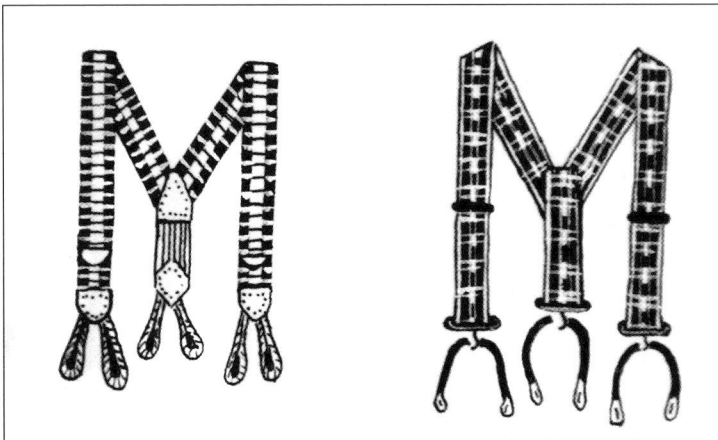

SUSPENDERS

All types were found to be universal.

TIES

The continental shape was much longer and wider than those made in Britain.

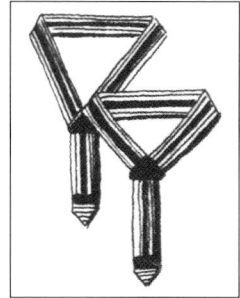

HANDKERCHIEFS

These were supplied in plain white with a hem or rolled edge. Coloured bordered handkerchiefs or all coloured ground shades were usable in the same variety of manufacture.

SCARVES

Supplied in woven and knitted fabrics. Various quantities widths, lengths, and patterns.

COMBS

Supplied in many shapes, colours, sizes, etc. All unmarked. There was no particular Continental style.

RUCKSACKS

Different qualities of canvas with the pockets staggered in all manner of ways. The majority made were of the frameless variety, but the Norwegian section always used a frame which was affixed on the back of the rucksack.

SNOW GOGGLES

Made to one standard pattern which could be folded up and put in a man's pocket with the minimum chance of breakage.

TURKISH TOWELS

Care had to be taken over the size of a continental towel, the most popular being 16-inch × 36-inch. This gave the appearance of a long tunnel shaped object and was quite the opposite to that which was used in England. The English most popular widths were 24-inch which gave an indication of the enormous difference in appearance. Several genuine Continental samples were obtained but were impossible to produce. Therefore, it was found advisable to concentrate on plain white towels with varied ends and fringes. Plain dyed towels in pastel shades could be used in order to increase the range.

Huckaback towels were not popular except where weight and room were the primary consideration. If, for instance, an Agent after having been dropped, had to live for one or two nights in hiding before making his contacts, a huckaback towel was issued in order to give him something to dry his hands on, and which he could bury afterwards with minimum of trouble.

STUDENT CLOTHING

The clothing and outfitting of a student can be said to be the final 'finishing' process before he proceeds to an assignment. It is the cloak which must conceal from the enemy and the people with whom he associates in the field, that he is other than a native of the locality, or a bona fide traveller. All his clothing and equipment must fit completely the cover story and status of the student. It is obvious that a student posing as a mechanic would arouse suspicion if under his veneer of dungarees and dirt, he was found to be wearing silk underclothes and a fine linen shirt.

This is a simple example, apparent to anybody, but the tell-tale points about clothes, patterns of shirts, underwear, toilet articles, etc., etc., are innumerable and require minute attention to ensure that no article is supplied to a student which would disclose to an expert examination, that it is other than genuine and of the type appropriate to the owner. The task of providing all the necessary variety of items of the correct type is formidable.

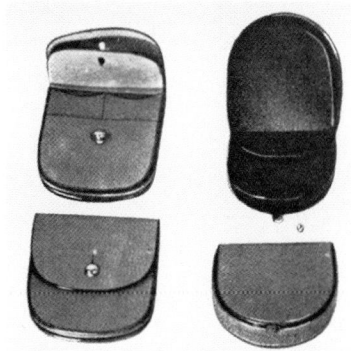

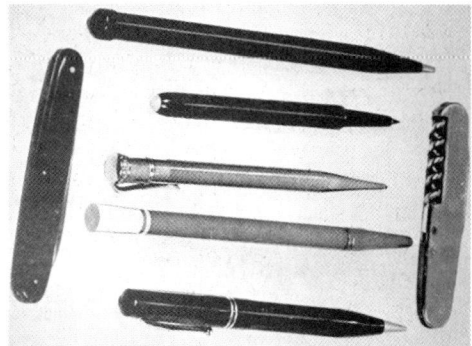

The following list shows a typical outfit for a male and female student proceeding to the Continent.

Male

Two Suitcases.
Two pairs shoes, one brown, one black.
One pair slippers.
One hat.
Two pair gloves.
Two towels.
One comb.
One toilet case.
Two sponge bags.
One nail brush.
One clothes brush.
One shoe brush.
One hair brush.
One overcoat.
One raincoat, with or without camel hair lining.

One working suit or sports suit.
One town suit.
Six shirts, poplin and/or woollen.
Three pairs pants.
Three vests.
One pullover or slipover.
One scarf.
Two pairs pyjamas.
One dressing gown.
Six pairs socks.
One pair braces.
One pair suspenders.
Three ties.
One dozen handkerchiefs.
One belt.
One wallet.
One pair cuff links.

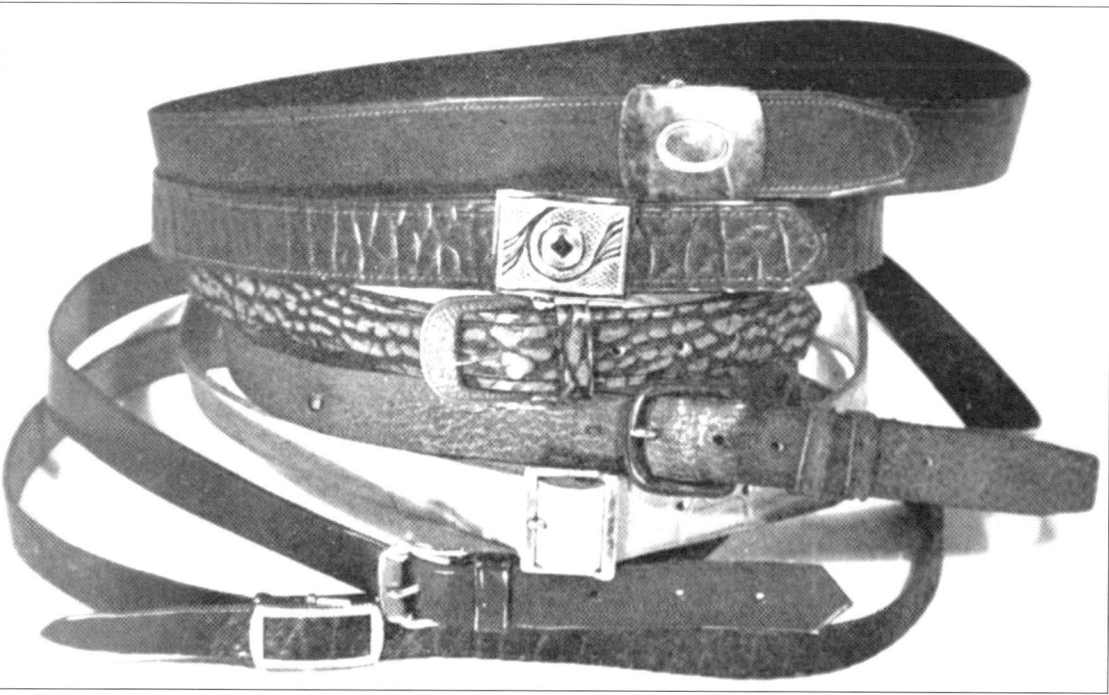

Female

Two Suitcases.

Two costumes, one town,
  one sports.

One overcoat, sports or travelling.

Three pairs of shoes, one sports, one
  walking, one dress.

One pair slippers.

Six pairs pure silk stockings or three
  silk, three Lisle.

Three slips.

Three slips.

Three pairs knickers.

Two nightgowns or pyjamas.

One woollen dress.

One silk dress.

One Wollen Blouse.

Two silk Blouses.

One twin set cashmere jumper and
  cardigan.

One corset.

Two Brassieres.

Two pairs gloves.

Two handbags, one sports, one dress.

One raincoat.

One scarf, silk, or wool.

One dozen linen handkerchiefs.

One dressing gown.

Two towels.

One face square.

One toilet case.

One nail brush.

One hair brush.

One clothes brush.

One shoe brush.

Despite the difficulties of supplying the students' necessities on the basis that he must be properly equipped, it is the policy and practice to go further in assisting the mission. It is a principle that if the student has complete confidence in his outfit, that very confidence is one of the finest tonics to his morale that could be administered. Everything is done to ensure that he is satisfied as well as properly outfitted according to his cover story.

Most of the clothing is new when taken from stock, but before it is issued to students it is 'aged' to produce the correct appearance of wear according to the student's cover

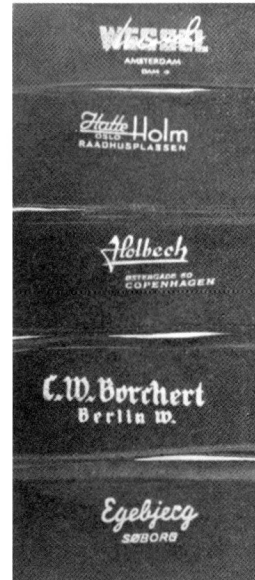

story. The appropriate state of wear can be perfectly simulated by the experienced men who do this work. Any article of equipment can be treated, but it is a skilled operation.

Final touches, are provided for the outfit in the form of watches, cigarette cases, wallets, penknives, fountain pens, etc., belts, purses, lighters, housewives, toilet and handbags as appropriate. All these items are procured through laborious and careful exploration of likely channels. Most of these items are found in the hands of pre-war importers or refugees, and some are obtained from other Government departments.

In addition there are special extras for those proceeding to join the Maquis. They have a choice of taking the following items, over and above, or in lieu of some of the foregoing.

One rucksack with or without frame or haversack.
One Canadienne jacket, or leather jacket, or wind jacket, or anorak, or sheepskin waistcoat with or without sleeves.
One pair corduroy or whipcord trousers, or plus-fours, or breeches.
One cap or beret.
One pair of ski or mountain boots studded with clingers, or fleece lined boots.
One pair of leather gauntlets, or fur lined gloves, or woollen gloves, or ski gloves in leather or proofed material.
One boilersuit or dungarees.
One ski cap.
One pair of ski trousers.
One ski jacket.
Three pairs of oiled woollen ski stockings and/or three pairs of golf stockings with elastic tops or turnovers.
One rubber water bottle.

Many students have to be equipped for countries where skiing is a necessary method of travel, and therefore they frequently require complete skiing outfits. Similarly seamen's outfits are often called for, and there are other less frequent special demands, not the least of which is the supply of enemy uniforms in a variety of ranks and services, complete down to the smallest detail.

To deal with the provision of this variety of requirements, a comprehensive range of men's clothing and personal equipment is held. The stock is comparatively large, because in addition to variety, there is the consideration of sizes to take into account. Given an idea of the volume of turnover, the number of articles issued in one month during 1944 was 8,665. The stock figure in that month was 20,040 articles.

No stock of women's clothing is held because fashion changes by district, and it has been found practicable to deal with women by selecting patterns for dresses, etc., from current foreign newspapers and periodicals appropriate to the country to be visited. The patterns, etc., are copied by selected tailors and suppliers. Individual 'shopping' for each woman student is necessary by this method, but it works well, and results in complete satisfaction of the student's requirements.

Continuous difficulty is experienced in obtaining suitable men's garments. This is to be expected, because clothing of normal British manufacture would not pass as

Continental on even casual examination. Contact has been made with civilian firms in this country who were either importers of genuine Continental articles of clothing, or who manufactured goods for continental sale and who still carry Continental tailors and cutters on their staffs.

Resort has had to be made to copying many articles. By the most careful attention to details, to weaves of materials, dyes, buttons, cottons, finish, shape, cut, trimmings, and all the numerous characteristics of clothing apparent to an expert, garments can be produced which are almost impossible to distinguish from Continental manufacture.

Clothing is issued without any makers or retailers marks, or mark showing sizes, because clothing may be traced back to the supposed supplier, and he may disclaim any knowledge, or even condemn the student by his assurance that he never stocked any such article. There are exceptions to these rules on some occasions because it is necessary as part of a student's cover story that he be definitely associated with some town, district, or firm, and then copied markings must be reproduced on his clothes. This process is difficult as it necessitates weaving trademarks, etc. A considerable amount of genuine continental second-hand clothing has also been obtained from refugees.

SUITCASES AND BRIEFCASES

A selection of different types and sizes of suitcases and briefcases were issued.

FACE SQUARES AND BAGS

Usually made from an oddment of towelling leftover from the manufacture of other articles. To obtain variety they were made in different sizes. Face bags were the most popular.

SPONGE BAGS

The most glaring designs were used with impunity. Many varieties could be obtained by employing different sizes, shapes, and contrasting bindings. Styles were altered by having bag and pochette shapes.

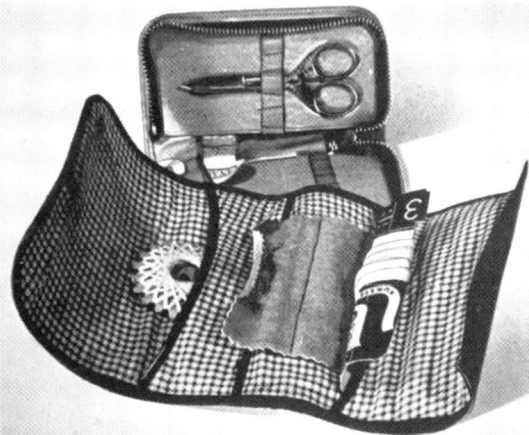

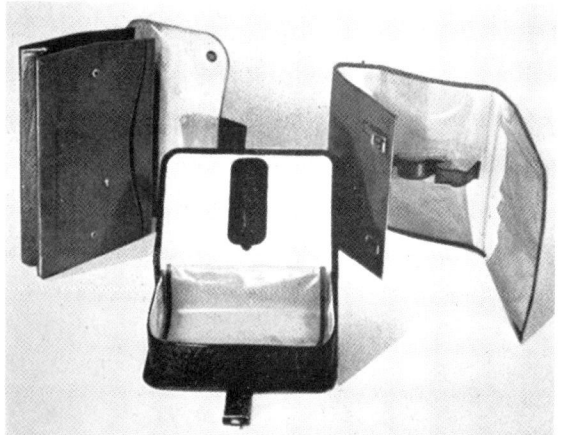

Above left: This shows the different types and sizes of brief cases issued.

Above right: This illustrates one half of a suitcase which is 'new' and the other half after being 'aged.'

Left: Suitcases can be supplied in various sizes as shown in this illustration.

Below left: These are two examples of German suitcases.

Below right: These are two examples of French suitcases.

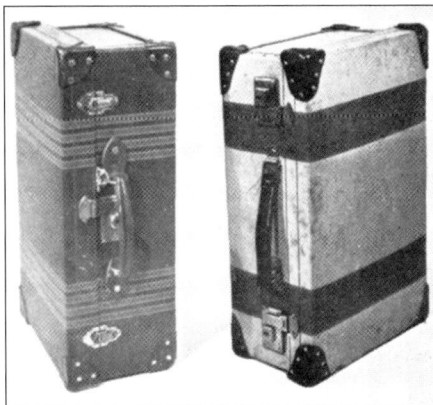

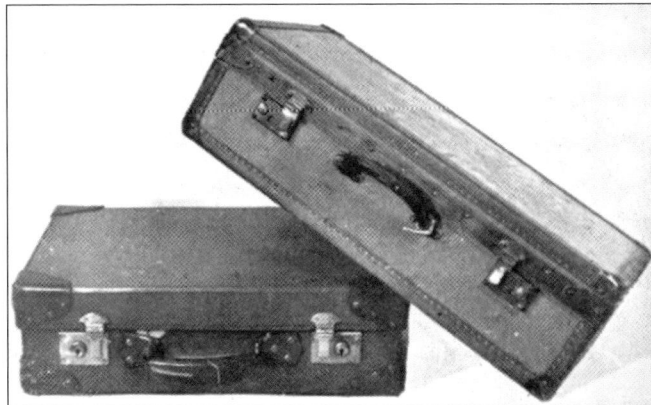

MAKE-UP

The Make-Up Department affords facilities for disguise and personal camouflage of the student. This is a process that cannot be hurried and sometimes involves weeks of specialised treatment including plastic surgery and dental operations. Make-up can be considered in three distinct classes:

Temporary—as a measure of emergency camouflage.

Semi-permanent—to cover the period of a short operation in the field.

Permanent—to obtain a complete change of personality which will last him indefinitely.

TEMPORARY MAKE-UP

This can be applied quite effectively by the student himself and has proved most useful in the Field to persons who require a quick change for a short period. Illustrations 1 and 2 show what can be done with a little shading, a theatrical moustache, and a pair of glasses.

Illustration No. 1.   Illustration No. 2.

SEMI-PERMANENT MAKE-UP

This requires more time and can be accomplished only by someone who has received instructions in makeup. Illustrations 3 and 4 show one type of semi-permanent make-up where the most obvious feature of the man is his bald head. This has been obviated by the use of a toupee. Illustrations 5, 6 and 7 show the method of measuring a man for a wig or toupee. Illustrations 8, 9 and 10 show how to take correct measurements for spectacles.

Illustration No. 3.

Illustration No. 4.

Illustration No. 5.

Illustration No. 6.

Illustration No. 7.

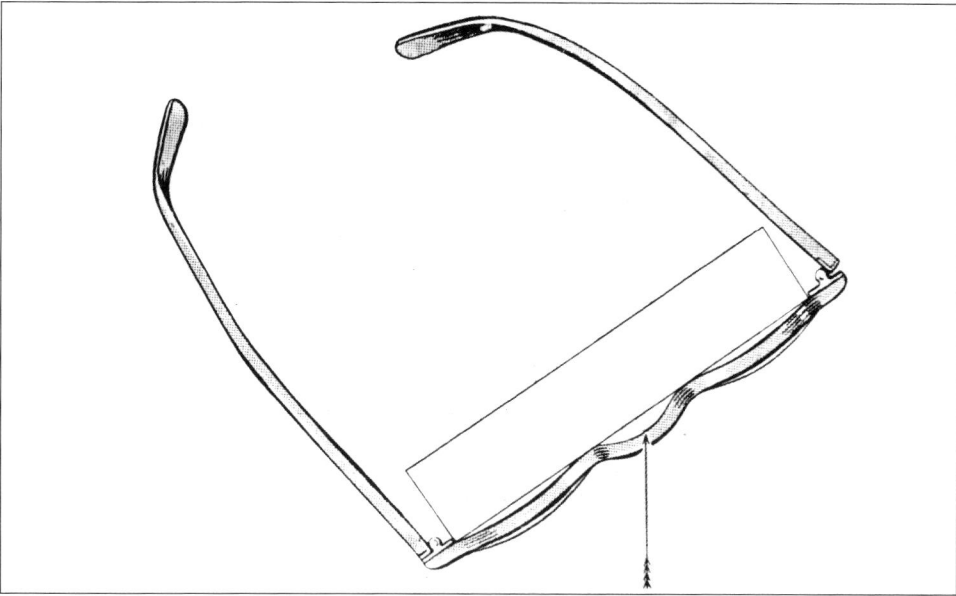

Illustration No. 8.

Illustration No. 9.

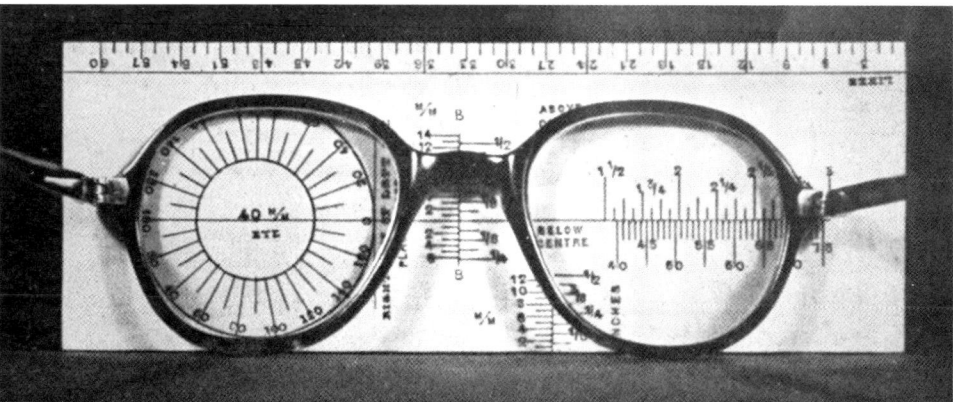

Illustration No. 10.

The Illustrations 11, 12, 13, 14, 15 and 16 show the use of gum pads and nose plugs, and the following instructions describe how impressions can be made. These instructions are given for the benefit of students who cannot avail themselves of local wig makers, opticians and dentists and who would have to rely on the Make-Up Department supplying them with their needs. If the instructions are carried out with care all the student's requirements can be met with first class results despite the distance between themselves and the Make-Up Department.

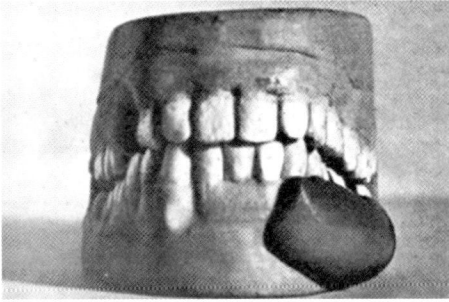

Illustration No. 11.

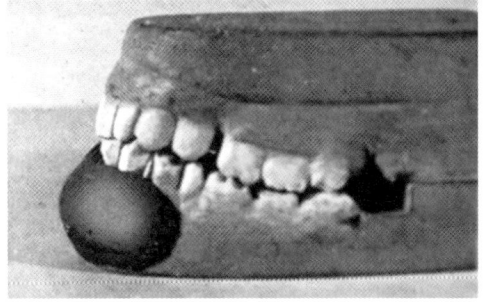

Illustration No. 12.

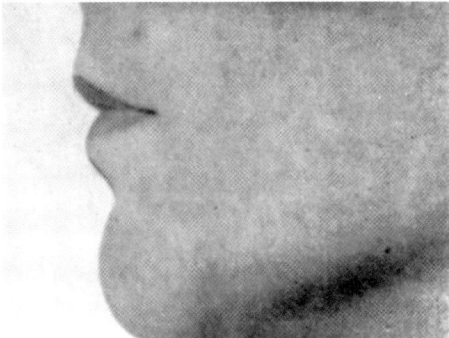

Illustration No. 13.

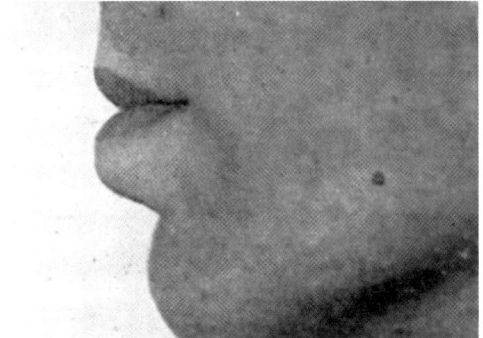

Illustration No. 14.

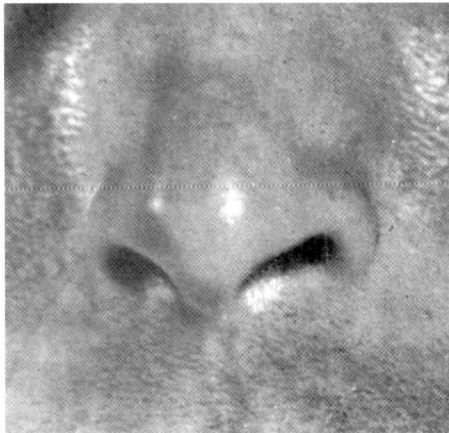

Illustration No. 15.

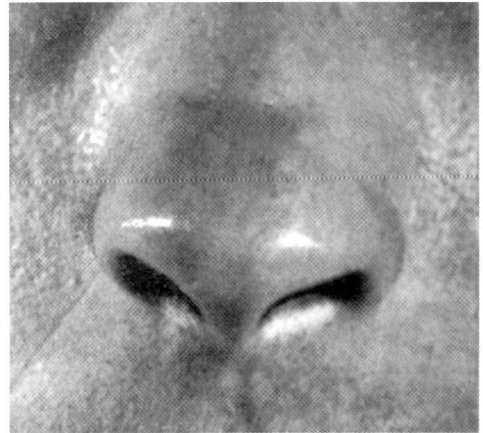

Illustration No. 16.

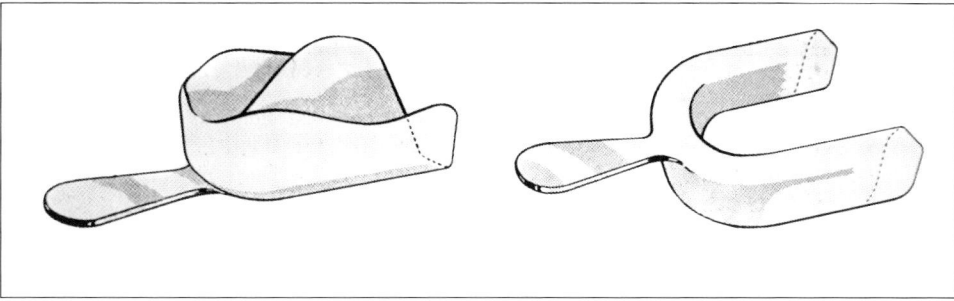

Illustration No. 17.

A fair range of impression trays (Illustration 17) should be available, 10 upper and 10 lower are suggested. With this range any size jaw may be dealt with. The size of trays can only be determined by experience and good judgement. Rehearse on a friend. Judge the size and shape, insert the tray, and see how it fits. Make sure the tray is large enough and see that there is a good clearance round all the teeth, and if necessary, bend to ensure that the muscle attachment or soft tissue are not displaced.

A composition is preferable to plaster for making impressions, as it is less messy and is much less unpleasant for the student. Also, impression taking from some people induces intense salivation which floods the floor of the mouth, and any attempt to take a good plaster impression with the mouth filled with saliva is a waste of time. The saliva mixes with the plaster and is inclined to crumble it. 'Stents Red' should be used. What follows is the procedure for this, The majority of compositions are set by cooling.

Place the composition in a bowl of hot water and when sufficiently pliable, knead well, and pass once or twice through a Bunsen flame to dry it and ensure that it is of a uniformly soft consistency. Make it into a roll and press in the previously warmed tray. Warming the tray ensures that the composition will adhere to the tray when removing from the mouth. Smooth out all wrinkles and dip in hot water, test on the side of the face to make sure it is not too hot, then place it in the student's mouth. Illustrations 18 and 19 show how to insert the tray for the bottom impression. When in position hold down with the left hand and with the right hand manipulate the cheeks. Allow approximately 5 minutes for setting and remove carefully. Follow the same directions for the upper jaw, illustrations 20 and 21. For the casting, use a fairly stiff mixture of plaster, well shaken down and allowed to set, place in warm water, and remove the composition. This should leave a perfect mould of the student's mouth. This is now ready for the dental surgeon and if the necessary care has been taken, he should be able to produce the required pads.

It is impossible to supply a fast dye for the skin, but there are several means of staining the skin for three or four days. Powder blocks can be supplied in three colours, brown, black, and green. These blocks can be impregnated with dimethyl phthalate as a repellent for mosquitoes. After approximately a dozen doses of Mepacreme, skin will turn a yellowish colour, turning into a fairly deep brown as the doses are continued. Carotene is the pigment of carrots and if taken internally will produce a staining of the body.

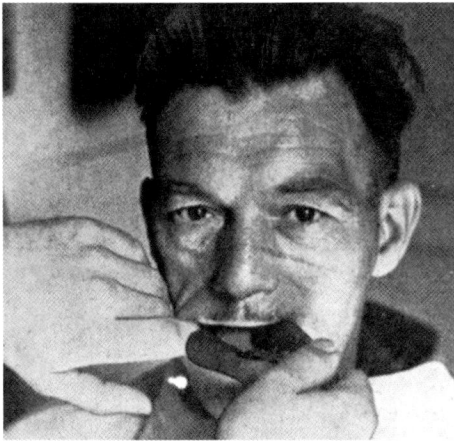

Illustration No. 18.

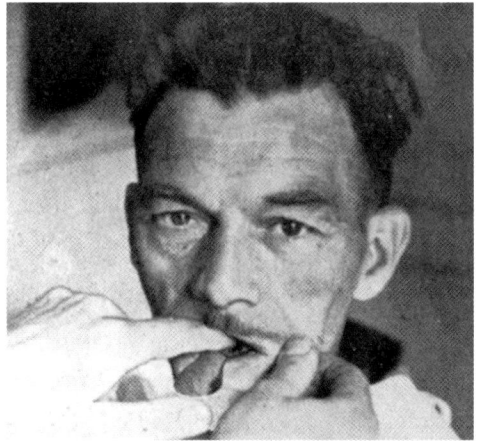

Illustration No. 19.

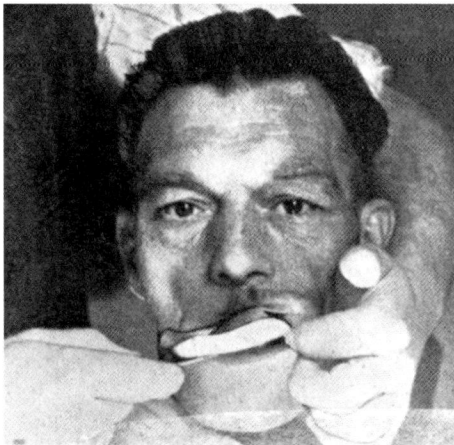

Illustration No. 20.

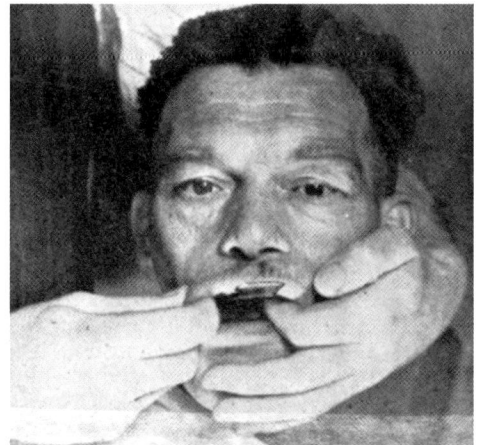

Illustration No. 21.

One gramme of silver nitrate in 100cc of water and 100cc of aqueous alcohol sprayed through a glass nozzle, will, after exposure to strong sunlight, produce a very strong dark brown stain that would last approximately 3 days in far east climates.

Permanganate of Potash, using two teaspoonfuls to a half pint of water and applied to the body with a cotton wool pad, will produce a brown stain that would last approximately two days. The following is a prescription for the production of a walnut dye: mix 17-drams of green walnut hulls, with 1 ¼-drams of Alum, 8-drams of Alcohol, and enough water to make 3ozs. Triturate the first two ingredients in a mortar, add the alcohol and let stand for four days. Filter and apply with a cotton wool pad.

Wrinkling cream is the name given to an ointment used for giving an aged appearance to the skin. It does not actually wrinkle the skin but produces an unhealthy pallor. Plastic noses and wigs can be supplied for distant use. For example, a white crew operating a native craft could be easily disguised in order to give the impression of natives if seen from a distance.

Contact lenses are useful camouflage for a person who has to wear very thick lenses in his spectacles. They may also be used to give the impression of a wall eye or a blind eye, and, if sufficient time is given they can be produced to alter the colour of the eyes.

PERMANENT CAMOUFLAGE

This can only be accomplished by alterations to the features and the removal of scars, which naturally has to be carried out by a qualified plastic surgeon. Appointments for permanent make-up and the necessary arrangements for the operation are made through the Make-Up Department, but it must be remembered that sufficient time must be given otherwise the application will have to be refused. An eminent plastic surgeon and his staff are at our disposal and have carried out a number of operations.

Some examples are shown in the following illustrations of what can be accomplished by facial surgery. Illustration 22 is a rebuilt broken nose. Illustration 23 shows the result of treatment of an unusually large and prominent nose. In illustration 24 the nose has been operated on to alter a typical Jewish character. This type of face presents a particular problem because their is something about the cheekbones, that although characteristic, cannot be clearly defined and the surgeon finds it impossible to make an alteration to the bones. The nose can be camouflaged by skilled surgery and the face can be altered to eliminate outstanding facial characteristics of the race of the owner.

Tattoo marks are most difficult to remove. The process is long and painful and recourse to removal is not recommended. By far the most satisfactory treatment has been found to be re tattooing with larger and more elaborate designs. Skilful blending can achieve amazing results and this method has the advantage of speed and there is much less discomfort to the subject.

A dental surgeon can achieve practically any alteration to the teeth and mouth. The methods used are many, but some examples can be given. Gum pads are within his province, and there uses have already been described. False teeth can of course be provided, or existing dental plates altered. Gold teeth should be removed. A hollow gold tooth in the form of a cap to slip over an existing tooth can be carried in a pocket ready for immediate use.

This article gives only examples of some methods of each type of personal camouflage. This important subject is one to which any student should give most careful consideration, and the best results will always be attained by cooperation between the subject and the make-up man.

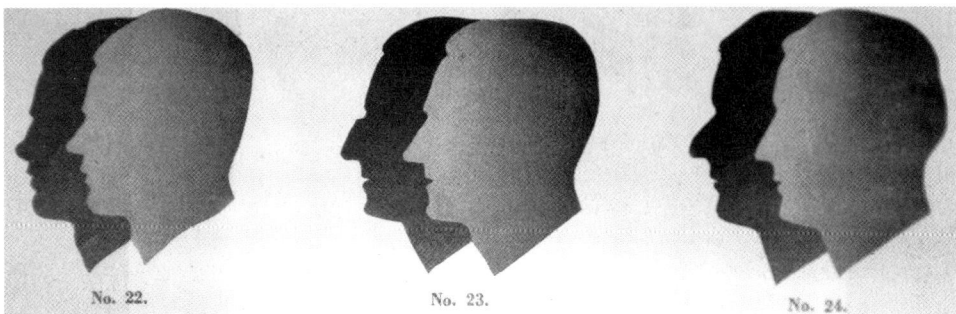

No. 22.　　　No. 23.　　　No. 24.

Illustrations Nos 22, 23 and 24.

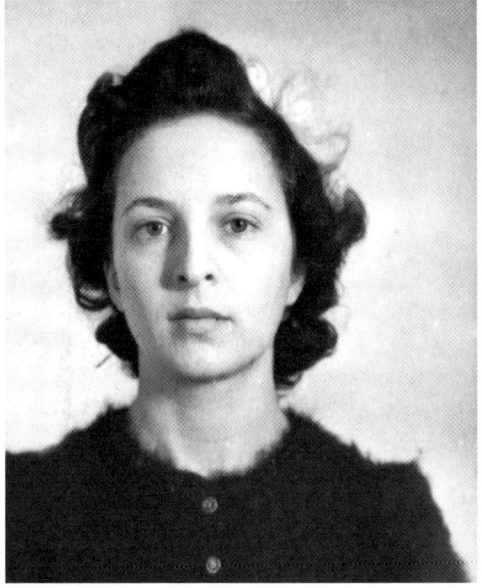

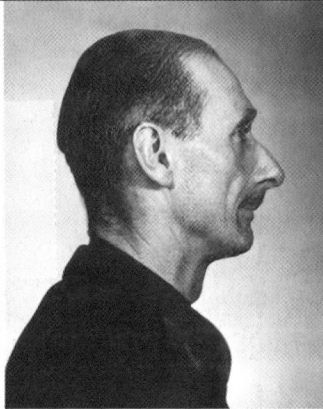

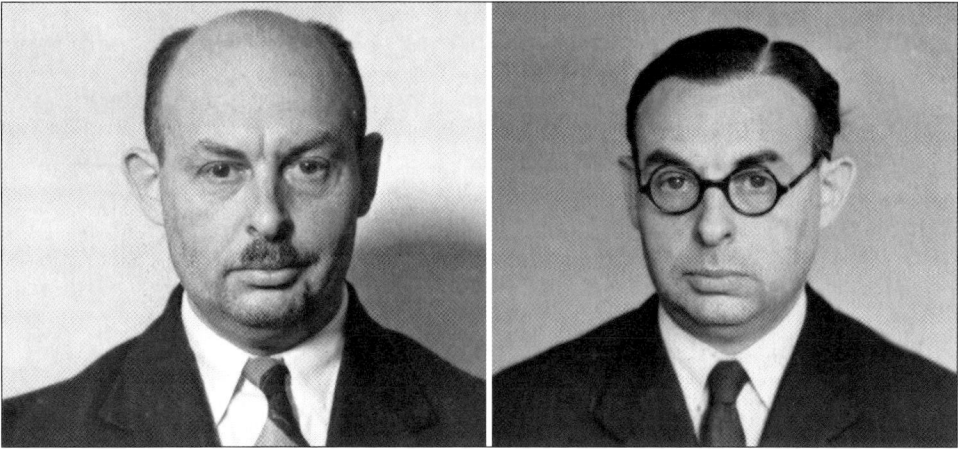

Above: The addition of a pair of glasses, a toupee and removal of the moustache changed this Agent's look.

Right: This Agent had nose and ear surgery to change their shape.

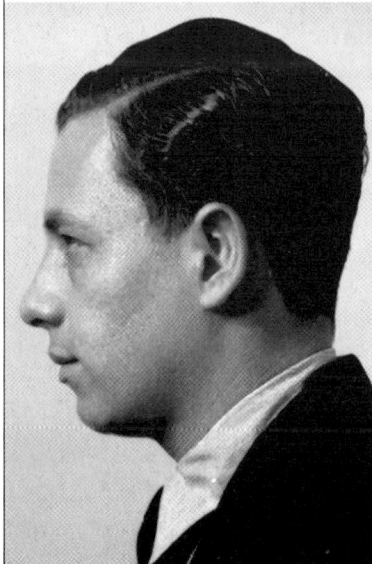

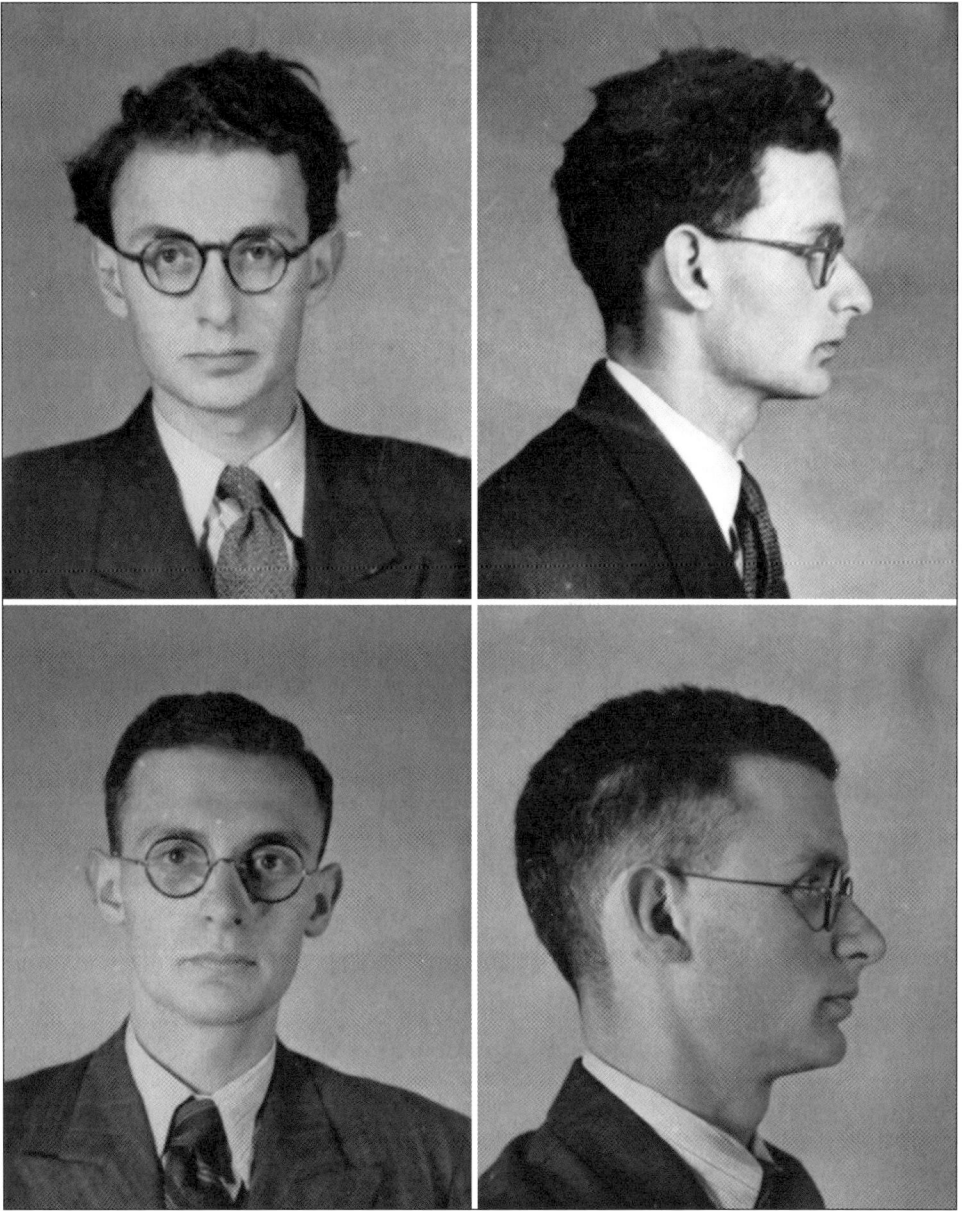

This Agent had nose surgery to change its shape.

FIELDCRAFT AND CAMOUFLAGE

The principles of Camouflage as used by the Armed Forces very rarely apply to the specialised forms of camouflage which are adopted for our specific purposes, where no attempt is made to render the object difficult to observe, but to present it openly to view as an entirely different object but usually of an innocent character; but there are occasions when we have to consider camouflage entirely from a Fieldcraft angle.

The aim of camouflage is to render the object inconspicuous and difficult to recognise; let us consider, therefore, the qualities which make an object conspicuous. These may be classified as under:

a) Movement
b) Colour: differentiation from the surrounding objects which form its background.
c) The general tone or texture of the object.
d) The form that the object takes: the contrast of light and shade.
e) The outline compared with its surroundings.
f) The form of the object's shadow.

It is obvious that the more one can eliminate the contrasting elements of an object with its background the more difficult it will become to recognise. Therefore, the fundamental steps towards effective camouflage are:

1. Absence of movement.
2. Colour resemblance.
3. Matching of tone and texture.
4. Destruction of the object's shape.
5. Disruption of the outline.
6. Elimination of its shadow.

Right: This image shows the contrast of colour to background.

Below left: This image shows nature's addition to disruptive pattern emulating immediate background of coral.

Below right: This image shows additional coloration blending with coral and background, and the elimination of shadow against broken ground.

SMALL CRAFT

We are all familiar with the common site of buildings, vehicles, and ships, painted in coloured designs. Disruption, as this patterning is called, functions to prevent or delay the recognition of an object by painting only. When the surface of an object is covered with these irregular patches of contrasting local colours and tones when, they assist the object so covered to blend into the existing background. The pattern is so designed that the shape of the object becomes disrupted and broken up. Set patterns can be supplied, but the study of the colour and tones used must be left to the user, who must make a careful analysis of the colours and tones in the location in which he is to operate, and have his paints carefully matched. Disruptive painting is not foolproof camouflage, but it is definitely an aid. Climatic conditions vary so much but apart from a guide as to patterning, no hard and fast rules can be made.

This method is chiefly used by us for the camouflage of small craft. Operating in water, the question of texture does not arise so long as the coloration matches the condition of the operation. The disruptive painting takes care of this, and also the breaking up of the shape, and as far as possible the elimination of shadow.

Left: An example of nature's method of fitting into existing background, i.e., a moth on a tree.

CLOTHING

Military operational clothing is also treated with these patterns. As these are generally needed for jungle warfare, the colours used are dark green and black. Colour is also applied to faces and hands. Suitable 'pancakes' can be supplied in various shades of black, green, and brown. (See Make-Up Section)

CONTAINERS

Parachute containers are painted in disruptive patterns according to the season, plus local coloration. This is only used as a temporary measure where the container has to be hidden quickly and for a short while.

A more elaborate form of camouflage is obtained in the form of rubber sheets representing tree trunks

Container with rubber sheet open.

Container with rubber sheet closed.

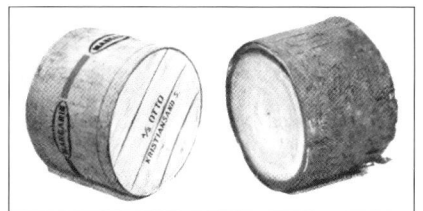

Container disguised as a keg of margarine and a container disguised as a wooden log.

which are wrapped around the container, giving the impression of a fallen tree. If the cells have to be carted away for some distance in order to be unpacked, they can be painted to appear as common objects, such as drums, logs, kegs of butter, etc.

Holdsworth containers having first been coated with a plastic paint to conform with local geological conditions, are also painted with a destructive pattern to give the requisite tone and texture to the surface.

Similar containers made from papier mâché and produced as rock boulders are also obtainable. These containers are exact representations of the various rock formations and embody all the six principles as laid down by camouflage. They are light to carry and are guaranteed damp proof.

CONTAINERS

Sneakers are in the form of a sandal carrying a sole bearing the imprint of a Japanese shoe or native foot. They are issued for use in raiding parties for operations in the Far East. They are easy to wear, and the track left by the wearer leaves faithful imprints, thus hiding all traces of the intruders having been other than Japanese or local natives.

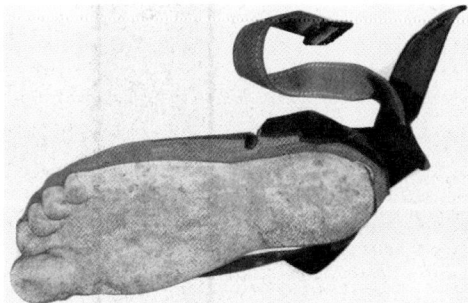

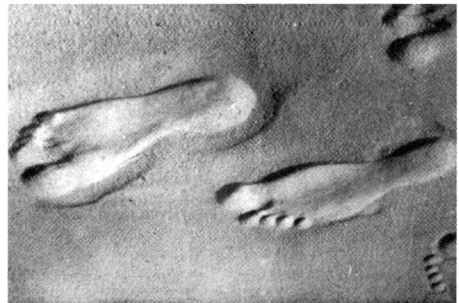

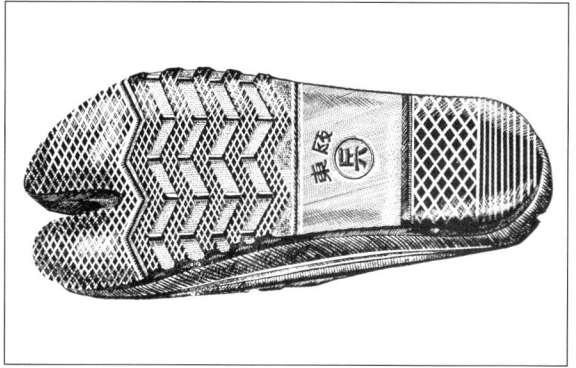

OBSERVATION POSTS

Various types of light portable observation posts are made for special operations. These are easily erected and afford enough room to hide two people. The below illustration shows an observation post treated with foam (Pyrene) to represent snow. Visibility is good from the interior while the exterior blends into the existing background.

SNIPER SUITS

Sniper suits can be provided for any location. The illustrations show one made of teak leaves for tropical use.

CAMOUFLAGE OF TYREBURSTERS

Three methods of camouflage of tyrebursters have been used; 1. Complete concealment of the device in a shell representing a stone, a lump of mud, or animal dropping. 2. Concealment of the Tyreburster in a cloth bag representing a stone. 3. Disruption in colour of the Tyreburster taped and painted.

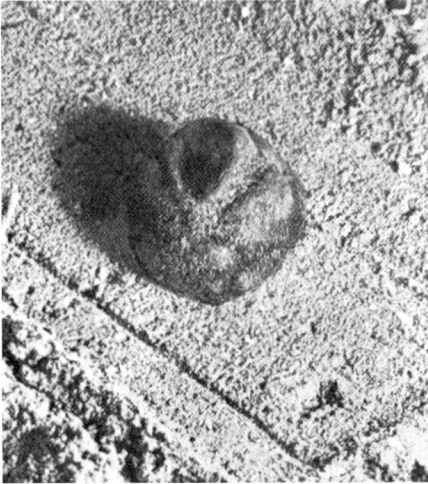

COMPLETE CONCEALMENT, NO. I

This type of camouflage is obviously the most satisfactory because, as in the case of stones, if the geological conditions of the place of operation are studied carefully, then the article fits completely into its own background, and in the case of animal droppings, the disguise is such that it will not attract undue attention because it is one of many objects with which the eye is unconsciously familiar.

Left: Tyreburster as a mule's dropping.

Below: Tyreburster, left to right, flintstone, sandstone, dry mud.

CONCEALMENT IN CLOTH BAGS, NO. 2

The illustrations show the method of concealing a Tyreburster in bags. The bags are made of rubberised canvas and are painted to resemble stones, two tone, with the geological colours of the locality in which the Tyrebursters are being used. The shapes of the bags differ in order to achieve a variety of outlines. This is a quick camouflage method and is a handy one because the space occupied by the actual camouflage material is very small.

Above left: Tyreburster concealed in an open cloth envelope.

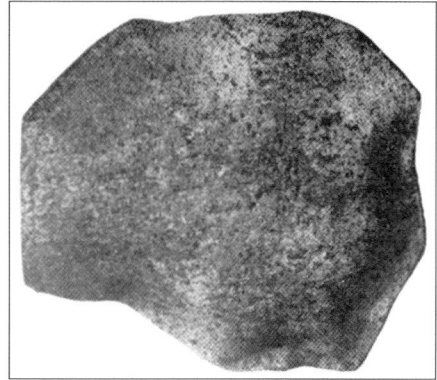

Above right: Tyreburster concealed in a closed cloth envelope.

TAPED TYREBURSTERS

The metal Tyreburster is completely covered within adhesive tape, a flap is left at the bottom so that the lead plug can be removed, and the detonator replaced. The whole is then painted with a disruptive pattern and coloured to conform with the geological type of the district. No paint can come into contact with the working parts, and apart from being a further precaution against damp, this type of painted burster takes up less space in packing.

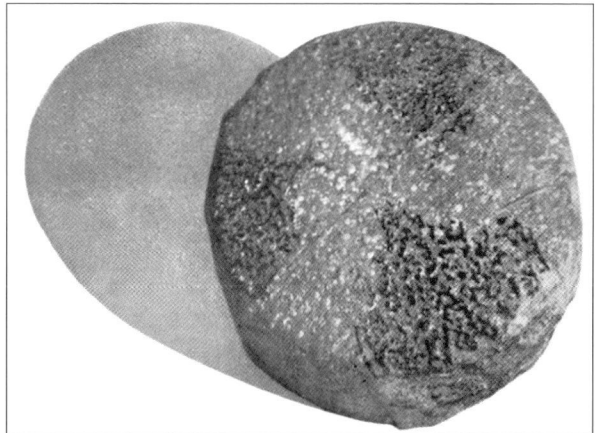

Tyreburster semi-camouflaged, i.e. covered with adhesive tape and painted disruptive patterns.

4

Printing Department

All the labels and printing matter necessary to complete the fake commodities as described in the previous sections are produced by the Printing and Art department. This also includes the production of armlets for invading forces, insignias for foreign uniforms and the printing of codes. The following pages give some idea of the assortment of work produced including reproductions of Continental luggage labels, which, when suitably aged, are attached to trunks, suitcases, etc., to give a genuine appearance or to bear out a cover story.

FAKE COMMODITIES LABELS

Above and opposite above: Above is reproduced a sample of a German food tin label. This is a Portuguese sardine tin label, which is normally printed on 'Flexglas'.

Above left: This is an example of a German bell battery label.

Above right: This is an example of a German tinned preserves label.

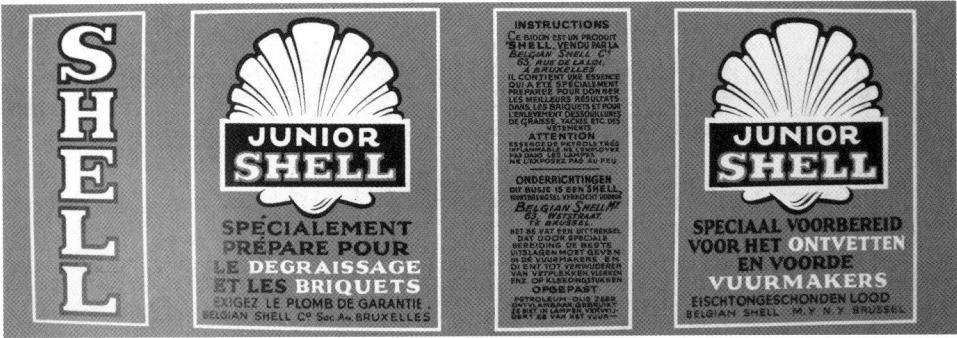

This is a reproduction label for a can of fluid used for degreasing and fire lighting.

A reproduction of a German vegetable tin label. The tins can be used for all normal types of concealment, such as ammunition, money, messages, codes, etc.

Above left: This is a reproduction of an Italian wine label used in the production of explosive Chianti bottles that goes above the straw basket.

Above right: This is a reproduction of an Italian wine label used in the production of explosive Chianti bottles that covers the cork.

This is a reproduction of an Italian wine label used in the production of explosive Chianti bottles that goes around the neck of the bottle.

FAKE LUGGAGE LABELS

FAKE MAPS

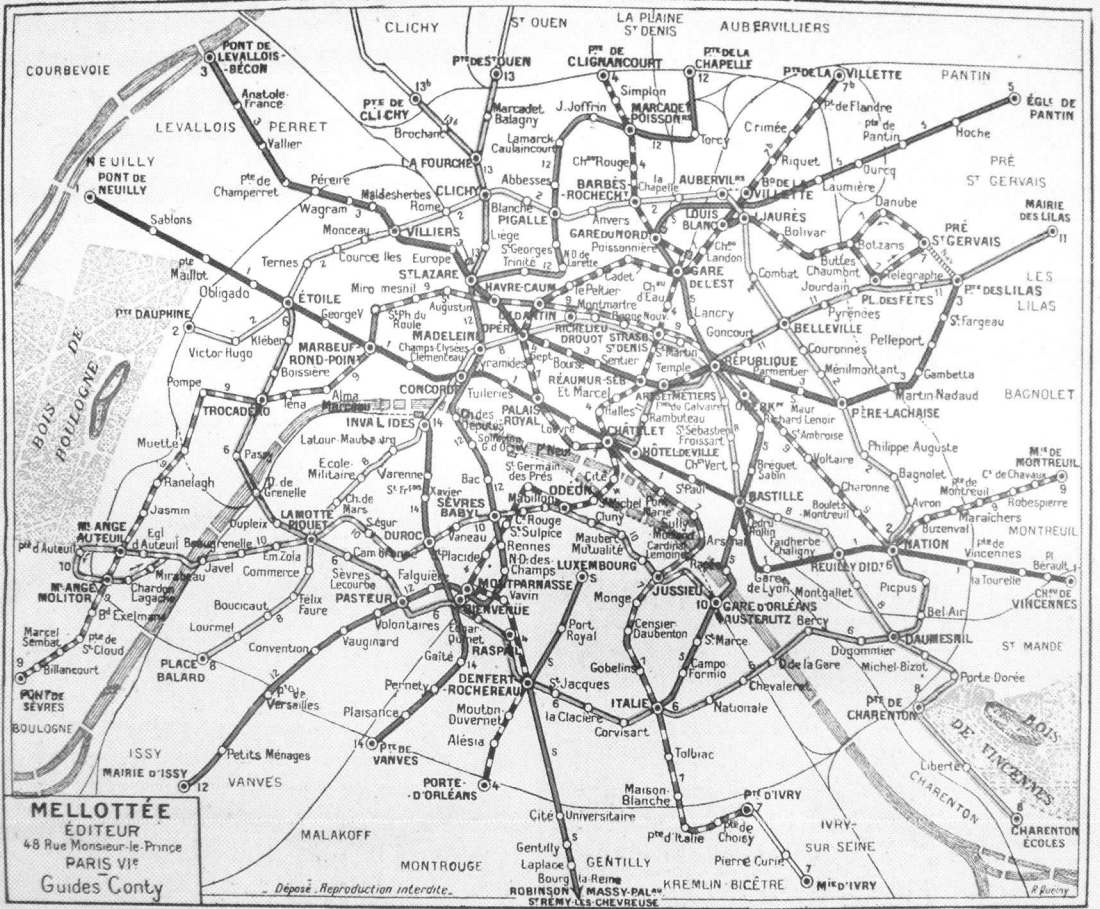

This is a reproduction of the Paris Metro map.

5

Photographic Section

AGENT'S PHOTOGRAPHIC SECTION

This section was formed in March 1943 in order to provide photographs for false identity papers of European origin and were required to be carried by the Agents proceeding to enemy occupied territory. These were produced for the following countries: France, Italy, Belgium, Norway, Denmark, Holland, Czechoslovakia, Germany, Austria, and Poland.

It was first of all essential to find original documents for all of the above-mentioned countries. This often meant that several types of documents for each country had to be procured. A study of these originals gave a general indication as to size, position of

The Photographic Section existed chiefly for the purpose of producing the necessary photographs for faked documents. These documents and photographs had to be of the highest standard to ensure the safe passage of SOE Field Agents through German check points.

head and shoulders, quality of paper used, and the method of printing. This enabled a dossier to be established for each country and each separate identity paper.

In October 1943, the Photographic Section was incorporated into the Camouflage Department together with the existing Makeup Section. This was an additional asset as in many cases the sitter had to appear older in one identity paper and younger in another. Therefore, only the best methods of makeup could be used, as anything phoney in the finished article would be endangering the life of the Agent. In some cases, it was possible to alter the sitter's age purely by lighting.

It must be remembered that the finished photographs were supposed to have originated from all over Europe, therefore each one had to be different, some giving the appearance of having been taken by second rate photographers, and others the work of good photographers. Imagination in the lighting, background, and printing, was the keynote for the staff. Features had to be clear, and the sitter could not be placed against a fancy background, or in any artistic position.

In some cases it was not possible to photograph the original subject, therefore the photographer had to resort to using an old photograph which was often a bad one, or possibly a group including the subject, and therefore the reproduction entailed a great deal of retouching. Another example shows how a man in uniform was re-dressed as a civilian. The following are some technical notes on the apparatus and methods used, together with the table showing the work produced from the 1st March 1943, to the 15th November 1944:

DRUMS

Ordinary photographic studio. Glass roof, if possible, for open air snapshot effect. A number of diffused lights, overhead lights, and spotlights. Backgrounds ranging from white to black, also some lengths of material for draping.

CAMERAS

Half plate and quarter plate studio cameras with different lenses, i.e., one soft-focus lens and one bad quality lens to help produce inferior photographs. Rollieiflex Cameras with supplementary lenses 1 and 11. (This kind of camera is very useful when many sitters have to be taken in a short time.) Contax Camera or Leica Cameras.

DARK ROOM EQUIPMENT

Films of any kind. They can be overexposed, under exposed, developed at different temperatures, and in different developers (chemicals) to produce the variety of results necessary. Printing papers: a variety of all available papers. The supply of foreign, especially cheap papers proved very difficult. When the paper had a watermark on the back, care was needed to ensure that the mark corresponded with the country for which the pass was intended. During the printing, all tricks of photography were employed, as well as different chemical mixtures. Temperature of developers, hot or cold water, particular development, all kinds of shading, etc.

ESSENTIAL EQUIPMENT

One Contax camera.
One Leica camera with 5 cm and 8 cm lens.
One Rolleiflex camera with supplementary lenses 1 and 11.
One half-plate camera, with quarter-plate adaptors, fitted with:
    11 1/3-inch Kershaw soft focus F5:6 lens.
    8-inch Cooke Anastigmat F4:5 lens.
    Ross Convertible F6:3 lens.
    Yellow, Red, and Green filters.
    One Miniature Enlarger.
    One whole plate Enlarger fitted with:
        15 cm Tessar F4:5, also
        2-inch Wray 'Super' F4:5 to reduce to 1x1 cm.
    One contact printer.
    Kodak films Panatomic X and Super XX.
    All available Kodak, Ilford, Agfa, and Lumiere film
    Bromide papers, etc.
Chemicals and dyes of all kinds.,

STATISTICAL STATEMENT OF WORK

From 1 March 1943 to 15 November 1944.

Agents photographed	1,620 men
Prints delivered	22,889
Reprints	11,335
Average per month: 80 Agents and 1,700 prints.	
Military Passes (British)	1,784 men
Prints delivered	11,197
Average per month: 89 men and 560 prints.	
Record Section (Enlargements only)	
Prints delivered	14,915
Average per month: 750 Enlargements	

EXAMPLES OF THE PHOTOGRAPHIC SECTION'S WORK

Nr 134600	Lijfrentekas. Wet van 10-12-24. Nr 134600		
Naam Lafont	Handteekening houder dezer Kaart		Boek Blad.
Voornamen Bernard	*Bernard Lafont*	te BRUGGE	
Burgerl. stand celibataire			Datum
			Nr
Nationaliteit: BELGISCHE			
geboren te 7/7/1895		Achtereenvolgende woningen	STRAAT
den Mahaut			
Beroep Brabant			
Vorig verblijf Behainte			
Tweede verblijf	Gestalte: Eén meter		
Ingeschreven. Boek 740 Blad 8	Brugge, 14/7/39		
Max Marks straat nr. 2	De Ambtenaar van den Burgerlijken Stand.		
den 4/3/39 19 39			

Wie onderhavige kaart vervalscht door uitschroppingen, doorhalingen, portretverwisseling, of anderszins stelt zich aan gerechtelijke vervolging bloot.

№ 4268729	Caisse de Retraite, Loi du 10-12-24, N° du Compte / Lijfrentekas. Wet van 10-12-24, N° der Rekening		DEMEURES SUCCESSIVES DANS LA COMMUNE ACHTEREENVOLGENDE WONINGEN IN DE GEMEENTE				
Nom / Naam Durand	Signature du porteur, / Handteeken des dragers			Vol. fol. Boek Blad.			
Prénoms / Voornamen Jean-Paul				Date Datum			
État civil / Burgerstand Veuf				Dm Afd.			
Nationalité: Belge / Nationaliteit: Belgische				N° N°			
né à / geboren te Athus			RUE. — STRAAT				
le / den 21 Mars 1884							
Profession / Beroep Banquier							
Résidence précédente / Vorig verblijf Ixelles	Taille: Un mètre cent.						
Seconde résidence / Tweede verblijf Bruxelles	Lengte: Een meter cent.						
Inscrit. Vol. 733 Fol. 175 / Ingeschreven. Boek Blad:	Délivré le 12/7/ 1947 / Afgeleverd, den						
Rue av. Bekhoud n° 3 / Straat, n°	L'Officier de l'État civil (ou son délégué): / De Ambtenaar van den Burgerstand (of zijn afgevaardigde):						
le / den 19/3/36							

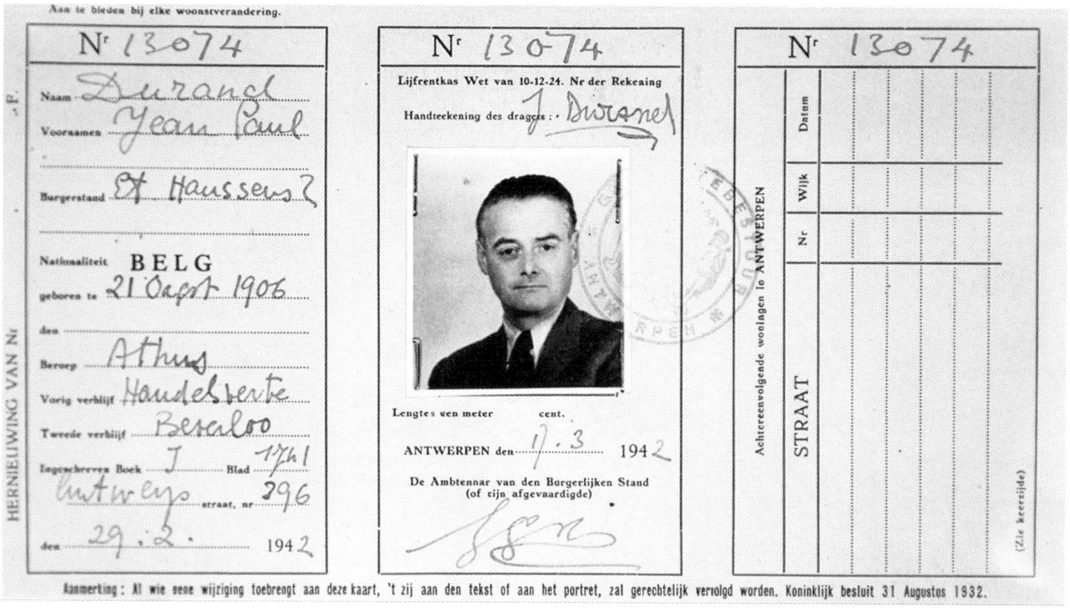

Aan te bieden bij elke woonstverandering.

Nr 13074

Naam Durand
Voornamen Jean Paul
Burgerstand Ep Haussens?
Nationaliteit BELG
geboren te 21 Oogst 1906
den
Beroep Athus
Vorig verblijf Handelsverte
Tweede verblijf Beseloo
Ingeschreven Boek J Blad 1741
Antwerps straat, nr 396
den 29.2. 1942

HERNIEUWING VAN Nr

Nr 13074

Lijfrentkas Wet van 10-12-24. Nr der Rekening

Handteekening des dragers: J. Durand

Lengte: een meter cent.

ANTWERPEN den 17.3 1942

De Ambtenaar van den Burgerlijken Stand
(of zijn afgevaardigde)

Nr 13074

Achtereenvolgende woningen te ANTWERPEN

Datum	Wijk	Nr	STRAAT

(Zie keerzijde)

Aanmerking: Al wie eene wijziging toebrengt aan deze kaart, 't zij aan den tekst of aan het portret, zal gerechtelijk vervolgd worden. Koninklijk besluit 31 Augustus 1932.

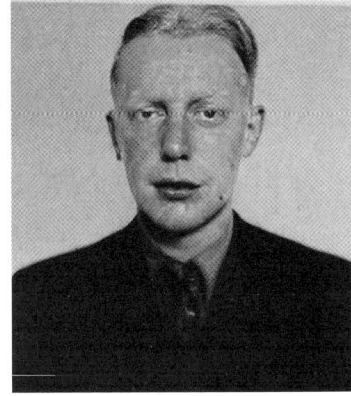

Suppliers

Suppliers	Commodity
Boxcraft Ltd., 19a Buckingham Road London N1	Cartons
C.T. Brock & Co, Hemmel Hempstead	Explosives
Bryant & May, Fairfield Works, Bow, London E3	Matches
Brilliant Signs Ltd., 131 Uxbridge Road, Shepherds Bush, London	Signs
Lewis Brooks & Co. Ltd., 112 Fenchurch Street, London EC3	Sacks and Sacking
Percy Baker, 28 Oarsman Road, London N1	Artists Brushes etc.
Arthur Beal & Co. 194 Shaftesbury Ave, WC2	Jute
Beetle Cement Co. Ideal House, 1 Argyle Street, W1	Cement
Belling & Co, Bridge Works, Southbury Road, Enfield	Electric heaters
Betts British Foil Factories, 241 City Road, EC1	Tinfoil
Borne & Co. Ltd. 71 Standen Road, SW18	Printing Inks
British Waxed Wrappings Ltd. Station Mills, NW10	Waxed Papers
Brown Bros. Ltd. 22 Great Eastern St, EC2	General Factors
Burt Bros (Bow) Ltd. Stoneleigh House, Stanfield Road, E3	Artificial Flowers
J & W Burt Ltd. 156 Caledonian Road, N1	Printing Machinery
A.E. Clarke Ltd. 120 Southwark Street, SE1	Materials, Canvas
A.H. Clarke, Warwick Road studios, Ealing	Silk Screen printing, Show cards, posters.
J. Collins & Son Ltd. 103 Cannon Street, EC1	Baskets
George Culver, White Lion Street, N1	Spectacles
Chance Brothers Ltd. Glass Works, Smethwick 40, Nr Birmingham	Glass filters
Cellon Ltd. Richmond Road, Kingston	Cellulose Paint
Canning Town Glassworks Ltd, Stephenson Street, Canning Town, E16	Glass Phials

Suppliers	Commodity
Carr Fasteners Co. Ltd. Stapleford, Nottingham	Dress & Bag fasteners, Electric fittings
Carto Containers Co. Ltd. Lonsdale Works, Lonsdale Square, Liverpool Road, N1	Cartons
Central Pulverizing Co. Ltd. 168 Burdett Road, E3	Mica
Courtaulds Ltd. 14 St Martins-le-Grand, EC1	Silks
T. Crowther & Son Ltd. 282 North End Road, Fulham, SW	Stone Ornaments
J. Dale Ltd, 14 Brunswick Park Road, New Southgate	Foil Tubes
John Deed & Sons ltd. 40 Osnaburgh Street NW9	Skins
L.S. Dixon & Co. Ltd. 22 Union Street, Barnet	Newspaper & Papers
Alfred Dunhill Ltd. 186 Campden Hill Road, London, W8	Special Pipes
J.A.P. Daborn, 9 Broadway, NW7	Picture Framers
Davis Services Ltd. Norwich Union House, Southampton Place, WC1	Glass Phials
Dysons Ltd. Gloucester Road, London	Make-up
Eyland & Sons Ltd. Rushall Street Works, Walsall	Buckles
Excelsior Printers Supply Co. Ltd. 41 Farringdon Street, London EC4	Printer's Equipment
John Edgington & Co. Ltd. 108 Old Kent Road, SE1	Drill & Tenting
Fassbender & Evans Ltd. 206 St John Street, EC1	Leather Goods
J. Feaver & Son Ltd. 120 Tower Bridge Road, SE1	Sheet metal workers and toolmakers
Franklin Iddins Ltd. North Circular Road, palmers Green	Cotton Materials
Fraser & Glass Ltd. Assembly Works, Woodside Lane, N12	Bakelite Razors
Joseph Freeman & Sons Ltd. 96 Garrett Lane, SW18	Cementone
Fulham Pottery & Cheavin Filter Co. Ltd. 210 New Kings Road, London SW6	Clay
C.G. Goord & Sons Ltd. 268 Holloway Road, N1	Leather Goods
General Optical Co. 120 Clerkenwell Road, EC	Lense Grinders
Gradton Paper Mfg. Co. Ltd. Dowses Yard, Charlton Terrace, N	Corrogated boxes
Griffin & Tatlock Ltd. Kemble Street, Kingsway, WC2	Artist Stationery
Harbutts Plasticine Ltd. 68 Victoria Street, SW1	Plasticine
William Howard, 240 St Annes Road, Tottenham	Dead Rats

Suppliers	Commodity
G. Harrison & Sons, 182 Drury Lane, WC2	Brass
R. Hovenden & Sons, 29 Berners Street, W1	Make-up
Halex Ltd. Larkshall Road, E4	Celluloid Brushes
Samuel Jones & Co. Ltd. 16 New Bridge Street, London EC4	Flexglass & Gummed Papers
Kodak Ltd, Wealdstone, Harrow	Photographic
Kings Cross & Attwood Plating Co. Pentonville Road, N1	Plating
A.F. Latton & Co. Ltd, 1 Devonshire square, Bishopsgate, EC2	Hessian
Louis Maurice & Co. Ltd. Lowther Road, London N7	Make-up
Sidney Levene, 255 Commercial Road, London E1	Embroidery
T.N. Lawrence, 4 Red Lion Court. EC4	Printers Boxwood
Mills Equipment Co. Ltd. Imperial Works, Fountayne Road, Broad Lane, N15	Webbing Equipment
Max Factor, North End, Croydon	Make-up
The Markham Trading Co. Ltd, 7 & 8 Norfolk Street, WC2	Adding machines
Mander Bros. ltd. 419 Old Ford Road, E3	Printer's Ink
Mentmore Mkg. Co. Ltd. Platignum House, Tudor Grove, E9	Pens & Pencils
Monotype Corperation Ltd, 14 Rosebery Ave, London EC1	Printer's Type
Ralph Neal, 32 Station Road, New Southgate	Engravers for medals and identity discs
Newbold & Bulford Ltd. 36/42 Clerkenwell Road, EC1	Spectacle frames
Nettlefold & Sons Ltd. Nettlefold House, Euston Road, N1	Screws, nails, etc.
Normand Electrical Co. Ltd, Neco Works, North Street, SW4	Electrical Equipment
Nicholls & Clarke Ltd. Neco Works, North Street, SW4	Paints etc.
O. Lierman Ltd, 12/14 Middle Street, Aldersgate	Beads
Old Time Furnishing Co. Victoria Street	Carpets
Osborne & Carret ltd. Firth Street, London	Wigmakers Blocks
C.J Plunckett & Co. Ltd. 38 Boland Street, W1	Dental Equipment
Properts Ltd. 142 Battersea Park Road, SW11	Polish & Leather dyes

Suppliers	Commodity
Plowish & Thompson Glass Ltd. Dial Works, Stourbridge, Worcs	Glass Phials
Phillips Mills & Co. 16 Hestor Road, SW11	Paper Shavings
F.T. Pillivant Ltd. Grammer Road, SW9	Cartons
Prestware Ltd. Lombard Road, Merton SW19	Pancake Containers
Plasticraft Ltd. Jubilee Close, Townsend Lane, NW9	Jewellery
Pinchin Johnson Ltd. Minerva Works, Silvertown	Paint
Reeves Ltd. 178 Kensington High St, London	Artists Equipment
Pymore Mill Co. Ltd. Bridport, Dorset	Hemp Twist
Rizla Cigarette Paper Mfrs. Beresford Avenue, Wembley	Photographers
Robinson Bros. 5 Hampstead Road. NW	Jewellery
S.D. Rand, 5 Argyll Street, W1	Bangles
Richfords, 9 Snow Hill, EC1	Stencils
Richmond and Chandler Ltd. Southall Street, Manchester 3	Paint Machinery
Rapidol Ltd. 27 Dover Street, W1	Hair Dyes
Silexine Ltd. Richford Street, Goldhawk Road, W6	Paints
Slick Brands Ltd. Stafford Road, Croydon	Cellulose Paint
Southall Timber Co. 86 High Street, Southall	Timber
G.H. Sanders & Co. Ltd. Victoria Works, Gordon Road, Southall	Tin coated tubes
Selectasine Silk Screens Ltd. 11 Southampton Row EC1	Silk Screen Material
J. Smith & Sons Ltd. 45 St Johns Square, EC1	Brass
Spicers & Co. Ltd. 19 New Bridge St. EC4	Paper
Spicket & Down Ltd. 79 Barnet Grove, E2	Cotton tapes
Stephenson & Blake Ltd. 33 Aldersgate Street, EC1	Printer's Type
Schori Metallising Process Ltd. Brent Crescent, NW10	Kuporisers
Skuse & Co. Ltd. 830 Harrow Road, NW10	Toothpaste
Shackell Edwards, 445 Hornsey Road, N19	Printing Ink
Stroud Bros. Ltd. Church Path Nurseries, Church Walk, N16	Grass mats
Starch Products Ltd. Gludox Works, Mill Street, Slough, Bucks	Dextrine
Sheath Bros. Ltd. 87 City Road, EC1	Rubber Goods
T. Abel Smith Ltd. Woodhall Park, Hertford	Faggots
Synthetic & industrial Finishers Ltd, Imperial Works, Balmoral Road, Watford	Synthetic Rubber

Suppliers	Commodity
Tress & Co, Stamford Street, London SE1	Ribbons
United Kingdom Optical Co. Bittacy Hill, Mill Hill, NW7	Glass Fitters
Union Glue & Gelatine Co. Ltd. Cransley Works, Garret Street, EC1	Glue & Gelatine
Vickers-Armstrongs Ltd, Chester Works, Broughton, Chester.	Aluminium Tubing
Chas. Wright Ltd. Edgeware, Middlesex	Dies & Engravers
E. Williams & Sons. Sandridge Road, St Albans, Herts	Steel Hardeners
Watson & Sons Ltd. Castle Street, Reading	Vibrator sets
Wilmotts Ltd. New House, 67 Hatton Gardens,	Spectacle Cases
Winsor & Newton, Bruce Road, Wealdstone	Artist Sundries
Wright & Mills Ltd, 11 The Parade, Hatfield	Spectacles
A. Warren Ltd. 50 St john Street, EC1	Book Binders
Yardley Ltd. 40 Piccadilly, W1	Chemists

Appendix B

List of Other SOE Stations

This is a list of other SOE Stations:

Station VI	Bride Hall. Near Ayot St Lawrence, Hertfordshire (Weapons Acquisition)
Station VIIa	Bontex Knitting Mills. Beresford Avenue, Wembley (Wireless Section: Production)
Station VIIb	Yeast-Vite Factory. Whippendell Road, Watford (Wireless Section: Packing & Dispatch)
Station VIIc	Allensor's Joinery Factory. King George's Avenue, Watford (Wireless Section: Research)
Section VIId	Kay's Garage, Bristol Street. Birmingham (Wireless Section: Production)
Station IX	The Frythe Estate. Near Welwyn Garden City (Wireless: Research; Special Signals) then (Weapons Development & Production)
Station IXa	P O Box 1. Ashford, Middlesex (Submersibles work at Staines reservoir)
Station IXc	Fishguard Bay Hotel. Goodwick, Pembrokeshire (Submersibles work in Fishguard Bay)
Station X	Bletchley Park. Bletchley, Milton Keynes (Code & Cypher School)
Station XI	Old Gorhambury House. Near St Albans, Hertfordshire (Accommodation)
Station XII	Aston House. Near Stevenage, Hertfordshire (Production, Packaging & Dispatch)
Station XIV	Briggens. Near Roydon, Essex (Forgery Section)

Appendix C

War Establishment of the Camouflage Section

Lieut. Colonel
Director of Camouflage
Policy, Direction, Supervision and Camouflage adviser to higher authority.
1 Cpl. ATS Shorthand Writer.
1 Driver I.C.—1 car utility.

STATION XV	
Commandant—Major	Responsible for work and administration of Station XV; deputies for Director of Camouflage. Administration of station personnel Under S.O. Admin. And Q. matters Q.M
1 Cpl. Clerk, ATS	
Colour Sergeant Major	
Sgt. Clerk. RASC	
Cooks, drivers, telephone orderlies, etc.	
S.O. Administration Capt.	Co-ordination and progress of works receipt and issue of works orders, and co-ordination with administration side. Inspection and dispatch.
W. C.I. R.E. Workshops foreman	
S/Sgt. ATS Clerk	
Stores	Ordering, purchasing, accounting, custody, and issue of all special operational and workshop stores. Q.M. deals with Q. personnel matters and transport. 1-15 cwt. 1-3 ton lorries 2 m/cs.
1 Lt (Q.M.)	
1 Cpl. Storeman	
1 L/Cpl. Clerk ATS	
2 Packers	
2 Civilian Buyers (also act for Stn. XVA)	
Captain i/c Workshops	Controlling painters, textile shop, compositing and printing shops, property shops, concealment devices for codes, micro-prints, etc.
1 S/Sgt. (Painter-artist) Assistant and deputy for OIC	

STATION XV	
Textiles	Production of special textile containers, sewing of silk codes, alteration and fitting of very special clothing (Uniforms). Canvas, network, and all textile camouflage work.
1 Sgt. ATS	
1 Cpl. ATS	
8 Tradeswomen	
Property Shop	The work consists of treating material to achieve appropriate appearance of age, special colouration, rusting of material, signs of wear, etc. Any type of material may require treatment—leather, clothing, woodwork, metal, textile, machines, suitcases, wallets, etc. Also packing of foodstuffs, cigarettes etc. both for students use and concealing materials. Alterations to insides of gramophones, etc. to conceal wireless sets money, etc.
Various appropriate tradesmen are drawn into this shop to deal with material to be handled.	
Printers—Machines	Machine men for printing of codes, etc. composed by compositors. Also printing of foreign labels for food, cigarettes and all types of commodities used for camouflage. Secret printing.
1 Sgt. i/c. also responsible for compositors.	
1 Cpl.	
2 Tradesmen	
Printers—Compositors	Composition of printed special books, codes, instructions for use of camouflaged materials for issue to students. Largest output is codes in fine-point type. Composing for secret printing.
1 Cpl.	
26 Tradesmen	
Special Drawing	Graded as painters, these NCOs are the artists who produce line drawings for labels and illustrations, touch up original samples, etc. They also undertake on the spot photography and make up material for printer's block-makers.
1 Sgt.	
1 l/Cpl. ATS	
Painters	General camouflage, painting of the larger types of product, including rubberised paint work, nets, canvas boxes.
1 Cpl. (L/Sgt). i/c	
1 Cpl. ATS	Note: Numbers are not constant, and craftsmen are split up under NCOs to deal with specific jobs in hand.
12 Tradesmen and tradeswomen painters	

STATION XV	
Painters	Small camouflage painting and painting explosive and incendiary camouflaged material under special conditions. See Note under Painters above.
1 Cpl.	
1 Cpl. ATS	
12 Tradesmen and tradeswomen painters	
Plasterers	Modelling, special work and prototypes.
S/Sgt. i/c. Plasterers	
Cpl. ATS	
Tradesmen and Tradeswomen	
1 Sgt.	Dealing with explosive filled plaster under special conditions. Finishing filled models.
1 Cpl. (ATS Tradesmen and Tradeswomen, all Plasterers)	
Captain i/c Workshops	Supervision of metal and woodwork shops. Invention and liaison with explosive officer on new camouflage devices. Mechanical side of explosive and incendiary material in addition to other camouflage metal and woodwork.
Metal Shop	Production of metal work camouflage material. Mechanical work for incendiary and explosive devices.
1 S/Sgt. Fitter i/c.	
1 Sgt. Sheet metal work.	
1 Cpl. Fitter.	
22 Tradesmen and Tradeswomen	
Carpenters Shop	Designs and invents woodwork devices. Doubles for WOI workshop foreman. Production of woodwork camouflage material. Woodwork for incendiary and explosive devices. Certain work on packing and sealing explosive, incendiary and other types of camouflage material.
W.O.II Artisan i/c Shop.	
1 Sgt.	
2 Cpls.	
13 Tradesmen.	
Captain i/c Explosive	Appropriate packers, etc. under supervision of OIC carry out work as above. Packing of explosives, etc. for all means of transport, examination, and repair of material in use. Making incendiary cigarettes, special filling and assisting male staff.
1 W.O.II Ammunition Examiner	
1 Sgt. Ammunition Examiner	
1 Cpl. Technical Storeman	
1 L/Cpl. Technical Storeman	
1 Cpl. ATS	
4 Ptes ATS	

Notes

1. 'Packer and Loaders' are the terms applied to the semi-skilled and specially skilled tradesmen for whom no appropriate trades exist. They are the 'blitz-squads' which are detailed for work in the shops wherever they are most needed according to the work in hand. They are also engaged in handling and checking incoming material and packing and loading finished products for transport by road, rail, air, or sea according to destination.

2. Lance appointments are distributed as follows:

2 Lance Sergeants	1 Painter
	1 Plasterer
11 Lance Corporals	2 Compositors
	2 Metal shop workers
	1 Carpenter (Station XVA)
	1 Tinsmith (Station XVA)
	1 Packer (Hairdresser) (Station XVC)
	1 Technical Storeman
	1 Packer
	1 Plasterer
	1 Carpenter
5 ATS Lance Corporals	1 Painter (special drawing)
	1 Painter
	1 Plasterer
	1 Textile Worker
	1 Clerk

3. Cooks and mess waiters are calculated separately under A.C.I. 346 of 1944.

4. The work of the Station is governed by operational demands and at certain rush periods personnel are switched to meet demands where they occur. The organisation is based on small parties of men and women under NCO experts, all trained in the special work of the Station, who can tackle specialised trade or general camouflage work according to the situation. An inflexible organisation on the lines of a static workshop, with Officers and NCOs to supervise set processes, would necessitate an establishment at least double the present size, on account of the peculiar and diverse nature of the work carried out.

STATION XVA	
1 S/Sgt. Fitter I/C Workshop	Prototypes and experiments with new devices.
6 Tradesmen (inc. 1 Cpl. 2 L/Cpls).	
2 Packers	
1 General Duty Man.	
1 Civilian Officer	
1 jnr. Cmdr. ATS (Tech)	Liaison with Country Sections on D/CAM work and material. Purchase, custody and issue of leather goods for all D/CAM sections. (Note: Turnover approx. 400 items monthly—suitcases, special wallets etc.)
1 Sub. ATS (Tech)	
1 Civilian Secretary	
1 Storeman	
1 Telephone orderly ATS	
1 Driver IC	
1 Car, 2 Seater 4x2	
1 M/C	
D/CAM.F (students clothing)	Procuring and purchase of students clothing and accessories. Searching for samples and sources.
1 Captain	
1 Civilian Officer Assistant	
1 Civilian Officer Admin	Paper work on orders, records, accounts, finance, progress of orders and general administration. Custody, issue, fitting and alteration of all clothing, etc.
3 Secretary Clerks	
1 Cpl RASC Clerk	
1 Cpl Storeman	
2 Storeman	
1 Cpl Tailor	
1 ATS Driver	1 car 2-seater 4x2

STATION XVB	
(Demonstration room and museum)	
1 Sgt. Instructor in Camouflage	Upkeep of ISRB Museum of devices and stores, demonstrations of material. Note: Supervised by Civilian Officer at Station XVA.
2 Cleaners Civilians	
2 Watchmen Civilians	
1 Fireman	

STATION XVC	
1 Civilian Officer (Hon. RAF F/O)	Photography of students for true and false identity documents. Photography of ISRB devices and material. Developing, printing, and copying, etc. Make-up and hairdressing etc. of students.
2 Civilians Photographers (Female)	
2 Pts. ATS Developers	
1 Civilian Secretary	
1 Civilian Watchman	
1 L/Cpl Packer for hairdressing and make-up	

Appendix D

List of Clothing Section Suppliers

LIST OF REGULAR DIRECT SUPPLIERS OF CLOTHING TO STATION XVA

M & N Hornes, 419/427 St Johns Street, Clarkenwell, EC1

Loroco Ltd, 19/20 Margaret St, W1

Anchor Models Ltd. 14 Gt. Tichfield St. W1

S. Fuss & Co. 140 Gt. Portland St, W1

Allard knitwear Co. Ltd. Audley House, 11 Margaret St, W1

Victor Jacobs Ltd. 19 Briset Street, St Johns Gate, EC1

Tress & Co, 3 Stamford St, SE1

Robert & John Ltd. 56 New Bond Street, London W1

Cortinnette Sports Ltd, 17/18 Margaret St, W1

Fineware Mfg. Co. 10/15 Chitty Street, Tottenham Court Road, W1

A & F Shoes, 6/9 Minerva Street, Hackney Road, E2

Dent Allcroft & Co. 189 Regent St. W1

L. Minc. 4 Saville Row. W1

LIST OF REGULAR DIRECT SUPPLIERS OF MATERIALS TO STATION XV

Supplier	Commodity
Adam & Lane & Neeve Ltd. 8 Copperfield Road E3	Brass eyelets, Blind cord, etc.
The Aerograph Co. Ltd. Lower Sudenham, SE26	Paint Sprayers
E.B. & N Atkins Ltd, Stewarts Lane Station, SW8	Plaster
Alderson & Tull Ltd, Sterling Works, Wansbeck Road, E9	Cotton Cords and Lines
Abdulla & Co. Ltd. 124 Commercial Street, E1	Making up of special cigarettes
Adana, 17 Church Street, Twickenham	Printing equipment
Amalgamated Dental Co. Ltd. 7 Swallow Street, W1	Zelex for Plaster work
Elizabeth Arden ltd. 76 Grosvenor Street, W1	Make-up
Avern & Bucknall (Corks) Ltd. 18 Whites Grounds, SE1	Corks

Baird 7 Tatlock Ltd. 14 St Cross Street, EC1	Chemicals and Chemical equipment
H Barnett & Co (London) Ltd. 63 Lowlands Road, Harrow	Twines and cords
N. Benjamin Ltd, 3 Shepherd Place, Mayfair, W1	Leather Goods
Blackwell & Co. Ltd. 24 Sugar House Lane, London E15	Poster Paints and paints

Monthly Work Reports Executed for Country Sections

REPORTS TAKEN AT RANDOM OF MONTHLY WORK EXECUTED FOR COUNTRY SECTIONS

GERMAN SECTION

5,000 Tyre Burster Bags made and camouflaged for use in Germany.

120 Malingerers Kits made up and packed in special cartons inside of German "Ciroga" coffee packets.

30 Black Wound Badges reproduced.

24 Benzedrine Tablets camouflaged as Swedish Throat Tablets.

4 Rosettes altered and affixed to German Caps.

8 Dinghies camouflaged and packed for Europe.

12 Copies reproduced of small badge for German Uniforms.

2 Special design Incendiary Boxes.

1 piece Explosive Boxes.

1 Explosive Rat.

1 each of Explosive Tins (electric).

1 Explosive Ration Tin.

1 Lever top explosive tin.

1 Box of 6 tins (electric).

1 of each kind of packet of German cigarettes.

1 Pr. Explosive Sabots.

1 Explosive Book.

1 Explosive Fish-plate.

1 Explosive Spar and 1 Explosive Log of Wood.

3 Wooden Boxes each containing 6 tins of food.

1 "People's Wireless Set" fitted with Transmitter.

1 Handbag repaired and mirror replaced.

6 Belts supplied.

6 Gestapo discs numbered.

1 Thermometer case in brass 13" long made up with screw cap.

3 "L" Tablets, 18 "E" Tablets and 18 "K" Tablets camouflaged as various German medicinal commodities.

12 Identity discs made and lettered according to details supplied.

The following concealments were carried out for Operation Ironside German Section

1 V.P. transmitter camouflaged in a Belgian Water Bottle, with instruction book, 2 serials, earth, 2-15 amp pins, lamp holder, 3 voltage selector plugs, range plunger, 4 W/T silk plans, 2 pilot lamps, and 25–100 dollar notes.

1 Polish M.O.R. set camouflaged in a German type of paint tin with battery pack, 4-H2 batteries, 1 H.T. battery, headphones, battery lead, serial and earth, 4 valves, 2 fuses, 1 silk code and 20,000 Reichsmarks.

1 German paint tin containing Mk.III Transmitter set, consisting of battery pack, spares box, 3 valves, 8 fuses, 1 Tuneon, 1 voltage selector plug, 1 universal plug, 1-6 volt vibrator, battery leads, 3 screwdrivers, 1 valve extrometer, headphones complete, key, instruction book, 7 pins, 2 Bulldog clips, 4 silk W/T plans, 20,000 Reichsmarks, key base, aerial and earth.

1 German paint tin containing generator, handle and lead, and further tin containing the generator stand.

15,000 Reichsmarks and codes camouflaged in a rucksack. 3 Gold Napoleons concealed in the heel of a boot. 2 Gold Napoleons concealed in a leather belt. SHAEF messages and time tables camouflaged in a match box.

The following concealments were carried out for Operation Times German Section

1 German paint tin concealing a Mk.III W/T set, tuneon, key, 2 fuses, adaptor pin, transformer terminals, aerial, earth, 4 silk W/T plans, 20,000 Reichsmarks, vibrator 6v, spare, valve extractor, 3 screwdrivers, universal adaptor, 2 Bulldog clips, 1 pr. Battery leads, 3 valves, instruction book, head band, head phones, key base, spares box.

1 German type of paint tin concealing Polish MOR set, headphones, battery pack, 4 valves, M.T. battery, 20,000 Reichsmarks, 4 U.2 batteries, lead, aerial, earth.

1 Belgian tea-can containing V.P. W/T set, aerial, earth, 3 connecting plugs, crystal adaptor, 2 plug in rods, screw in plug, 1,500 dollars.

2 German type tins, one concealing hand generator, lead and handle, and the other the stand of generator.

15,500 Reichsmarks and 1 silk one time pad concealed in a rucksack.

1 code concealed in a wallet.

1,5000 dollars concealed in a Thermos flask.

B.B.C. Broadcast plan and B.B.C. strip camouflaged in a tube of German toothpaste "Blendax."

5 Gold Napoleons concealed in a cap.

SHAEF messages and Broadcast times camouflaged in a small leather book.

The following concealments were carried out for Operation Bruno German Section

15,500 Reichsmarks and one time pad camouflaged in a Rucksack.

3 Gold Napoleons concealed in a heel of boot.

2 Gold Napoleons concealed in a leather belt.

2 Codes concealed in a tube of "Nivea" toothpaste.

SHAEF messages and Broadcast times camouflaged in a matchbox.

The following concealments were carried out for Operation Jaeger German Section

2 Microphones concealed in a Belgian tea-can with B.B.C. call signs, black and red substitution square, 1 silk and one time pad.

The following concealments were carried out for Operation Penda German Section

1 Australian pack containing a Mk.III set.

1 Further Australian pack containing 1 spares box, 1 key base, phones, headband, instruction book, 3 valves, 1 pr. Battery leads, 2 crocodile clips, universal adaptor, 3 screwdrivers, valve extractor, tuneon, key, 8 fuses, 7 adaptor pins, transformer terminal, aerial, earth, crystal, adaptor, generator, cable.

1 gallon German paint tin concealing M.O.R. battery pack, phones complete 4 valves, H.T. battery, 4 U.2 batteries, aerial, earth, set of battery leads, 9 crystal adaptor.

1 H.T. battery containing 1 W.P. set, aerial, earth, universal plug, crystal adaptor, 3 pilot bulbs, 3 plugs, 2 pins, range plunger, instruction book.

1 German type of tin containing 3 legs of generator and 1 handle.

1 Sardine tin made to conceal miniature crystals B.H.I. crystal adaptor and signal plan.

The following concealments were carried out for Operation Aidan German Section

1 Australian pack containing spares box, key base, phones, headband, instruction book, 3 valves, battery leads, 2 Bulldog clips, universal adaptor, 3 screwdrivers, valve

contractor, tuneon, key, 8 fuses, 7 adaptor pins, transformer terminal, aerial wire, earth wire, crystal adaptor, generator, cable.

1 Belgian tea-can made up concealing V.P. set, instruction book, aerial, earth, 15 amp, pins, 2 lamp adaptor, crystal adaptor, selector plugs, ranger plunger, pilot bulbs.

1 German type of paint tin concealing Polish M.O.R. set, 4 valves, aerial, earth, battery leads, 1 pr. headphones complete, 2 fuses.

1 German type of paint tin concealing battery pack, crystal adaptor, 12 crystals, N.T. battery, 4 U.2 batteries, 4 silk plans, 1 6 volt 30 A/H accumulator charged and filled, camouflaged in a German type waterproof tin.

1 Notebook concealing transparent photos of Birlies Signal Plan. 4 photos of B.B.C. programmes, 1 silk strip giving B.B.C. call signs.

2 Microphotos SHAEF, B.B.C. messages and B.B.C. programme, black and red substitution squares, 12 silks of one time pad camouflaged in a Belgian tea-can for Operation Matita.

White piping altered in black on shoulder tabs, and braid sewn round them.

Numbers embroidered in cotton on shoulder pads removed, and braid added.

30 ration cards and 500 Reichsmarks concealed in a dressing case. 1 powder carton concealing 20 × 20 Reichsmarks and 2 × 100 Reichsmarks 80 × 20 in a first aid pack. All of these articles were supplied, and were already aged.

1 Australian pack concealing a Mk.III set.

1 Sardine tin made to conceal 4 crystals, crystal adaptor and 4 silk plans.

The following clothing was aged, German Section

2 Suits of clothes and 1 trilby hat. 2 overalls, 1 leather jacket, 2 collars, 1 pr. French trousers. 2 shirts, 2 vests, 2 underpants, 6 handkerchiefs, 2 towels, 1 pr. braces, 3 prs socks, 1 pr. gloves, 1 cap.

Alterations carried out on:

2 Air Force jackets. 2 suitcases aged, 6 leather belts supplied.

The following clothing and items were supplied, German Section

2 Leather wallet sabotage outfits supplied. 12 tins of food packed in 3 wooden boxes. Badges and braid sewn on to 4 German uniforms, these were also slightly aged. 1 bakelite razor, 1 shaving brush, 1 toothbrush, 1 pocket knife, 1 aluminium mug, all of German origin supplied.

The following clothing repaired (i.e. buttons sewn on, dummy darns added, boots repaired with odd scraps of leather) and then aged accordingly: 1 cap, 2 towels, 4 sponge bags, 8 prs. pants, 9 vests, 5 pullovers, 7 shirts, 13 prs. socks, 17 handkerchiefs, 5 scarves, 6 prs. boots, 6 prs. gloves, 9 ties, 1 jacket, 5 prs. trousers, 3 raincoats, 1 hat, 1 pr. braces, 4 leather jackets, 2 pr. shoes, 2 berets, 1 belt, 1 blouse jacket, 1 balaclava, muffler and hat.

11 shaving brushes aged. Oiled silk lining removed from sponge bag. 6 belts, 6 suitcases, 2 wallets, 15 German briefcases, 8 German lighters supplied.

1 Prisoner of War parcel made up containing 2,000 cigarettes.

Samples of various German and Belgian articles brought back from the Continent supplied as specimens for future use: Zahn Crème, Identity card cases, Ecko tobacco packets, Luna matches, Elnove matches, spade matches, 7 assorted packets of razor blades.

250 packets of incendiary cigarettes completed. 65 explosive rats, 16 pieces of explosive coal, 4 explosive logs and 50 explosive fish-plates completed and despatched. 2 V.Ps. camouflaged, one in a Belgian Army type water-bottle, and one in a workman's tea caddy. 21 students fitted up with clothing and equipment consisting of 649 items.

NORWEGIAN SECTION

25 white kid money belts made up to sizes as requested. 25 bags made of waterproof material for containing papers, etc.

130 cardboard carton size 7″ × 12″ × 17″ supplied from stock.

1,000 Boxes Norwegian matches made up and supplied.

16 carrying toboggans completed and despatched.

210 tin-lined wooden camouflaged boxes completed for the packing of stores.

25 uncamouflaged tin lined S.D.U. boxes produced.

1 sample tin lined box made up to contain 20 WD 24 hour rations, 20 dehydrated 'A' packs and 20 × 2 3/4 oz tins margarine.

Supplied 27 wallets, 2 briefcases, 11 belts.

Supplied and aged 22 suitcases, 4 briefcases, 7 wallets.

46 students fitted up with articles of clothing and equipment consisting of 2,180 items.

DUTCH SECTION

8 crystals camouflaged in a packet of "Ciroga" coffee.

11 microprints and 5 silks camouflaged in a wallet, and 1 one time pad and substitution square camouflaged in a notebook.

12 page M.P. one time pad, 1 substitution square, and 2 microprints of B.B.B. conventions concealed in one pencil notebook.

12 page one time pad and 1 substitution square concealed in large wallet.

Utility markings removed from 40 prs. stockings.

6 cigarette cases, 2 tobacco pouches and 2 chess sets supplied.

15 suitcases and 1 belt supplied and aged.

11 students fitted up with clothing and equipment consisting of 351 items.

POLISH SECTION

Waterproof pocket inserted in briefcase with zip fastener.

7 leather money belts, each with 3 pockets and press stud fasteners.

5 wallets, 4 briefcases and 4 cigarette cases supplied.

1 special magnetised needle for use as a compass.

1 Jedborough W/T set camouflaged in tins, in 3 coal sacks.

1 map case dyed.

1 housewife supplied.

26 articles of clothing supplied to section.

2 students fitted out with clothing consisting of 93 items.

BELGIAN SECTION

Microprints concealed in spool of Elastoplast.

Money and codes concealed in three small toilet cases.

Money concealed in briefcases.

Money and codes concealed in Belgian tea-can.

Money concealed in Junior Shell Tin.

Money concealed in loose leaf notebook.

Money concealed in one set of brushes.

Money concealed in writing case.

Money and codes concealed in large petrol lighter.

Funds and codes concealed in small ink stand.

Funds and codes concealed in folding mirror.

10,000 dollars and microprints concealed in Portuguese sardine tin.

Marks removed from 10 shirts.

6 French fountain pens supplied.

Microprints concealed in talcum powder box.

1 'L' tablet concealed in India rubber.

Crystals and microphotographs concealed in wooden box.

10 crystals concealed in wooden box.

267 articles of clothing supplied to Section.

8 French cigarettes lighters and 6 suitcases supplied.

10 crystals and microprints of codes concealed in wooden box.

FRENCH SECTION

1 pr. boots softened and broken in.

Heel grips and socks fitted to one pair shoes.

12 three-pocket calico money belts made and supplied.

1 pr. shoes repaired with iron tips and English marks removed.

Marks removed from Military helmet, and knife cleaned and sharpened.

9,000 Gauloises cigarettes and 45 boxes of French matches supplied.

1 pistol holder repaired.

Marks removed from photograph.

Marks removed from one pair scissors, and sharpened.

12 three-pocket calico money belts with braces.

52 suitcases supplied and aged.

11 wallets, 1 purse, 1 briefcases, 9 belts supplied and aged.

15 cigarette lighters supplied.

1 toilet case and make up supplied.

12 students fitted out with clothing consisting of 1,158 items.

DANISH SECTION

WD markings removed from 40 car tyres and tubes.

1 ultra-violet bulb and choke supplied for use with invisible writing.

Supplied and aged 7 suitcases, 2 wallets, 2 belts.

1 briefcase supplied.

Nasal operation carried out on a student to enable him to return to the field without fear of recognition.

Gold tooth concealed with porcelain.

1,400,000 rounds of .303 S.A.A., 1,300 Mk.4 rifles and 300 Bren guns packed into wooden boxes camouflaged as various size foreign machinery cases.

4 students fitted up with articles of clothing and equipment consisting of 107 items.

AMERICAN SECTION

1 proofed cotton money belt and 2 white kid money belts made up to measurements specified.

Marks removed from 5 car tyres and inner tubes, and 5 bicycle tyres and inner tubes.

1 German Identity Disc and 12 Gestapo discs made up and lettered.

6 belts aged.

14 fluorescent pencils supplied.

1 sewing machine.

1 French brush and comb.

10 balloons.

10 oiled silk containers for protection of papers, messages, etc.

2 jars toothpaste.

2 code pipes.

2 Kensington Pins.

12 infra-red filters for small torches.

12 infra-red filters for large torches.

2 hair brushes.

4 small wallets.

16 Belgian tea-cans.

5 large Wallets.

5 ladies' handbags.

24 toothpaste tubes with 24 ballons.

9 shaving brushes.

2 photo wallets.

4 small corks.

4 double-bottom suitcases supplied and aged.

36 double-bottom briefcases supplied and aged.

9 German penknives.

5 fountain pens.

2 German paint tins made up with false bottoms for carrying purposes.

36 boxes of German matches supplied.

1 student fitted out with clothing and equipment and 329 various items supplied.

FAR EAST GROUP

250 copies each of trade cloth tabs supplied.

150 Holsworth containers camouflaged and packed for transit overseas.

255 unmarked tubes of glass frosting ointment awaiting dispatched and a further 60 tubes dispatched to complete order for 375 tubes.

98 'Y' type dinghies dispatched, complete with all accessories.

8 incendiary briefcases, 8 incendiary suitcases, 8 incendiary deed boxes completed as dummies and dispatched.

267 tubes of frosting ointment camouflaged as pigmentan awaiting dispatch.

3 cases of rubberized paint supplied and dispatched.

12 incendiary briefcases and 12 small incendiary boxes completed.

48 black stockinette masks dispatched.

100 assorted bridge limpets, 50 pieces explosive mango wood, 50 post boxes camouflaged as boulders, and 50 Holdsworth containers completed and dispatched.

PHOTOGRAPHY AND ILLUSTRATION SECTION

114 students photographed for fake passes. (2,135 prints delivered).

155 students photographed for ordinary military passes (1,070 prints delivered).

71 reprinting orders (562 prints delivered).

A total number of 2,347 enlargements were made, and 5 films developed.

20 lantern slides were completed for Camouflage Section. A number of camouflage photographs were taken in the studio for experimental purposes, and 12 copies made of them. 3 Catalogues of Camouflage Devices completed and dispatched to Station XV.

MI9 RAF Secret Air Crew Pencils

This appendix is not a part of the original SOE report.
It has been researched and written by Craig Moore, the editor of this book.

During the Second World War the Derwent Pencil Company in Keswick, Cumbria, was chosen by MI9, the British Directorate for Military Intelligence, Section 9, to manufacture a secret pencil that contained a rolled-up map of Europe and a very small compass. These were issued to RAF bomber crews to aid them in escape and evasion in the event of being shot down. If they were captured and sent to a German prisoner of war camp, it was hoped the men would be allowed to keep a simple pencil. The map and compass would then come in useful for planning future escapes.

Very few British troops, sailors and airmen captured in the First World War managed to escape successfully back to their own lines. They lacked the tools and training as well as any established escape routes in occupied Europe. With the threat of another war with Germany looming, the War Office consulted the director of naval intelligence, the director of military intelligence, and the director of intelligence at the Air Ministry. These discussions resulted in the recognition of a need for a joint service approach.

On 23 December 1939 Section 9 was newly formed within the Directorate of Military Intelligence under the leadership of Brigadier Norman Crockatt DSO, MC. This section was to work in close connection with and act as an agent for the Admiralty, Air Ministry and Army. MI9 was responsible for the preparation and execution of plans to facilitate the escape of British prisoners of war of all three services in Germany and elsewhere. It was also tasked with arranging instruction in escape and evasion techniques as well as 'making other advance provisions as considered necessary'. (The Charter. Conduct of Work No. 48 MI9.)

Room 424 in the London Metropole Hotel in Northumberland Avenue was chosen as the headquarters of this new clandestine organisation. No one would notice the comings and goings of uniformed personnel in a hotel during the war, so the location provided anonymity and convenience, being only a short walk from the War Office. On 14 February 1940, after the Metropole Hotel suffered bomb damage during the London Blitz, the MI9 technical section moved to the Wilton Park country estate near Beaconsfield in Buckinghamshire.

As it expanded, MI9 was reorganised into different sub-departments. In January 1942 MI9 Intelligence School 9 Section Z was given the responsibility for the production and distribution of escape and evasion equipment. IS9 (Z) also conducted experimental work and prepared prisoner of war parcels that contained hidden maps and escape aids. After the war, MI9 was assimilated into the British Special Intelligence Service (SIS), often referred to incorrectly as MI6.

Charles Fraser-Smith's wartime job was to source and supply equipment and gadgets for MI9 and the Special Operations Executive (SOE). These included items such as concealable knives and maps, tiny compasses, forged foreign currency and documents, edible notepaper, surgical saws, and miniature cameras. He also had to conceive of ways to hide these items inside everyday things that would pass unnoticed by enemy soldiers. He could be compared to the fictional character 'Q' in the James Bond 007 spy movies. Fraser-Smith had already put secret compartments in shaving brushes, golf balls, pens and tobacco pipes. He would contact the companies that manufactured these objects and place a special order for their products with specific modifications. Most companies were pleased to be helping the war effort, even if it was in secret.

Fraser-Smith started most concealment projects by looking at the items most commonly carried by civilians in occupied countries. He also considered what equipment aircrew usually carried. Pilots, navigators, and flight engineers used pencils rather than pens as the ink in pens would freeze at high altitudes, making them useless. Fraser-Smith approached the managers of the Cumberland Pencil Company in Keswick, Cumbria, the oldest manufacturer of pencils in Great Britain. They accepted the difficult task of trying to develop a special escape aid pencil that could conceal a map and compass. The project had to be kept secret, so all members of staff involved in its manufacture were sworn to secrecy under the Official Secrets Act.

The Cumberland Pencil Company Ltd factory in Keswick, Cumbria.

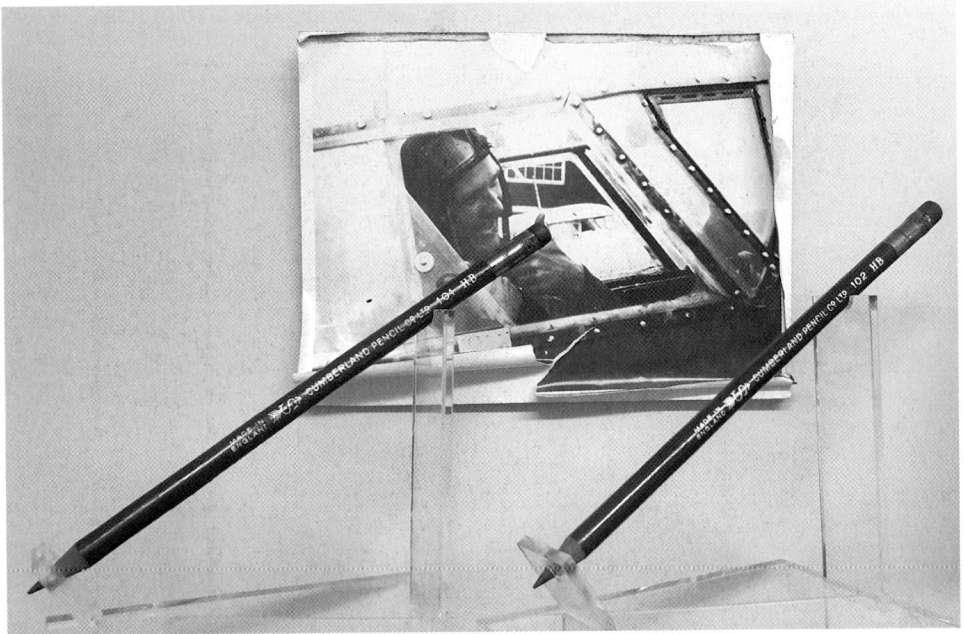

Original Second World War escape pencils on display at the Derwent Pencil Museum.

A glimpse of the secret escape map hidden inside the pencil.

All members of the Cumberland Pencil management team had to act as normal. Only a few of the hundred-strong workforce were involved, while the others had to be kept in the dark about what was happening. At 5.30 p.m., team members left work as normal and returned home, but later in the day they would return to the factory laboratory through the back door. They also crept back into the factory at weekends to work on the project.

The first part of the conversion process required the removal of the metal ferrule and rubber attached to the end of each pencil. The team would then carefully drill out the inside using a large drill bit that would extract most of the lead and more of the wood. This would make a tube large enough to accommodate a rolled map. A short section of lead would be left at the working end of the pencil. A small brass compass

The escape map in 1:600,000 scale showing the distance in kilometres between towns in blue.

would be inserted into the opening of the metal ferrule before it was glued back onto the top of the pencil. The final job was to glue the eraser back into the ferrule. When the work was complete, the pencil looked exactly the same as any other without a secret concealment compartment.

The technical manager at Cumberland Pencil Co., Fred Tee, had first considered making a new set of pencils from scratch with a larger central tube. The width of the tool that was used to chisel out the grooves in the cedar wood slats used to make normal pencils could be adjusted to make a larger groove. The problem was that the factory was a tight-knit community. The changes to the tooling equipment, the use of additional cedar wood slates from the storeroom and the appearance of extra boxes of pencils overnight would be noticed, and questions would be asked. This is why Tee decided that the extra steps needed to create the secret escape pencil should be done on completed pencils after normal working hours.

THE SECRET WW2 PENCIL

DERWENT PENCIL MUSEUM

Derwent Pencil Museum logo.

THE REPLICA

In recent years, to honour the achievements of the factory workers during the Second World War, the company decided to produce a limited-edition replica of the RAF bomber crew escape pencil in its own presentation box called the Borrowdale Box. This was not an easy task. The factory team made thousands of pencils of several types each month, so it was assumed that using modern machinery to make one more type of pencil would not be difficult. However, the process of inserting a map and compass inside a pencil was much harder than it first appeared, making the staff at Derwent Pencil Company, the new name of the Cumberland Pencil Co., appreciate the extraordinary workmanship carried out by the factory staff back in the 1940s. Detailed information on how the RAF escape pencil was made during the war was

——— THE CUMBERLAND PENCIL C⁰ LTᴰ ———
SECRET MAP AND COMPASS PENCIL

PRINTED ON VERY FINE PAPER, THE MAPS WERE ROLLED AND INSERTED INTO THE
PENCIL BARREL CAVITY. 4 MAPS WERE PRINTED DETAILING ESCAPE ROUTES
THROUGH GERMANY AND WEST TO THE NETHERLANDS, BELGIUM AND SOUTH TO
SWITZERLAND. THE METAL FERRULE, COMPASS AND ERASER WERE THEN FITTED.
A STAMPED CODE DENOTED WHICH MAP WAS ENCLOSED. PENCILS WERE ISSUED
TO BOMBER COMMAND AIRCREW IN THE ROYAL AIR FORCE AND SENT TO POW
CAMPS. THEY WERE A VITAL PART OF THE WAR TIME ESCAPE NETWORK.

Above: The replica
RAF escape pencil
presentation box
produced by the
Cumberland Pencil
Company Ltd.

Right: Cumberland
Pencil Company Ltd
factory van.

restricted under the Official Secrets Act and had never been made public. And the men
who had made the pencils were no longer around to ask; they had taken their secrets
to the grave.

The team first tried to construct a new pencil from scratch. They adjusted the width
of the blades that cut out the grooves to cut a wider groove for the pencil lead on both
halves of the cedar wood slats, but when these two halves were glued together they
were crushed during the shaping process.

The technical manager remembered being told by his father, who had been part of
the 1940s management team and involved in the escape pencil's nocturnal production,

Boxed sets of the replica WW2 secret escape pencil.

that they had drilled out the centre of completed 8mm pencils for most of the pencil's length to allow it to take the rolled-up map. The team tried this approach, but it was very messy as sawdust mixed with fine graphite powder flew into the air as the drill bit went through the centre of the pencil.

It was decided to try the procedure again but to use a batch of specially manufactured pencils that only had a small quantity of lead in the tip. The pencil was hollow for most of its length. When the centres of these pencils were drilled, there was no longer messy fine graphite powder to contend with, just sawdust. Another problem that had to be overcome was sourcing a tiny 7.8mm-diameter compass. This proved impossible. The smallest compass that could be found was 9.5mm in diameter. That meant that the replica pencil was going to have to be slightly bigger than the typical 8mm diameter. Other than that unavoidable difference, these pencils had to look and feel the same as standard pencils.

The replicas were painted with four coats of green and one coat of gloss paint to match the wartime pencils, but adding the lettering on the side presented a problem. Normally this was done by hot silver-foil imprinting using an engraved metal die that was pushed into the surface of the pencil. However, because the pencil was now a thin, hollow wooden tube, it broke. A different method had to be found, and screen printing was the answer.

Instead of manufacturing a small tissue or silk map of north-west Europe for the replica escape pencils, the company decided to print a map that showed the location of the graphite mine, the Cumberland Pencil Factory and the Pencil Museum in the Lake District. The first few attempts to roll up the small map by hand so that it was tight enough to fit inside the pencil failed. The team tried using a Rizla cigarette rolling machine, but that was not tight enough. They then examined a surviving wartime escape pencil and discovered that the managers in the 1940s had used a piece of thin wire with what looked like a small fishhook at one end and a circle at the other. The map was wound by hand very tightly around the wire and then tied off with three pieces of cotton to prevent it unravelling. The fishhook and circle end not only helped in winding up the map, but when inserted into the hollowed-out pencil, they kept the map from moving around internally if the pencil was shaken, thus preventing any hint that the pencil was not absolutely normal. This approach was copied.

A larger metal ferrule had to be manufactured to fit the 9.5mm-diameter compass and the standard 8mm pencil end rubbers. Despite the company's modern machinery and the lack of any need for secrecy, the Derwent team still could not replicate exactly what those special men did when they came back to the factory in the dead of night to make the escape pencils in secret.

It is possible to see the original escape pencils, and the replicas, at the Cumberland Pencil Company's Pencil Museum in Keswick, Cumbria. This is a fascinating museum—perhaps not the adjective you would expect to use when describing a museum about the humble pencil, but it will surprise you. It is the ideal location to visit on a rainy day in the Lake District.

CHARLES FRASER-SMITH

Charles Fraser-Smith was born on 26 January 1904. He was the son of a solicitor, and the family also owned a wholesale grocery business. He became an orphan at the tender age of 7 and was taken in by a Christian missionary family who lived in Hertfordshire. He was not very academic but loved science and making things, and

he had an unusual early working life. His first job was as a prep-school teacher in Portsmouth, and then he became a motorcycle messenger rider. He gave this up to work in an aircraft factory but later decided to become a Christian missionary in Morocco.

In 1939 he returned to Britain. One Sunday he was asked to give a sermon about his missionary work to the congregation of the Open Brethren Evangelical Church in Leeds. He did not realise that two civil servants from the Ministry of Supply were sitting in the church pews in front of him. His sermon concentrated on his practice of bricolage in North Africa, the necessity of obtaining supplies from all available sources. The men from the ministry were impressed, and he was offered a job using those skills.

Charles Fraser-Smith was 36 when war broke out in 1939. He had not passed the Civil Service examinations, so he was only classed as a temporary civil servant. He was assigned to the Ministry of Supply's Clothing and Textiles Department (CT6)

This photograph of Charles Fraiser-Smith was used on his wartime identity card for the Ministry of Supply, Clothing and Textiles, Department 6.

and commuted by train from his Hertfordshire house to the offices of the Ministry of Supply near St James's Park in London. At the beginning of his tenure, with no explanation, he was summoned to an office and asked to sign the Official Secrets Act. This was to force him to remain silent about his work for the next thirty years. He was given a new office and a personal assistant, but he never knew the people who gave him instructions. They would phone his office, asking for 'CT6'. He would then receive details of the requirement for a new gadget, a fake uniform, forged documents, or a piece of escape equipment. Details on how the items were to be concealed, manufactured and sourced were not supplied, however. Those decisions were left to Fraser-Smith to work out.

During the war he used over 300 companies to produce special equipment and secret gadgets. Very few of them received the recognition they deserved because of the secret nature of the work. Sourcing the tiny compass to be inserted into the top of the escape pencil's metal ferrule proved particularly problematic. Fraser-Smith approached the Baker Brothers who worked in a back alley in Clerkenwell, London. Surprisingly, this small company had the contract to make large ship compasses for the Royal Navy. They found it amusing when they heard the specifications for the new compasses they were being asked to manufacture. The maximum diameter had to be no more than one-quarter of an inch. A compass that small had not been made before. The Baker brothers were up for the technical challenge and managed to come up with a design and prototype that worked. Once approved, work started on fulfilling the first order. It was these compasses along with the thin maps printed on tissue paper or silk that Fraser-Smith took with him on the train to Keswick.

Fraser-Smith referred to the top-secret equipment he produced as 'Q' gadgets. The designation was borrowed from the Royal Navy's anti-submarine ships in the First World War, known as 'Q ships', which were disguised to look like unarmed merchant ships. When German submarines surfaced, the covers over the main guns were quickly pulled away, and the prey became the hunter. It followed that unmarked police cars in London were known as 'Q boats' for many years. Ian Fleming's knowledge of Q ships and their deceptive role may have been the reason he gave the quartermaster in James Bond's fictitious world the name 'Q'. (The heads of government departments were often referred to by one letter.)

Fraser-Smith was one of a number of suppliers of Q gadgets working for the War Office's Ministry of Intelligence during the Second World War. After the war, he purchased a dairy farm in Bratton Fleming, Devon, where he died in November 1992. More information about the secret gadgets of the Second World War can be found in the book *The Secret War of Charles Fraser-Smith: The 'Q' Gaget Wizard of World War II* (Michael Joseph Ltd, 1981) by Charles Fraser-Smith with Gerald McKnight and Sandy Lesberg.

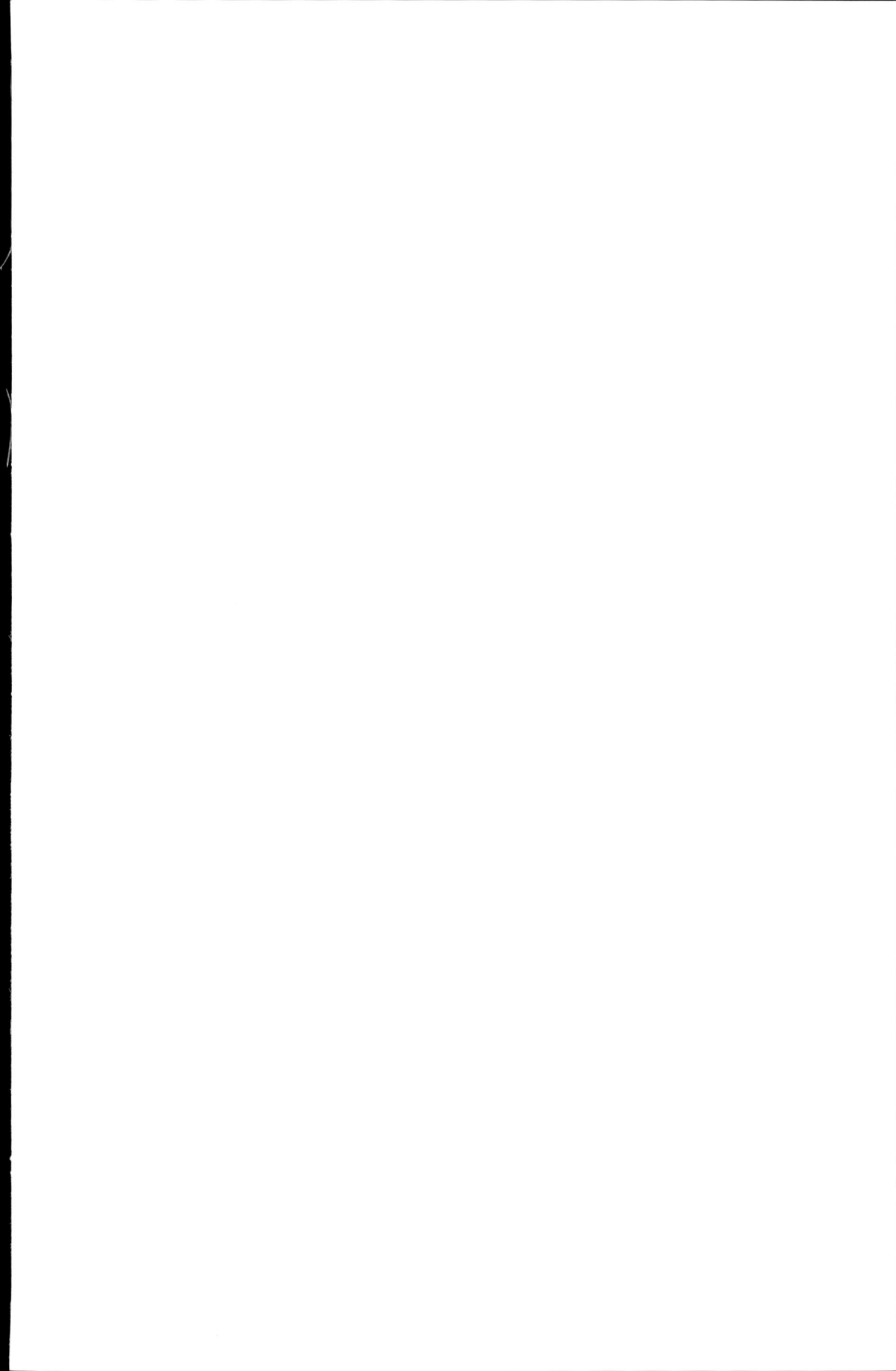